HISTORY OF THE GREAT WAR

BASED ON OFFICIAL DOCUMENTS

BY DIRECTION OF THE HISTORICAL SECTION OF THE COMMITTEE OF IMPERIAL DEFENCE

ORDER OF BATTLE OF DIVISIONS

• PART 4 •

The Army Council, G.H.Q.s, Armies, and Corps 1914–1918

Compiled by

MAJOR A. F. BECKE

R.F.A. (Retired), Hon. M.A. (Oxon.)

The Naval & Military Press Ltd

Published by

The Naval & Military Press Ltd

Unit 10, Ridgewood Industrial Park,

Uckfield, East Sussex,

TN22 5QE England

Tel: +44 (0) 1825 749494

Fax: +44 (0) 1825 765701

www.naval–military-press.com

www.military-genealogy.com

ORDER OF BATTLE OF DIVISIONS

Part 1   The Regular British Divisions

Part 2a   The Territorial Force Mounted Divisions and
The 1st-Line Territorial Force Divisions (42-56)

Part 2b   The 2nd-Line Territorial Force Divisions (57th-69th),
with The Home-Service Divisions (71st-73rd)
and 74th and 75th Divisions

Part 3   New Army Divisions (9-26 and 30-41)
and 63rd (R.N.) Division

Part 4   The Army Council, G.H.Q.s, Armies, and Corps 1914–1918

*In reprinting in facsimile from the original, any imperfections are inevitably reproduced
and the quality may fall short of modern type and cartographic standards.*

Printed and bound by Antony Rowe Ltd, Eastbourne

PREFACE

This is the concluding Part of the Order of Battle of the British Forces which were engaged in the Great War of 1914–1918. The previous five parts* gave the Orders of Battle of the 90 British Divisions which were formed by these islands :—3 Cavalry, 5 Mounted, 12 Regular, 36 New Army, 28 Territorial Force, and 6 other** Divisions.

This Part opens with the composition of the Army Council and shows its expansion during the Great War. The Army Council is followed by G.H.Q. Home Forces ; and then come the G.H.Q.s in France, Egypt, Gallipoli, Salonika, and Italy, and in each case the locations of their headquarters are given.*** In addition, for each of these five theatres a table is given which shows all the battles and engagements fought in the particular theatre, and the formations engaged in each operation.

After the G.H.Q. lists are the orders of battle of the five British Armies which fought on the Western Front. Each Army order of battle gives the Army Commander and Staff, location of Army Headquarters, the battles and actions in which the Army fought, and the Corps and other formations which were engaged under the Army in each of these operations.

Then follow the Tables of the twenty-eight British Corps, all formed during the Great War. Each Corps Table gives the Corps Commander and Staff, all the battles and actions in which the Corps took part, the divisions and other formations which fought under the Corps on each occasion, and, in France, the Army in which the Corps was serving at the time.

To complete this record of the Great War, Appendix 1 sets forth the Commanders of the Central Force (in England) and the Commanders of the Home Defence Armies ; in Appendix 2 are the G.O.C.s of the seven Home Commands and of the London District. Appendix 3 gives the six Groups of the G.H.Q. (France) Heavy Artillery Reserve which in 1916 became the Headquarters of six Corps heavy artilleries†. In Appendix 4 are the different natures of Ordnance with the B.E.F. (France) : at Mons on the 23rd August 1914 and on Armistice Day the 11th November 1918, as well as the yearly output of new guns and the war-time increase in the strength of the Royal Artillery. In Appendix 5 are the Commanders, Staff, and Composition of the three Tank Groups, formed shortly after Armistice ; and, to conclude, Appendix 6 gives the British Section of the Supreme War Council, as it was two months after its formation.

The period covered by this Part includes two major developments in the progress of warfare which it is right to notice.

The First, is the use, and on a steadily increasing scale during the four-and-a-quarter years of hostilities, of Air Forces by both sides††. Beginning in a small way in 1914, Air Forces gradually exerted increasing influence on ground operations, and this led to the co-operation of ground defences, in order to minimize the effective use of the hostile aircraft. To achieve this on the Western Front, towards the end of 1916 an Anti-Aircraft Defence Commander was added to the Staff of each Army, although the relatively junior

---

* Parts 1 ; 2A and 2B ; 3A and 3B.
** 63rd (Royal Naval) Division ; and 71st, 72nd, 73rd, 74th, and 75th Divisions.
*** The Table (pp. 24 and 25) showing locations of G.H.Q. British Armies in France 1914–1918, has in addition the contemporary locations of British Advanced G.H.Q., as well as the French G.Q.G. 1914–1918, and G.Q.G.A. in 1918.[1]
† The other fourteen Corps Heavy Artillery Headquarters were formed in France or Palestine, for the particular Corps with which they served.
†† The History of the Royal Flying Corps (Royal Air Force from 1/4/18) is given in the Official History of the Royal Air Force.
[1] G.Q.G.A. opened on 29/3/18. (For List of Abbreviations see pp. ix & x.)

A*

rank of the officer appointed to this post and the comparatively small force of light ordnance which was allotted to his command, both emphasize that this development was still in an early stage of evolution. Nevertheless it was a beginning, and is rightly alluded to in this work. Furthermore, in February, 1916, the Director-General of Military Aeronautics had been added to the Army Council.

The Second, is the introduction and employment of a new ground-weapon—The Tank. From their first engagement on the 15th September, 1916 (in the Battles of the Somme), tanks exerted a gradually increasing effect. On the 20th November, 1917, the opening day of the Battle of Cambrai, the tank was directly responsible for a change in the method hitherto generally employed in trench-warfare assaults. To mark the intervention of this new land-weapon, the engagements in which the Tank Corps* took part are all enumerated, together with the troops with whom the tanks co-operated in each fight, likewise the Army in which the tanks fought on each occasion is stated, and as far as possible the number of tanks taking part in each action.**

A short allusion is also made to the Tank Repair Shops whose strenuous efforts kept in action as many as possible of these landships for the almost continuous operations undertaken by the Tank Corps.***

Limitations of space have prevented the inclusion of lists of the Army Troops which formed part of the Armies on the Western Front. As the Great War went on these Army Troops naturally became more numerous, and there were constant changes to suit the needs of the different sectors of the front, as the Armies which held them became engaged in the great battles which were fought. To have included the Army Troops would have almost doubled the size of this Part. The Army Troops being omitted, no useful purpose could be served by enumerating the comparatively few units comprised under Corps Troops.

The War Diaries and official documents have provided the principal sources of information on which this Part is built up. Unfortunately, during the Great War, the formations serving in England kept no official diaries ; consequently for the necessary facts about Home-Service formations, resort has been made to monthly and quarterly Army Lists and to the few official documents which exist : Composition of Headquarters, and Order of Battle, Home Forces, etc.

Whereas in the compilation of the divisional orders of battle considerable assistance could be obtained from published divisional histories,† there exists little similar material for the compiler of this Part to use. It is true, there is a valuable and well-mapped *Record of the Advance of the Egyptian Expeditionary Force, July* 1917—*October* 1918, and it contains a wealth of facts ; also two of the Armies which fought on the Western Front have published histories which deal with part of their activities.†† There is a short history of the Tank Corps, and full ones of the Indian Corps in France, the Anzac Corps, and the Canadian Corps,††† otherwise no other Corps histories have appeared.

This lack of published material about the war activities of the higher formations renders necessary a work of reference which will furnish, at any rate, a short summary of each of the G.H.Q.s, Armies, and Corps which were formed between 1914 and 1918 : showing their commanders and their staffs, narrating shortly their story, tabulating the engagements in which they fought, and detailing the formations they controlled during active operations. In this way the names of their Commanders and their historic battle honours will be preserved for reference in the future.

---

* This title is used for clarity and for brevity, although it was not officially adopted until 27/7/17 (see p. 267).
** The co-operation of the 8 tanks of E. Company in the 2nd and 3rd Battles of Gaza is recorded under G.H.Q., E.E.F. and under XXI Corps (pp. 38 and 39 ; and 253).
*** See footnote on p. 268.
† 41, out of the 90 war-time divisions had published divisional histories by 1939
†† These are : " Fourth Army in the Battles of the Hundred Days, 1918 ; " and " Fifth Army for the period of General Sir H. Gough's Command."
††† Up to 1939 only one volume of the Canadian Corps History had been published. For the identification, etc., of the French formations, which co-operated with British forces in the Great War, reliance has been placed on the two parts, forming Volume 10, of the French Official History of the Great War, entitled *Ordres de Bataille des Grandes Unités* (published in 1923 and 1924).

ii

The lists of General Officers Commanding and of Staff Officers do not show temporary changes, due to absences on short leave, etc.

In compiling the lists of Battles and Engagements the previous custom has been followed, and deviations have been made from the *Report of the Battles Nomenclature Committee* (published in 1921), so as to include any fights of which particular formations have reason to be proud.*

Although the Operations in Mesopotamia came under the War Office in February, 1916, the Official History of the operations in that theatre was written under the direction of the India Office, consequently the composition, etc., of G.H.Q. Mesopotamia is not included in this Part.

The words " Action " and " Affair " are generally omitted in the lists of Engagements, and only the date and name of the Engagement are given.**

In the event of any formation not being engaged in a definite action during a whole year, then only the year is shown, and this signifies that the particular formation was on active service in the specified theatre of operations, during the indicated period.

When the five parts of the Divisional Orders of Battle were being compiled, the engagements of the various divisions and the higher formations in which the divisions served at those times were all checked by representatives of the division concerned. It is mainly on this sound basis that the whole structure of the engagements of all the British Armies and Corps has been built up.

I am glad to record that in the case of the Tank Corps, for which there was no such checked record available, I have received the most valuable help from General Sir H. J. Elles, K.C.B., K.C.M.G., K.C.V.O., D.S.O., Major-General Sir E. D. Swinton, K.B.E., C.B., D.S.O., and Major-General J. F. C. Fuller, C.B., C.B.E., D.S.O. For this most opportune assistance I am deeply grateful.

With regard to the Table showing the Supreme War Council, British Section, in January, 1918,*** I am indebted to the research undertaken by the Staff of the War Cabinet Secretariat.

My deep gratitude is also due to the Staff of the War Office Library for essential help over the dates of appointment of several members of the Army Council.

The evacuation of the documents held by the Military Branch has not tended to lighten in any way the work of compilation, but it has made more valuable than ever the skilled help I have received from members of the Historical Section. Especially it is my welcome duty to record my most grateful thanks to Mr. S. Woolgar, late, R.F.A. (i/c of the evacuated documents) for his ready and most efficient support in constantly providing me with the appropriate diaries and papers, and for tirelessly assisting me in reaching the solutions of the many difficulties which so regularly confront the compiler of such a work as this.

Any corrections or amendments to this Part should be sent to the Secretary, Historical Section, Cabinet Secretariat, Great George Street, S.W.1.

A. F. B.

London.
June, 1944.

---

*This procedure was adopted in the previous five Parts of this series.
** For example : " The Action of Tieghem, 31st October [1918]," will appear as " Tieghem, 31 October [1918]."
*** Given in Appendix 6.

CONTENTS

A**

---

* Formed from II Anzac Corps.
** At first entitled Machine Gun Corps (Heavy Section) ; this became Machine Gun Corps (Heavy Branch) on 18/11/16, and Tank Corps on 27/7/17.

LIST OF ABBREVIATIONS

NOTE.—For the period of the Great War, 1914–1918, the titles of regiments have been taken from the 1914–1918 Army Lists.

A

A.-A.	Anti-Aircraft.
A.-A. & Q.-M.-G.	Assistant-Adjutant & Quartermaster-General.
A. & N.Z.	Australian & New Zealand.
A. & Q.	Adjutant & Quartermaster-General.
A.C.	Armoured Car.
A.-D.	Assistant-Director.
Advd.	Advanced.
A.H.Q.	Army Headquarters.
A.L.H.	Australian Light Horse.
Am.	American.
Ammn.	Ammunition.
Anzac.	Australian & New Zealand Army Corps.
A.O.	Army Order.
A.O.C.	Army Ordnance Corps.
A.S.C.	Army Service Corps.
A. & S.H.	Argyll and Sutherland Highlanders.
Aus.	Australian.
A.V.C.	Army Veterinary Corps.

B

Bde.	Brigade.
B.E.F.	British Expeditionary Force.
Berks.	Berkshire.
B.-G., or Brig.-Gen.	Brigadier-General.
B.-G.G.S.	Brigadier-General General Staff.
B.-G.R.A.	Brigadier-General Royal Artillery (Commander of the Artillery of the Corps).
B.-G.R.E.	Brigadier-General Royal Engineers.
B.-M.	Brigade-Major.
Bn. (Bns.)	Battalion (Battalions).
Border.	Border Regiment.
Bty. (Bties).	Battery (Batteries).
Bucks.	Buckinghamshire.
B.W.I.	British West Indies Regiment.

C.

Capt.	Captain.
Cav.	Cavalry.
Cdn.	Canadian.
Cdr.	Commander.
C.E.	Chief Engineer.
C.E.D.	Corps Expéditionnaire des Dardanelles.
C.E.O.	Corps Expéditionnaire d'Orient.
C.H.A.	Commander of Corps Heavy Artillery.
C.G.S.	Chief of the General Staff.
Ches.	Cheshire.
C.I.G.S.	Chief of the Imperial General Staff.
C.-in-C.	Commander-in-Chief.
Col.	Colonel.
Coll.	Colonial.
Comp.	Composite.
Conn. Rgrs.	Connaught Rangers.
Coy. (Cos.)	Company (Companies).
C.R.E.	Commanding Royal Engineers.

D.

D.	Director.
D.A.C.	Divisional Ammunition Column.
D.-A.-D.	Deputy-Assistant-Director.
D.-A.-G.	Deputy-Adjutant-General.
D.-A. & Q.-M.-G.	Deputy-Adjutant & Quartermaster-General.
D.A.N.	Détachement d'Armée du Nord
D.C.L.I.	Duke of Cornwall's Light Infantry.
D.-D.	Deputy-Director.
D.-D.M.S.	Deputy-Director Medical Services.
D.-D.V.S.	Deputy-Director Veterinary Services.
Devon.	Devonshire.
Detnt.	Detachment.
D.F.P.S.	Détachement Français de Palestine et Syrie.
D.G.	Dragoon Guards.
Dgn. (Dgns.)	Dragoon (Dragoons).
Dismtd.	Dismounted.
Div.	Division.
D.L.I.	Durham Light Infantry
D.L.O.	Duke of Lancaster's Own Yeomanry.
D.M.C.	Desert Mounted Corps.
Dorset	Dorsetshire.
D.-Q.-M.-G.	Deputy-Quartermaster General.

E.

E.E.F.	Egyptian Expeditionary Force.
E.F.	Expeditionary Force.
E.-in-C.	Chief Engineer (General Headquarters).
E. York.	East Yorkshire Regiment.

F.

Fd.	Field.
Fd. Amb.	Field Ambulance.
Fr.	French

G.

Garr.	Garrison.
Gds.	Guards.
G.H.Q.	General Headquarters.
G.O.C.	General Officer Commanding.
G.O.C.-in-C.	General Officer Commanding-in-Chief.
Gordon H.	Gordon Highlanders.
G.Q.G.	Grand Quartier Général des Armées Françaises.
G.Q.G.A.	Grand Quartier Général des Armées Alliées en France.
G.R.O.	General Routine Order.
G.S.	General Staff.
G.S.O.1.	General Staff Officer (1st Grade).

H.

H., or How.	Howitzer.
H.A., or Hy.Arty.	Heavy Artillery.
H.A.C.	Honourable Artillery Company.

ix

H.A.G.	... ...	Heavy Artillery Group.
Hants.	... ...	Hampshire.
H.A.R.	... ...	Heavy Artillery Reserve.
Herts.	... ...	Hertfordshire.
H.F.	... ...	Home Forces.
H.Q.	... ...	Headquarters.
Hsrs.	... ...	Hussars.
Hy.	... ...	Heavy.

I

I.	... ...	Intelligence.
I.-G.	... ...	Inspector-General.
Impl.	... ...	Imperial.
Ind.	... ...	Indian.
Inf.	... ...	Infantry.
I.S.	... ...	Imperial Service.
It.	... ...	Italian.

K.

King's	... ...	King's (Liverpool Regiment).
K.O.	... ...	King's Own (Royal Lancaster Regiment).
K.O.S.B.	... ...	King's Own Scottish Borderers.
K.O.Y.L.I.	... ...	King's Own (Yorkshire Light Infantry).

L.

L., or Lt.	... ...	Light (Whippets, if referring to Tank Bns.)
L.A.	... ...	Light Armoured.
L.C.	... ...	Light Car.
L.F. (or Lanc. Fus.)		Lancashire Fusiliers.
L.G.	... ...	Lewis Gun.
L.H.	... ...	Light Horse.
Lanc.	... ...	Lancashire.
Lanc. Fus. Bde.	...	Lancashire Fusilier Brigade.
Lcrs.	... ...	Lancers.
Leicester.	... ...	Leicestershire.
Lieut.-General.	...	Lieutenant-General.
L. of C.	... ...	Line of Communications.
Lond.	... ...	London.
Lt.-Col.	... ...	Lieutenant-Colonel.

M.

M.E.F.	... ...	Mediterranean Expeditionary Force.
M.G.C.(H.B.)	...	Machine-Gun Corps (Heavy Branch).
M.-G.G.S.	... ...	Major-General General Staff.
M.G.O.	... ...	Machine-Gun Officer.
M.-G.R.A. (Army).		Major-General Royal Artillery (G.O.C. R.A. of Army).
M.-G.R.A. (G.H.Q.).		Major-General Royal Artillery (of Expeditionary Force).
M.M.G.	... ...	Motor-Machine-Gun.
M.O.	... ...	Medical Officer.
M.S.	... ...	Medical Services.
Maj.	... ...	Major.
Maj.-Gen.	... ...	Major-General.
m.g.	... ...	machine gun.
M.G. Sqdn.	...	Machine-Gun Squadron.
Middx.	... ...	Middlesex Regiment.
Mk.	... ...	Mark.
Mn.	... ...	Midnight.
Mtd.	... ...	Mounted.
Mtn.	... ...	Mountain.

N.

N.F.	... ...	Northumberland Fusiliers.
N.Z.	... ...	New Zealand.
N.Z.M.R.	... ...	New Zealand Mounted Rifles.
Norf.	... ...	Norfolk.
North'n.	... ...	Northamptonshire Regiment.
Notts.	... ...	Nottinghamshire.

O.

O.	... ...	Operations.
O.B.	... ...	Order of Battle.
O.S.	... ...	Ordnance Services.

x

opp.	... ...	opposite.
Oxf.	... ...	Oxfordshire.

P.

P.	... ...	Pioneers.
-pdr.	... ...	-pounder.
Pltn. (Pltns.)	...	Platoon (Platoons).
Port.	... ...	Portuguese.

Q.

Q.-F.	... ...	Quick-Firer.
Q.-M.-G.	... ...	Quartermaster-General.
Q.O.	... ...	Queen's Own.

R.

R.	... ...	Royal.
R.A.	... ...	Royal Artillery.
R.A.F.	... ...	Royal Air Force.
R.A.M.C.	... ...	Royal Army Medical Corps.
R.B.	... ...	Rifle Brigade.
R.D.F.	... ...	Royal Dublin Fusiliers.
R.E.	... ...	Royal Engineers.
R.F.	... ...	Royal Fusiliers.
R.F.A.	... ...	Royal Field Artillery.
R.F.C.	... ...	Royal Flying Corps.
R.G.A.	... ...	Royal Garrison Artillery.
R.H.A.	... ...	Royal Horse Artillery.
R.M.	... ...	Royal Marines.
R.M.F.	... ...	Royal Munster Fusiliers.
R.M.L.I.	... ...	Royal Marine Light Infantry.
R.M..M.C.	... ...	*Régiment mixte de marche de Cavalerie.*
R.N.A.C.D.	...	Royal Naval Armoured-Car Detachment.
R.N.A.S.	... ...	Royal Naval Air Service.
R.S.	... ...	Royal Scots (Lothian Regiment).
R.W.F.	... ...	Royal Welch Fusiliers.
Regt.	... ...	Regiment.
Régt.	... ...	*Régiment.*
Rgrs.	... ...	Rangers.
Rif.	... ...	Rifles.
R.Innis.F.	... ...	Royal Inniskilling Fusiliers.
R.N.Div.	... ...	Royal Naval Division.
R.Sec.	... ...	Right Section.

S.

S. & M.	... ...	Sappers & Miners.
S. & T.	... ...	Supply & Transport.
S.S.O.	... ...	Senior Staff Officer.
S.W.B.	... ...	South Wales Borderers.
S.Afr.	... ...	South African.
Sco. Rif.	... ...	The Cameronians (Scottish Rifles).
Sea.H.	... ...	Seaforth Highlanders.
Sec.	... ...	Section.
Ser.	... ...	Service.
Sqdn.	... ...	Squadron.
Stn.	... ...	Station.

T.

T.M.	... ...	Trench Mortar.
Tempy.	... ...	Temporary.
Terrtl.	... ...	Territorial.
Tpt.	... ...	Transport.

U

U.K.	... ...	United Kingdom.

V.

V.S.	... ...	Veterinary Services.

W.

War.	... ...	Warwickshire.
Wh.	... ...	Whippets (Light Tanks).
Worc.	... ...	Worcestershire.

Y.

Y. & L.	... ...	York & Lancaster Regiment.
Yeo.	... ...	Yeomanry.

THE ARMY COUNCIL
1914—1918

SECRETARY OF STATE FOR WAR[1].	CHIEF OF THE IMPERIAL GENERAL STAFF.	ADJUTANT-GENERAL TO THE FORCES.
[31 March, 1914]. Rt. Hon. H. H. ASQUITH,[4] K.C., M.P.	[6 April, 1914]. General Sir C. W. H. DOUGLAS, G.C.B., A.D.C. (died, 25/10/14).	[9 April, 1914]. Lieut.-Gen. Sir H. C. SCLATER, K.C.B.
6 Aug., 1914. Field-Marshal Rt. Hon. EARL KITCHENER OF KHARTOUM, K.G., K.P., G.C.B., O.M., G.C.S.I., G.C.M.G., G.C.I.E. (lost at sea, 5/6/1916).	25 Oct., 1914. Lieut.-Gen. Sir J. WOLFE MURRAY, K.C.B.	22 Feb., 1916. Lieut.-Gen. Sir C. F. N. MACREADY, K.C.B., K.C.M.G.
7 July, 1916. Rt. Hon. D. LLOYD GEORGE,[5] M.P.	23 Dec., 1915. General Sir W. R. ROBERTSON, K.C.B., K.C.V.O., D.S.O.	11 Sept., 1918. Lieut.-Gen. Sir G. M. W. MACDONOGH, K.C.M.G., C.B.
11 Dec., 1916. Rt. Hon. EARL OF DERBY, K.G., G.C.V.O., C.B.	19 Feb., 1918. General Sir H. H. WILSON, K.C.B., D.S.O.	
20 April, 1918. Rt. Hon. VISCOUNT MILNER, G.C.B., G.C.M.G.		

DIRECTOR-GENERAL OF MILITARY AERONAUTICS.[7]	DEPUTY-CHIEF OF THE IMPERIAL GENERAL STAFF.[8]	[15 January,
22 Feb., 1916. Lieut.-Gen. Sir D. HENDERSON, K.C.B., D.S.O.	23 Dec., 1915. Maj.-Gen. R. D. WHIGHAM, C.B., D.S.O.	
18 Oct., 1917 } Maj.-Gen. J. M. SALMOND, –31 March, 1918 } C.M.G., D.S.O.	29 April, 1918. Maj.-Gen. C. H. HARINGTON, C.B., D.S.O.	
NOTE—On 1/4/18 the ROYAL AIR FORCE was established by the amalgamation of the ROYAL FLYING CORPS and the ROYAL NAVAL AIR SERVICES.		

[1] President of t
[2] Vice-President f
[3] Finance Memr.
[4] Prime Ministe
[5] Appointed Pre
[6] Also Secretary f

ADDED TO THE ARMY COUNC-

[7] On 22 Febru.
[8] On 15 Decemr.
[9] On 10 Febru.
[10] On 4 May, 1

2

QUARTERMASTER-GENERAL TO THE FORCES.	MASTER-GENERAL OF THE ORDNANCE.	PARLIAMENTARY UNDER-SECRETARY OF STATE FOR WAR.[2]	FINANCIAL SECRETARY[3].
[April, 1914]. Maj.-Gen. Sir J. S. Cowans, K.C B., M.V.O. [Sept., 1915. Lieut.-Gen. Sir J. S. Cowans, K.C.B., M.V.O.	[8 Feb., 1913]. Maj.-Gen. Sir S. B. Von Donop, K.C.B. 4 Dec., 1916. Maj.-Gen. Sir W. T. Furse, K.C.B., D.S.O.	[14 June, 1912]. Rt. Hon. H. J. Tennant, M.P. 7 July, 1916. Rt. Hon. Earl of Derby, K.G., G.C.V.O., C.B. 14 Dec., 1916. Rt. Hon. I. Macpherson, M.P.	[14 June, 1912]. Rt. Hon. H T. Baker, M.P. 19 June, 1915. Rt. Hon. H. W. Forster, M.P.

SECRETARY.	DIRECTOR-GENERAL OF MOVEMENTS AND RAILWAYS.[9]	SURVEYOR-GENERAL OF SUPPLY.[10]
[1914]. Sir R. H. Brade,[6] K.C.B.	10 Feb., 1917. Sir W. G. Granet, Knt. 21 March, 1918. Sir S. Fay, Knt.	4 May, 1917. A. Weir, Esq.

NES.

Army Council.
  the Army Council.

8/4/1908–4/12/1916.
  Minister, 7/12/1916.
  the War Office.

DURING THE GREAT WAR :—

1916.
.1915.
1917.

G. H. Q.s

HOME FORCES*
G.H.Q.

COMMANDER-IN-CHIEF

(H.Q.—Horse Guards, Whitehall).

5 August, 1914	General Sir I. S. M. HAMILTON.**
13 March, 1915	General Sir H. M. L. RUNDLE.
19 December, 1915	Field-Marshal Viscount FRENCH.***
30 May, 1918	General Sir W. R. ROBERTSON.

M.-G.G.S.

5 Aug., 1914...Maj.-Gen. G. F. ELLISON.
14 July, 1915...Col. A. HINDE.
19 Dec., 1915 ⎱
—12 May 1918 ⎰ Maj.-Gen. F. C. SHAW.†

G.S.O.1.

5 Aug., 1914...Col. C. ROSS.
30 Dec., 1914...Maj. F. G. FULLER.
17 June, 1915 ⎱
—14 July 1915 ⎰ Maj. A. HINDE.

C.G.S.

4 June, 1918...Maj.-Gen. C. F. ROMER.

B.-G.G.S.

19 Dec., 1915...Br.-Gen. H. C. LOWTHER.
4 Oct., 1917...Maj.-Gen. H. C. LOWTHER.

D.-A.-G.

5 Aug., 1914...Col. Sir H. A. W.
JOHNSON, Bt. (A.-A.-G.)
29 May, 1915...Br.-Gen. Sir H. A. W.
JOHNSON, Bt.

D.-Q.-M.-G.

5 Aug., 1914...Br.-Gen. S. H. WINTER.
15 March, 1915...Br.-Gen. C. W.
GARTSIDE-SPAIGHT.

D.-A. & Q.-M.-G.

19 Dec., 1915	Br.-Gen. F. R. C. CARLETON.
31 May, 1916 ... ... ⎱	
—20 July, 1918 ⎰	Maj.-Gen. H. A. L. TAGART.

D.-A.-G.

21 July, 1918...Br.-Gen. E. R.
FITZPATRICK.

D.-Q.-M.-G.

21 July, 1918...Br.-Gen. H. A. JONES.

Q.-M.-G.

1 September, 1918 ... ... Maj.-Gen. G. F. ELLISON.

---

* From August, 1914—December, 1915 it was called G.H.Q. Central Force ; then until June, 1916 it was G.H.Q. Forces at Home ; thence onward, until August, 1918, it was G.H.Q. Home Forces, and from August, 1918, it was G.H.Q. Forces in Great Britain. From December, 1915, until it was dissolved in March, 1916, Central Force was a separate command.
** Became G.O.C. M.E.F. (Gallipoli) on 11/3/1915.
*** Became Governor-General of Ireland on 9/5/1918.
† Became G.O.C.-in-C. Forces in Ireland on 13/5/1918.

Inspector-General R.A.

11 Jan., 1917...Maj.-Gen. C. C. Van
STRAUBENZEE.
9 July, 1918...Maj.-Gen. G. McK.
FRANKS.

Inspectors R. H. & R.F.A.

24 Oct., 1915 { Maj.-Gen. J. M. S.
BRUNKER,
Br.-Gen. R. W. BREEKS.
20 April, 1916...Maj.-Gen. J. M. S.
BRUNKER.
20 July, 1916 { Maj.-Gen. J. M. S.
BRUNKER,
Br.-Gen. R. F. FOX.
31 Oct., 1917...Maj.-Gen. Sir J. M. S.
BRUNKER.
9 Aug., 1918...Br.-Gen. D. J. M.
FASSON.

Inspector R.G.A.

24 Oct., 1915...Br.-Gen. E. G. NICHOLLS.
6 Feb., 1917...Br.-Gen. P. de S. BURNEY.
21 Dec., 1917...Br.-Gen. C. J. PERCEVAL.

Inspector of Artillery & A.-A. Artillery.

17 April, 1915...Br.-Gen. B. F. DRAKE.

Chief Engineer.

22 Oct., 1914...Maj.-Gen. R. M. RUCK.
28 June, 1917...Br.-Gen. S. H. POWELL.

Inspector R.E.

18 Nov., 1915...Br.-Gen. A. W. ROPER.

Staff Officer for Emergency Measures.

25 April, 1917...Maj.-Gen. E. O. HAY.

Director Army Signals.

[14 July, 1913] Br.-Gen. A. J. M.
OGILVIE.

D.-D. Army Signals.

5 August, 1914
—Dec., 1915 } ... ... Col. R. L. HIPPISLEY.

6 May, 1918 ... ... Br.-Gen. R. H. H. BOYS.

D. Medical Services.

5 Aug., 1914...Maj.-Gen. J. G. MacNEECE.
April, 1916...Maj.-Gen. Sir T. J.
GALLWEY.
27 Jan., 1918...Maj.-Gen. J. J. GERRARD.
10 Aug., 1918...Col. H. A. HINGE.

A.-D. Veterinary Services.

5 Aug., 1914...Col. C. RUTHERFORD.
June, 1916...Lt.-Col. R. H. HOLMES.
24 March, 1918...Col. R. H. HOLMES.

A.-D. Supplies.

5 Aug., 1914...Col. H. G. MORGAN.
1 April, 1915 ⎱ Col. A. H. THOMAS
—Dec., 1915 ⎰   (A.-D.S. & T.).

———————

12 Dec., 1917...Lt.-Col. J. C. M. DORAN.

A.-D. Ordnance Services.

5 Aug., 1914...Col. T. W. HALE.
7 Oct., 1914...Col. R. CRAWFORD.
29 April, 1918 ⎰ Col. E. A. MOULTON-
              ⎱   BARRETT,
              ⎱ Col. M. H. KNAGGS.

Inspector-General of Communications.

29 Jan., 1915...Br.-Gen. Hon. R. A.
              MONTAGU-STUART-WORTLEY.
17 March, 1917...Br.-Gen. H. C. SUTTON.
8 Nov., 1917 ⎱ Maj.-Gen. G. F. ELLISON.
—31 Aug., 1918 ⎰

A.-D. Transport.

5 Aug., 1914 ⎱ Col. F. W. B. KOE.
—31 March, 1915 ⎰

D.-D. Railway Transport.

5 Aug., 1914...Col. J. W. PRINGLE.
March, 1918...Col. C. H. COWIE
              (Railway Adviser).

Embarkation Commandants.

5 Aug., 1914...Br.-Gen. A. B. HAMILTON
11 March, 1915...Br.-Gen. F. B
              MATTHEWS,
5 Sept., 1915...Br.-Gen. A. G.
              BALFOUR,
26 Jan., 1916...Br.-Gen. A. W.
              FORBES.

BRITISH ARMIES IN FRANCE
G.H.Q.

COMMANDER-IN-CHIEF.

5 August, 1914	Field-Marshal Sir J. D. P. FRENCH.
Noon, 19 December, 1915 ...	General Sir D. HAIG.
1 January, 1917	Field-Marshal Sir D. HAIG.

Military Secretary.

5 August, 1914	Col. Hon. W. LAMBTON.
6 September, 1915	Br.-Gen. H. C. LOWTHER.
27 December, 1915	Br.-Gen. H. H. DUKE OF TECK.*
8 May, 1916	Maj.-Gen. W. E. PEYTON.
22 March, 1918	Maj.-Gen. H. G. RUGGLES-BRISE.

Chief of the General Staff

5 Aug., 1914...Lt.-Gen. Sir A. J. MURRAY.
25 Jan., 1915...Lt.-Gen. Sir W. R. ROBERTSON.**
22 Dec., 1915...Lt.-Gen. Sir L. E. KIGGELL.
24 Jan., 1918...Lt.-Gen. Hon. Sir H. A. LAWRENCE.

M.-G.G.S.

5 Aug., 1914 ⎱ Maj.-Gen. H. H.
25 Jan., 1915 ⎰ WILSON.***
15 Feb., 1918...Maj.-Gen. G. P. DAWNAY.
14 Mar., 1918...Maj.-Gen. J. H. DAVIDSON (M.-G.G.S.—O.)

Deputy-Chief G.S.

26 Jan., 1915...Br.-Gen. E. M. PERCEVAL (Sub-Chief).
17 July, 1915...Br.-Gen. R. D. WHIGHAM (Sub-Chief).
22 Dec., 1915 ⎱ Maj-Gen. R. H. K. BUTLER
–25 Feb., 1918 ⎰ (Deputy-Chief).

M.-G.G.S. (Staff Duties)

14 March, 1918...Maj.-Gen. G. P. DAWNAY.

---

* Created Marquess of Cambridge on 16/7/17, and took the surname of Cambridge.

** Became C.I.G.S. on 23/12/15.

*** From 26/1/15–21/12/15 Maj.-Gen. H. H. Wilson[1] was Chief Liaison Officer with General Foch, who commanded *Groupe Provisoire du Nord;* this *Groupe* on 13/6/15 was redesignated *Groupe d'Armées du Nord.*[2]

[1] Became Lieut.-General on 18/2/15. On 22/12/15 General Wilson took over the command of IV Corps.

[2] General Foch held this command from 4/10/14–26/12/16.

G.H.Q. (FRANCE)

B.-G.G.S. (O.a).

7 Nov., 1914...Br.-Gen. G. M. HARPER.
20 Feb., 1915...Br.-Gen. F. B. MAURICE.
22 Dec., 1915...Br.-Gen. J. H. DAVIDSON.
14 Mar., 1918...Br.-Gen. J. G. DILL.

B.-G.G.S. (O.b).

28 July, 1915...Lt.-Col. R. HUTCHISON
(G.S.O.I.—O.b.).
2 Feb., 1916...Br.-Gen. J. T. BURNETT-
STUART.
4 Feb., 1917...Br.-Gen. K. WIGRAM.
30 Sept., 1918...Br.-Gen. W. ROBERTSON.

B.-G.G.S. (Intelligence).

5 Aug., 1914...Col. G. M. W. MACDONOGH
(G.S.O.1—I.d.).
7 Nov., 1914...Br.-Gen. G. M. W.
MACDONOGH.
3 Jan., 1915...Br.-Gen. J. CHARTERIS.
24 Jan., 1918...Br.-Gen. E. W. COX
(drowned, 26/8/18).
16 Sept., 1918...Br.-Gen. G. S. CLIVE.

B.-G.G.S. (Training).

30 Jan., 1917...Br.-Gen. A. SOLLY-
FLOOD.
15 Oct., 1917...Br.-Gen. C. BONHAM-
CARTER.
15 July, 1918...Col. D. J. C. K. BERNARD
(A.-D.—Training).
2 Aug., 1918...Col. H. F. BAILLIE
(A.-D.—Training).

Adjutant-General.

5 Aug., 1914...Maj.-Gen. Sir C. F. N.
MACREADY.
22 Feb., 1916...Lt.-Gen. G. H. FOWKE.

Quartermaster-General.

5 Aug., 1914...Maj.-Gen. Sir W. R.
ROBERTSON.
27 Jan., 1915...Lt.-Gen. R. C.
MAXWELL.
23 Dec., 1917...Lt.-Gen. TRAVERS E.
CLARKE.

Director-General (Transportation).
(Put under Q.-M.-G., June 1918).

20 October, 1916 ... ... Maj.-Gen. Sir ERIC GEDDES (I.-G. Transportation, France),
3 December, 1916 ... ... Maj.-Gen. Sir ERIC GEDDES.
7 June, 1917 ... ... Maj.-Gen. P. A. M. NASH.
19 March, 1918 ... ... Maj.-Gen. S. D' A. CROOKSHANK.

M.-G.R.A.

5 Aug., 1914...Maj.-Gen. W. F. L.
LINDSAY.
25 Jan., 1915...Maj.-Gen. J. P. DUCANE.
12 Dec., 1915...Maj.-Gen. J. E. W.
HEADLAM.
28 May, 1916...Maj.-Gen. J. F. N. BIRCH.

A.-D. (A.-A.)*

Nov., 1917...Lt.-Col. N. W. WEBBER
(G.S.O.1—A.-A.).
30 Mar., 1918...Br.-Gen. C. EVANS
(B.-G.G.S.—A.-A.).
18 July, 1918...Col. V. M. C. NAPIER.

B.-G.R.A.

15 April, 1918...Br.-Gen. C. G. PRITCHARD.

A.-D. of Artillery.

7 Nov., 1916...Col. C. W. SCOTT.
6 Mar., 1918...Col. J. T. DREYER.

---

* The A.-A. Artillery available at G.H.Q. was No. 14 Sec. (2, 13-pdrs.) and No. 75 Sec. (2, 3″ A.-A. guns). The A.-A. School of Gunnery was also in the G.H.Q. area.

Engineer-in-Chief.
5 Aug., 1914...Br.-Gen. G. H. FOWKE
(B.-G.R.E.)
20 April, 1915...Maj.-Gen. G. H. FOWKE.
5 Mar., 1916...Maj.-Gen. S. R. RICE.
1 Nov., 1917...Maj.-Gen. G. M. HEATH.

Director of Gas Services.
7 Mar., 1916...Br.-Gen. H. F. THUILLIER.
17 June, 1917...Br.-Gen. C. H. FOULKES
(Also Commdg. Special Bde.).

Inspector-General of Training
3 July, 1918...Lt.-Gen. Sir F. I. MAXSE.

Director of Supplies.
5 Aug., 1914...Br.-Gen. C. W. KING.
27 Jan., 1915...Br.-Gen. E. E. CARTER.

Director of Transport.
5 Aug., 1914...Br.-Gen. F. C. A. GILPIN.
30 Nov., 1914...Br.-Gen. W. G. B. BOYCE.

Director of Roads.
20 Oct., 1916...Br.-Gen. H. P. MAYBURY
(Depy.-Director).
26 April, 1917...Br.-Gen. H. P. MAYBURY.

Director, Army Signals.
5 Aug., 1914...Col. J. S. FOWLER.
26 Oct., 1914...Br.-Gen. J. S. FOWLER.
1 Jan., 1917...Maj.-Gen. J. S. FOWLER.

Inspector of Mines.
2 Jan., 1916...Br.-Gen. R. N. HARVEY.
4 Jan., 1918...Br.-Gen. D. S. MacINNES
(died, 23/5/18).
4 June, 1918...Br.-Gen. H. BIDDULPH.

Inspector M.G. Corps.
30 Mar., 1918...Br.-Gen. C. H. T. LUCAS
(B.-G.G.S.—M.G.s).
Sept., 1918...Br.-Gen. C. H. T. LUCAS.
Oct., 1918...Br.-Gen. L. F. RENNY.

Director Ordnance Services.
5 Aug., 1914...Br.-Gen. H. W. PERRY.
10 Oct., 1914...Br.-Gen. H. D. E. PARSONS.
1 June, 1918...Br.-Gen. Sir C. M. MATHEW.

Director of Railways.
5 Aug., 1914...Col. J. H. TWISS.
22 Nov., 1916 } Br.-Gen. W. D.
—2 May, 1917 } WAGHORN.

Director of Railway Traffic.
1 Mar., 1918...Br.-Gen. V. MURRAY
(Director of Transportation,
23/2/17—28/2/18).

G.H.Q. (FRANCE)

Director-General Medical Services
5 Aug., 1914...Maj.-Gen. T. P.
WOODHOUSE.
1 Jan., 1915...Lt.-Gen. Sir A. T. SLOGGETT.
1 June, 1918...Lt.-Gen. C. H. BURTCHAELL.

Director Veterinary Services.
5 Aug., 1914...Br.-Gen. J. MOORE.
1 Jan., 1918...Maj.-Gen. J. MOORE.

Director of Remounts.
5 August, 1914 ... ... Br.-Gen. F. S. GARRATT.

B.-G. Personal Services.
Sept., 1917...Col. J. B. WROUGHTON
(A.-A.-G.—P.S.).
10 Nov., 1917...Br.-Gen. J. B. WROUGHTON.

B.-G. Demobilization.
Oct., 1918 ...Br.-Gen. G. N. T.
SMYTH-OSBOURNE.

Paymaster-in-Chief.
5 Aug., 1914...Br.-Gen. C. A. BRAY.
1 Jan., 1916...Maj.-Gen. C. A. BRAY.

Director Army Postal Services.
5 Aug., 1914...Col. W. PRICE.
27 May, 1918...Br.-Gen. W. PRICE.

Director of Forestry.
1 May, 1916...Maj. G. M. OLDHAM.
14 July, 1916...Lt. Col. G. M. OLDHAM
(C.R.E Forests).
10 Mar., 1917...Br.-Gen. LORD LOVAT.

Director Hirings & Requisitions.
1 Jan., 1915...Lt.-Col. E. A. W.
COURTNEY (A.-D., Requisitions).
7 June, 1915...Col. E. A. W. COURTNEY
(D.-D., Requisitions).
21 Mar., 1916...Col. E. A. W. COURTNEY
(D., Requisitions).
10 May, 1918...Maj.-Gen. Rt. Hon. L. B.
FRIEND.

Director of Works.
5 Aug., 1914...Br.-Gen. A. M. STUART.
3 June, 1916...Maj.-Gen. A. M. STUART.

Director of Engineering Stores.
24 June, 1918...Br.-Gen. J. W. S. SEWELL.

Director of Docks.

20 Oct., 1916...Br.-Gen. R. L. WEDGWOOD.

Controller of Labour.

4 Dec., 1916...Br.-Gen. E. GIBB
(Director).
11 Feb., 1918...Col. E. G. WACE.

President Claims Commission.

23 June, 1916...Maj.-Gen. Rt. Hon. L. B.
FRIEND
(Also, from 10/5/18,
Director of Hirings &
Requisitions, q.v.).

British Mission with G.Q.G. des Armées Alliées en France.

12 April, 1918...Lt.-Gen. Sir J. P. DUCANE.

Director Inland Water Transport.

28 Dec., 1914...Lt.-Col. G. E. HOLLAND
(D.-D.).
Nov., 1915...Col. G. E. HOLLAND.
27 June, 1917...Br.-Gen. C. M. LUCK.

Controller of Salvage.

11 Feb., 1918...Br.-Gen. E. GIBB.

D.-A.-G. Base (3rd Echelon).

5 Aug., 1914...Maj.-Gen. E. R. C.
GRAHAM.

British Mission with G.Q.G. des Armées Françaises.

18 Aug., 1914...Lt.-Gen. Sir J. MAXWELL.
6 Sept., 1914...Br.-Gen. Hon. H.
YARDE-BULLER.
28 Dec., 1916...Br.-Gen. G. S. CLIVE.
17 Mar., 1917...General Sir H. H.
WILSON.
26 June, 1917...Br.-Gen. G. S. CLIVE.
16 Sept., 1918...Br.-Gen. F. W. L. S. H.
CAVENDISH.

NOTE—The Heads of the French Mission (attached to G.H.Q. France) from August, 1914 until 11 November, 1918 were, in succession : Colonel Huguet*; Colonel des Vallières ; Colonel de Bellaigue de Bughas ; and Général de Division de Laguiche.
* Colonel Huguet left London with G.H.Q. on 14/8/14, and remained until December, 1915.

G.H.Q. (FRANCE)

L. of C. Area.

Inspector-General of Communications.

5 August, 1914	Lt.-Gen. F. S. ROBB.
19 September, 1914	Lt.-Gen. R. C. MAXWELL.
27 January, 1915	Lt.-Gen. F. T. CLAYTON.
2 December, 1916	Lt.-Gen. J. J. ASSER (Cdr., L. of C. Area).

August 1914*.

No. 1 Base.

5 Aug., 1914...Col. F. J. PARKER.

No. 2 Base.

5 Aug., 1914...Col. A. G. MARRABLE.

No. 3 Base.

5 Aug., 1914...Col. J. J. ASSER.

Advd. Base (Amiens).

5 Aug., 1914...Col. A. G. THOMSON.

1914*—1918.

Boulogne Base.

13 Oct., 1914...Col. J. J. ASSER.
18 July, 1915...Col. H. W. WILBERFORCE.
6 July, 1917...Br.-Gen. H. W. WILBERFORCE.

Calais Base.

24 April, 1915...Col. J. S. NICHOLSON.
2 Dec., 1916...Col. H. D' A. P. TAYLOR.
7 Dec., 1917...Br.-Gen. R. L. ADLERCRON.
22 Jan., 1918...Br.-Gen. F. W. RADCLIFFE.

Le Havre Base.

13 Oct., 1914...Col. H. B. WILLIAMS.
23 Nov., 1914...Br.-Gen. H. B. WILLIAMS.
18 July, 1915...Br.-Gen. J. J. ASSER.
3 June, 1916...Maj.-Gen. J. J. ASSER.
2 Dec., 1916...Br.-Gen. J. S. NICHOLSON.

Rouen Base.

13 Oct., 1914...Col. A. G. MARRABLE.
23 Nov., 1914...Br.-Gen. A. G. MARRABLE.
8 Dec., 1916...Br.-Gen. F. J. DE GEX.
April, 1917...Br.-Gen. C. L. MACNAB.
31 Oct., 1917...Br.-Gen. L. F. PHILIPS.

Advanced Base.

13 Oct., 1914...Lt.-Col. F. C. L. HULTON.
3 June, 1916...Col. F. C. L. HULTON.

Marseilles Base.

3 Nov., 1914...Col. G. F. N. TINLEY.
3 Mar., 1918...Br.-Gen. R. C. B. LAWRENCE.

---

* British Bases on the North Coast of France became unsafe during the Retreat from Mons, and St. Nazaire (on the Loire) was selected on 29/8/14 to replace the north coast Bases. On 3/9/14 No. 6 Base Depot left Le Havre and arrived at St. Nazaire on 5/9/14. Col. P. Bulman became Commandant at St. Nazaire.

Subsequent operations made it safe on 13/10/14 to reopen the Bases—on the North Coast of France—Le Havre, Boulogne, and Rouen.

NOTE—There were also Bases at Amiens, Brest, Cherbourg, Dieppe, and Dunkirk. Abancourt, Abbeville, Arras, Paris, and Trouville were L. of C. areas, and Étaples was an Administrative District.

BRITISH ARMIES IN FRANCE

BATTLES (WESTERN FRONT)

1914

23 & 24 August ... ... **Battle of Mons** [I & II Corps, Cav. Div., 5th Cav. Bde., & 19th Inf. Bde.].

24 Aug –5 Sept. ... ... **RETREAT FROM MONS** [I, II, & III* Corps, Cav. Div.,* & 5th Cav. Bde.].

26 August ... ... **Battle of Le Cateau** [II Corps, with 4th Div. & 19th Inf. Bde. and Cav. Div.].

7–10 September ... ... **Battle of the Marne** [I, II, & III Corps, and 1st* & 2nd* Cav. Divs.].

12–15 September ... **Battle of the Aisne** [I, II, & III Corps, and 1st & 2nd Cav. Divs.].

4–10 October ... ... **Defence of Antwerp** [R.N. Div. & IV** Corps].

10 Oct.–2 Nov. ... ... **Battle of La Bassée** [II Corps & Indian Corps, and 2nd Cav. Bde., and Secunderabad Cav. Bde.].

12 Oct.–2 Nov. ... ... **Battle of Messines** [Cavalry Corps, *** and attached troops].

13 Oct.–2 Nov. ... ... **Battle of Armentières** [III Corps].

19 Oct.—22 Nov. ... **BATTLES OF YPRES** [I & IV Corps, and 2nd & 3rd Cav. Divs.].

NOTE—On the 26th December the British First Army and Second Army began to form in France.

---

* III Corps (4th Div. and 19th Inf. Bde.) formed in France on 31/8/14.
    The 6th Div. fought on the Aisne on 19 and 20/9/14, under I Corps ; but the division only joined III Corps in October, before the move to the North.
    On 6/9/14 the 3rd and 5th Cav. Bdes. were combined and placed under Br.-Gen. H. Gough ; on 13/9/14 the two brigades became the 2nd Cav. Div. under Major-General H. Gough. The Cavalry Division (less 3rd Cav. Bde.) became 1st Cav. Div. on 13/9/14.
** IV Corps (3rd Cav. Div. and 7th Div.) was formed in Belgium, on 5–10/10/14.
*** Cavalry Corps was formed in France on 10/10/14 ; and, at first, consisted of 1st and 2nd Cav. Divs.

1915

10–13 March	**Battle of Neuve Chapelle** [First Army].
22 April–25 May ...	**BATTLES OF YPRES** [Second Army].

---

9 May	**Battle of Aubers Ridge** [First Army].
15–25 May	**Battle of Festubert** [First Army].
25 Sept.–8 Oct.	**Battle of Loos** [First Army].

NOTE—On the 13th July the Third Army had been formed in France.

1916

NOTE—On the 5th February the Fourth Army was formed in France.

2–13 June	Battle of Mount Sorrel* [Cdn. & XIV Corps: Second Army].
1 July–18 November	**BATTLES OF THE SOMME** [Third, Fourth, & Reserve (later Fifth)** Armies].

---

* 1¾ miles south of Hooge.
** Reserve Army was formed in France on 22/5/16 (from H.Q. of Reserve Corps) ; and on 30/10/16 Reserve Army was renamed Fifth Army.

1917

11 Jan.–13 March ...	**Operations on the Ancre** [Fifth Army].
14 March–5 April	**German Retreat to the Hindenburg Line** [Third, Fourth, & Fifth Armies].
9 April–4 May	**BATTLES OF ARRAS** [First & Third Armies].

3–17 May	**Battle of Bullecourt** [Fifth Army].
7–14 June	**Battle of Messines** [Second Army].
21 June–18 November	**Operations on the Flanders Coast** [XV Corps : Fourth Army].
31 July–10 November	**BATTLES OF YPRES** [Second & Fifth Armies].

15–25 August	**Battle of Hill 70** [First Army].
20 Nov –3 Dec.	**BATTLE OF CAMBRAI** [Third Army].

1918

21 March–5 April ... **FIRST BATTLES OF THE SOMME** [First, Third, Fourth, & Fifth Armies].

9–29 April ... ... **BATTLES OF THE LYS** [First & Second Armies].

27 May–6 June ... ... **Battle of the Aisne** [IX Corps: under Sixth (Fr.) Army (until 29/5), then under Fifth (Fr.) Army].

THE ADVANCE TO VICTORY.

20 July—2 August ... **BATTLES OF THE MARNE** [XXII Corps: under Fifth (Fr.) Army].*

8–11 August ... ... **Battle of Amiens** [Fourth Army].

18 Aug.–6 Sept. ... **The Advance in Flanders** [Second & Fifth Armies].

21 Aug.–3 Sept. ... **SECOND BATTLES OF THE SOMME** [Third & Fourth Armies].

26 Aug.–3 Sept. ... **SECOND BATTLES OF ARRAS** [First & Third Armies].

12 Sept.–9 Oct. ... ... **BATTLES OF THE HINDENBURG LINE** [First, Third, & Fourth Armies].

9–12 October ... ... **Pursuit to the Selle** [First, Third, & Fourth Armies].

---

* 51st and 62nd Divs. acted directly under XXII; but the 15th and 34th Divs. attacked under French Tenth Army—15th in Fr. XX Corps and 34th in Fr. XXX Corps.

1918 *(Contd.)*

THE FINAL ADVANCE.

28 Sept.–11 Nov.   ...   **IN FLANDERS** [Second Army].

28 Sept.–2 Oct. ...   ...   **Battle of Ypres** [Second Army].

14–19 October   ...   ...   **Battle of Courtrai** [Second Army].

2 Oct.–11 Nov. ...   ...   **IN ARTOIS** [Fifth Army and VIII Corps, First Army].

17 Oct.–11 Nov.   ...   **IN PICARDY** [First, Third, & Fourth Armies].

17–25 October   ...   ...   **Battle of the Selle** [First, Third, & Fourth Armies].

1 & 2 November   ...   **Battle of Valenciennes** [First & Third Armies].

4 November   ...   ...   **Battle of the Sambre** [First, Third, & Fourth Armies].

11 November   ...   ...   **Capture of Mons** [First Army].

11 a.m., 11 NOVEMBER—ARMISTICE.

FRANCE
(WESTERN FRONT)

LOCATIONS

G.H.Q., B.E.F., and ADVD. G.H.Q.; G.Q.G., and G.Q.G.A.

	1914	1915	

G.H.Q., B.E.F.	London 5/8
	Embarked
	   3.30 p.m. 14/8
	Boulogne
	   5.15 p.m. 14/8
	Amiens 14/8
	Paris 15/8
	Le Cateau ... 16/8
	St. Quentin
	   6 p.m. 25/8
	Noyon 5 p.m. 26/8
	Compiègne
	   4.30 p.m. 28/8
	Dammartin ... 31/8
	Lagny 10 p.m. 1/9
	Melun 2/9
	Coulommiers ... 9/9
	Fère en Tardenois 12/9
	Abbeville 5 p.m. 8/10
	St. Omer ...13/10
		St. Omer
		
		Hazebrouck
		   28/4–28/5
		Merville 15–20/6
			St. Omer
			Montreuil
			(Pas de

	1914*	1915	
G.Q.G. DES ARMÉES FRANÇAISES (Of the North & North-East)	Vitry le François (Marne) ... 5/8 Bar sur Aube ... ... 31/8 Châtillon sur Seine ... ... 6/9 Romilly sur Seine ... ... 28/9 Chantilly (Oise) 29/11	Chantilly.	Chantilly.

	1914	1915	
G.Q.G. DES ARMÉES ALLIÉES EN FRANCE	....	....	

ARMISTICE

* COMMANDANTS-EN-CHIEF :—
  2/8/14—Général Joffre.
17/12/16—Général Nivelle.
17/5/17—Général Pétain.

1916	1917	1918
		Montreuil.
		G.H.Q. Train (Thourotte) 10 p.m., 6 & 7/3
		G.H.Q. Train (Curchy) 8 & 9/3
.30/3 (is). Beauquesne 27/6–23/11	Montreuil. Bavincourt 3 p.m. 22/4–6/6 G.H.Q. Train 6–8/6 (Godewaersvelde) Blendecques 9/6–18/11 Bavincourt. 19/11–3/12	G.H.Q. Train : ⎡ Wiry 8–18/8 ⎢ Boubers sur ⎢ Canche ⎢ 18/8–4/9 ⎨ Gouy ⎢ 25/9–14/10 ⎢ Bertincourt ⎢ 15/10–9/11 ⎢ Iwuy ⎣ 10–19/11

1916	1917	1918
	Chantilly. Beauvais (Oise) ... ... 10/1 Compiègne (Oise) 4/4	Compiègne. Provins ... ... 26/3 (Seine et Marne).

1916	1917	1918
		**
....	....	Beauvais (Oise) ... ... 29/3 Sarcus (Seine Inférieure) ... 7/4 Mouchy le Châtel (Oise) ... 1/6 Bombon (Seine et Marne) ... 5/6 Senlis (Oise) 18/10

A.M. 11/11/1918.

** On 26/3/18 Général Foch was appointed to co-ordinate the action of the Allied Armies on the Western Front ; on 3/4/18, in addition, he was directed to be responsible for the general strategy of the military operations ; and on 14/4/18 he was officially appointed " Général en Chief des Armées Alliées en France."

LOCATION OF ADVANCED G.H.Q.

Bavincourt	... ...	10 miles S.W. of Arras.
Beauquesne	... ...	5 miles S.S.E. of Doullens.
Bertincourt	... ...	5 miles E. of Bapaume.
Blendecques	... ...	2 miles S.S.E. of St. Omer.
Boubers sur Canche	...	3 miles W.N.W. of Frévent.
Curchy	... ...	2½ miles N.W. of Nesle.
Godewaersvelde	...	11 miles S.W. of Ypres.
Gouy	... ...	6 miles S.W. of Arras.
Hazebrouck	... ...	17 miles S.W. of Ypres.
Iwuy	....	5 miles N.E. of Cambrai.
Merville	_. ...	7 miles N.W. of Béthune.
Thourotte	... ...	5 miles N. of Compiègne.
Wiry	... ...	10 miles S. of Abbeville.

EGYPTIAN EXPEDITIONARY FORCE*
G.H.Q.

COMMANDER-IN-CHIEF.

[30 October, 1912]	Major-General Hon. J. H. G. BYNG.**
8 September, 1914	Lieut.-General Sir J. G. MAXWELL.**
27 October, 1915	General Sir C. C. MONRO.***
9 January, 1916	General Sir A. J. MURRAY.
Mn. 28 June, 1917	General Sir E. H. H. ALLENBY.

C.G.S.
27 Oct., 1915...Maj.-Gen. A. L. LYNDEN-BELL.

16 Sept., 1917...Maj.-Gen. L. J. BOLS.

B.-G.G.S.
23 Nov., 1915⎱
–2 June, 1916⎰ Br.-Gen. W. GILLMAN.

13 Aug., 1917...Br.-Gen. G. P. DAWNAY.
20 Feb., 1918...Br.-Gen. A. B. ROBERTSON.
16 April, 1918...Br.-Gen. W. H. BARTHOLOMEW.

B.-G.G.S. (I).
8 August, 1918   ... ...   Br. Gen. B. T. BUCKLEY.

A. & Q.

D.-A.-G.
23 Oct., 1915...Maj.-Gen. E. M. WOODWARD.
1 Feb., 1916...Lt.-Col. J. B. WELLS (acting).
9 Mar., 1916...Lt.-Col. C. P. SCUDAMORE (acting).
1 April, 1916...Lt.-Col. W. J. AINSWORTH (acting).
6 April, 1916...Maj.-Gen. J. ADYE.
23 Mar., 1918...Maj.-Gen. W. G. B. WESTERN.

D.-Q.-M.-G.
23 Oct., 1915...Maj.-Gen. W. CAMPBELL.

Assistant to D.-Q.-M.-G.
2 August, 1917   ... ...   Br.-Gen. E. F. O. GASCOIGNE.
27 January, 1918   ... ...   Br.-Gen. E. EVANS.

---

* This title was adopted on 20/3/1916, when General Sir A. J. Murray assumed command of the Mediterranean Expeditionary Force and the Force in Egypt.
** G.O.C. of the British Force in Egypt.
*** General Sir C. C. Monro left Alexandria on 11/1/16, and returned to France to command First Army, B.E.F. (4/2/16).

C

M.-G.R.A.

23 Nov., 1915...Maj.-Gen. S. C. U. SMITH.

E.-in-C.

23 Nov., 1915...Maj.-Gen. G. WILLIAMS.
14 May, 1916...Maj.-Gen. H. B. H. WRIGHT.

D. Army Signals.

23 November, 1915 ... ... Br.-Gen. M.G.E. BOWMAN-MANIFOLD.

Force in Egypt.

7 Jan., 1918...Maj.-Gen. H. D. WATSON.

Western Frontier Force*.

13 May, 1916...Lt.-Gen. Sir B. T. MAHON.
21 June, 1916...Maj.-Gen. Sir C. M. DOBELL.
19 Sept., 1916...Lt.-Gen. Sir C. M. DOBELL.
4 Oct., 1916...Maj.-Gen. W. A. WATSON.
6 Mar., 1917 ⎫
–21 Mar., 1918 ⎬ Br.-Gen. H. G. CASSON.

Coastal Section, Western Force.

22 Mar., 1917 ⎫
— Jan., 1918 ⎬ Br.-Gen. R. M. YORKE.

Southern Section, Western Force.

22 Mar., 1917...Col. R. W. H. WILLIAMS-WYNN.

Canal Zone.

— Sept., 1918...Br -Gen. A. H. O. LLOYD.

Desert Column.**

7 Dec., 1916...Lt.-Gen. Sir P. W. CHETWODE, Bt.
21 April, 1917 ⎫ Maj.-Gen. Sir H. G.
–2 Aug., 1917 ⎬ CHAUVEL.

Southern Canal Section.

4 Feb., 1917...Br.-Gen. P. C. PALIN.
25 June, 1917 ⎫ Br.-Gen. E. R. B.
— Mar., 1918 ⎬ MURRAY.

Eastern Force.***

18 Oct., 1916...Lt.-Gen. Sir C. M. DOBELL.
21 April, 1917 ⎫ Lt.-Gen. Sir P. W.
–2 Aug., 1917 ⎬ CHETWODE, Bt.

---

* Became Delta and Western Force on 6/3/17 ; ceased to exist on 21/3/18.
** The Staff of the Desert Column consisted of : Lt.-Col. V. M. Fergusson (G.S.O.1), Lt.-Col. E. F. Trew (A.-A. & Q.-M.-G.), Br.-Gen. A. D'A. King (B.-G., R.A.), and Br.-Gen. R. L. Waller (C.E. until 28/2/17 ; then Br.-Gen. R. E. M. Russell). Desert Column disappeared in August, 1917, on reorganization of E.E.F.
*** The Staff of Eastern Force consisted of : Br.-Gen. G. P. Dawnay (B.-G.G.S.), Br.-Gen. E. F. O. Gascoigne (D.-A. & Q.-M.-G.), Br.-Gen. A. H. Short (B.-G. R.A.), and Br.-Gen. E. Mc L. Blair (C.E. until 1/3/17 ; then Br.-Gen. R. L. Waller). Eastern Force disappeared in August, 1917, on reorganization of E.E.F.

D. Supplies & Transport.
23 Nov., 1915...Br.-Gen. F. W. B. KOE.
26 July, 1916...Br.-Gen. G. F. DAVIES.

D. Ordnance Services.
23 Nov., 1915...Br.-Gen. H. W. PERRY.
22 Aug., 1916...Br.-Gen. P. A.
BAINBRIDGE.

D. Works.
23 Nov., 1915...Br.-Gen. E. M. PAUL.

D. Labour.
16 Aug., 1917...Br.-Gen. R. C.
JELLICOE.

D.M.S.
23 Nov., 1915...Maj.-Gen. W. BABTIE, V.C.
17 Mar., 1916...Maj.-Gen. W. G. A.
BEDFORD (sick, 7/4/16).
11 April, 1916...Maj.-Gen. J. MAHER.
9 Oct., 1917...Maj.-Gen. A. E. C. KEBLE
(tempy.).
2 Feb., 1918...Maj.-Gen. W. T. SWAN.
19 Sept., 1918...Maj.-Gen. R. H. LUCE.

D.V.S.
7 Nov., 1915...Br.-Gen. E. R. C.
BUTLER.

D. Remounts.
23 October, 1915 ... ... Lt.-Col. V. R. HINE-HAYCOCK
(Asst.-Dir., acting).
28 October, 1915 ... ... Br.-Gen. C. L. BATES.

D. Railway Traffic.
7 Dec., 1915...Col. Sir G. B. MACAULEY.
10 April, 1917...Br.-Gen. Sir G. B.
MACAULEY.

D. Inland Water Transport.
10 Feb., 1917...Lt.-Col. W. H. COYSH
(A.-D.).
23 July, 1918...Col. W. N. BICKET
(D.-D.).
30 Oct., 1918...Br.-Gen. W. N. BICKET.

Training Directorate.
16 April, 1918 ... ... Br.-Gen. A. B. ROBERTSON.

Alexandria District.

9 Dec., 1915...Br.-Gen. R. C. BOYLE.

Sollum District.

15 July, 1916...Br.-Gen. H. W. HODGSON.

8 Feb., 1918...Br.-Gen. R. M. YORKE.

L. of C. Defences.

28 Jan., 1916...Maj.-Gen. W. A. WATSON.
4 Oct., 1916 ⎱
–6 Mar., 1917 ⎰ Br.-Gen. H. G. CASSON.

Levant Base.

Cdt. & I.G. Cmns. :
24 Dec., 1915...Lt.-Gen. E. A. ALTHAM.
15 Nov., 1916 ⎱ Lt.-Col. St. G. B.
–29 Jan., 1917 ⎰ ARMSTRONG (A.-A.-G.).

Palestine L. of C. Defences.

2 May., 1917 ⎱ Br.-Gen. H. D. WATSON.
–6 Jan., 1918 ⎰

Inspector, Palestine L. of C.

2 May, 1917...Br.-Gen. E. N. BROADBENT.

Military Governor, Jerusalem.

9 Dec., 1917...Br.-Gen. R. M. BORTON.
27 Dec., 1917...Col. RONALD STORRS.

Hejaz Operations.

6 Dec., 1916...Lt.-Col. T. E. LAWRENCE* (S.S.O.).

Occupied Enemy Territory Admn.

16 Jan., 1917...Br.-Gen. G. F. CLAYTON.
16 April, 1918...Maj.-Gen. Sir A. W. MONEY.

Chief Political Officer.

25 Mar., 1918...Br.-Gen. G. F. CLAYTON.

CYPRUS.

High Commissioner & C.-in-C.

5 August, 1914 ... ... Major Sir H. G. GOOLD-ADAMS.
January, 1915 ... ... Major Sir J. E. CLAUSON.

Commandant, Troops.

December, 1916 ... ... Col. Sir H. G. DIXON.
June, 1918 ... ... Maj. J. G. B. LETHBRIDGE.

---

* In April, 1918, became S.S.O. Northern Hejaz Operations. Lt.-Col. A. G. C. Dawnay was appointed G.S.O.1.H.Q. Hejaz Operations on 5/11/17.

Ordnance Base Depot, Alexandria.*

22 Feb., 1915...Br.-Gen. R. W. M.
JACKSON.

G.H.Q. (3rd Echelon).*

28 July, 1915...Br.-Gen. T. E. O'LEARY
(D.-A.-G.).
8 Mar., 1916...Lt.-Col. G. N. FITZJOHN
(A.-A.-G.).
6 April, 1916...Lt.-Col. C. P.
SCUDAMORE (A.-A.-G.).
10 Oct., 1917...Br.-Gen. C. P.
SCUDAMORE (D.-A.-G.).

Liaison Officer with War Office.

13 June, 1917...Lt.-Col. A. P. WAVELL.
29 Dec., 1917...Lt.-Col. A. C. M.
WATERFIELD.

Liaison Officer with French E.F.

29 March, 1916...Lt.-Col. G. E. TYRRELL.
7 July, 1916...Lt.-Col. E. L. STRUTT.
4 Nov., 1916 ⎱ Capt. I. M. SMITH
–9 Jan., 1918 ⎰ (with French Navy).

**Liaison Officer
with French Contingent.**

28 Dec., 1916...Lieut. G. J. A. MARC.
14 Feb., 1918...Maj. R. H. ST. MAUR.

**Liaison Officer
with Italian Contingent.**

June, 1917...Lieut. F. J. R. RODD.
29 April, 1918...Capt. R. B. MITFORD.
Aug., 1918...Lieut. J. D. O. MURRAY.

---

* Served both the Mediterranean Expeditionary Force and the Force in Egypt until 20/3/1916, when the Egyptian Expeditionary Force came into being.

G.H.Q., E.E.F.

LOCATION OF G.H.Q., E.E.F.*

4 August, 1914   ...   **Cairo.***

25 January, 1916   ...   **Ismailia.***

Noon, 23 October, 1916.   **Cairo.**

        [On 28/6/17 General Sir E. H. H. Allenby assumed Command of the E.E.F. General Allenby visited Khan Yunis (Palestine) on 27/7/17 ; Shellal and Rafa on 29/7/17 ; Deir el Balah on 30/7/17 ; Qantara on 31/7/17, and returned on the same day to Cairo.]

11 August, 1917   ...   **Kelab** (Palestine : 2 miles S.W. of Khan Yunis).

21 January, 1918   ...   **Bir Salem** (near Er Ramle).

Noon, 31 October, 1918.   **Armistice with Turkey came into force.**

---

   * Headquarters of the Force in Egypt, as well as of the M.E.F., until 20/3/16, when the Force in Egypt and the M.E.F. merged and were known henceforward as the E.E.F.

   oTE—It is 200 miles from Cairo to Khan Yunis, and 50 miles from Khan Yunis to Bir Salem.

EGYPTIAN EXPEDITIONARY FORCE

FORMATION.

In August, 1914, Turkey was still regarded by Egypt as the suzerain power, although for some years there had been a British occupation of the country. When war broke out between England and Germany on the 4th August* the British Force in Egypt was 1 Cavalry Regiment, 1 R.H.A. Battery, 1 Mountain Battery, R.G.A., 1 Field Company R.E., 4 Infantry Battalions, and detachments of A.S.C., R.A.M.C., A.V.C., A.O.C., and Military Mounted Police.** In addition, one Battalion*** and detachments of R.G.A., A.S.C., and R.A.M.C. were stationed at Khartoum, under the command of General Sir F. R. Wingate, Governor-General of the Anglo-Egyptian Sudan. This Battalion furnished half-a-company to garrison Cyprus.

Relations with Turkey soon became strained, and on the 30th October the Allies presented an ultimatum to her, and at the same time severed diplomatic relations. On the 5th November a formal declaration of war followed.

The Khedive of Egypt was openly pro-Turk, and he had been in Turkey since August, 1914. In order to secure Egypt and retain control over the all-important Suez Canal, the British Government deposed the Khedive on the 18th December, declared a protectorate over Egypt, and raised the Khedive's Uncle to the throne, with the title of Sultan of Egypt. At the same time the title of the British Representative was changed from Consul-General to High Commissioner.

Briefly, this was the sequence of events which led, as troops became available, to the gradual building-up of a considerable expeditionary force in this near-eastern theatre of war, and led in turn to Egypt, Sinai, and eventually Palestine and Syria becoming battle-grounds in the Great War.

At the end of August the Egyptian Camel Corps was moved to the eastern boundary to cover the Suez Canal. When early in September the Lahore Division passed through the Canal on its way from India to France it dropped the III Mountain Artillery Brigade and the Sirhind Infantry Brigade to reinforce the garrison of the Canal Zone. It became possible, therefore, to release the seasoned regular units which had formed the peace-time garrison, and they all returned to England and joined new divisions, which were assembling there, prior to reinforcing the B.E.F. on the Western Front.† On the 25th September, 42nd (East Lancashire) T.F. Division†† reached Alexandria. The division was sent to Egypt for two reasons: to strengthen the garrison and to complete its war-training. Some six weeks later the Indian troops allocated for the defence of Egypt

---

* Two days previously Germany and Turkey signed an offensive and defensive treaty.
** The units were: 3/Dragoon Gds., " T " Battery (XI Bde. R.H.A.), No. 7 Mtn. Bty. R.G.A No. 2 Fd. Coy. R.E., 2/Devon., 1/Worc., 2/North'n., and 2/Gordon H.
Since 30/10/12 the Force in Egypt had been commanded by Major-General Hon. J. H. G. Byng. On 8/9/14 Lieut.-General Sir John G. Maxwell took over command of the Force in Egypt and Maj.-Gen. Byng then returned to England, and proceeded to raise the 3rd Cavalry Division at Ludgershall; this Cavalry Division disembarked at Ostend on 8/10/14.
*** 1/Suffolk Regt.
† 3/Dgn. Gds. joined 3rd Cavalry Division; " T " R.H.A. and 2/Gordon H. the 7th Division; 2nd Fd. Coy. R.E., 2/Devon., 1/Worc., and 2/North'n. the 8th Division; and the 1/Suffolk the 28th Division.
†† Received the number 42nd on 26/5/15.

began to disembark at Suez : Imperial Service Cavalry Brigade, Bikanir Camel Corps, Lucknow Infantry Brigade (from Lucknow Division), and the Imperial Service Infantry Brigade. This released the Sirhind Infantry Brigade, which left to rejoin the Lahore Division in France. The Indian garrison in Egypt was now organized in two divisions (10th & 11th Indian), and the defence of the Canal was entrusted to them and the Imperial Service Cavalry Brigade, together with 3 mountain batteries from India, two field artillery brigades of the 42nd Division, a pack-gun battery from the Egyptian Army, and the guns of those English and French warships which were anchored in the canal to serve as floating batteries. Early in December a partly-trained Australian and New Zealand contingent also reached Egypt and reinforced the hurriedly assembled garrison.

Meanwhile, during November, 1914, the Turks occupied el 'Arish (in Sinai), and the immediate threat to the Canal line was only too clear ; whilst in Southern Arabia the opposing forces had already clashed. From this time onwards the British forces which were assembled in Egypt were continuously engaged : at first in localized operations to cover that country and the Canal Zone ; then, in 1917, in delivering those blows which, by the end of the following year, resulted in Turkey suing for peace.

BATTLES AND ENGAGEMENTS.

1914

Operations in the Bab el Mandeb.

10 November ... ... **Capture of Sheikh Sa'id** [29th Ind. Inf. Bde. & 23/Sikh P.].

1915

DEFENCE OF EGYPT.

3 & 4 February ... **Actions on the Suez Canal** [10th Ind. & 11th Ind. Divs., N.Z. Inf. Bde., Impl. Ser. Cav. Bde., Herts. Yeo., West-minster Dgns., A Sqdn. D.L.O. Yeo., Bikanir Camel Corps, III E. Lanc. R.F.A., 5th Egyptian Bty., 1st E. Lanc. Fd. Coy., E. Lanc. Sig. Coy., with 1 Flight R.F.C., & 1 French Seaplane Flight.].

Operations in the Bab el Mandeb.

14 & 15 June ... ... **Turkish Attack on Perim** [Detnt., 23/Sikh Pioneers].

Defence of Aden.

4 and 5 July ... ... **Lahaj** (20 miles N.N.W. of Aden), [Aden Troop, Camel Bty. R.G.A., 23/Fortress Coy., 3/S. and M., S.W.B. (Brecknock Bn.), 23/Sikh P., 126/Baluchis].

20 July ... ... **Sheikh 'Othman** (7 miles N.N.W. of Aden) [From Egypt : B.Bty., H.A.C., Berks. Bty., 28th Ind. Inf. Bde. ; and from Aden : Aden Troop, Camel Bty., 23/Fortress Coy., and 3/S. & M.].

Western Frontier—Senussi Operations.

11–13 December ... **Wadi Senab** [Notts. Bty., 2/Comp. Yeo. Regt., R.N.A.C.D., 6/R.S., and 15/Sikhs.].

25 December ... ... **Wadi Majid** [Notts. Bty., Comp. Yeo. Bde., 2/8/Middx., 15/Sikhs, 1st N.Z. Rif. Bde.].

---

* This table of battles and engagements, which embraces some seven different theatres of activity, is given chronologically, in order to emphasize the numerous demands made on G.H.Q. E.E.F. to meet the calls of the wide-spread local operations. This table also emphasizes the change-over from merely defensive operations to those active operations which culminated in the invasion of the enemy territories—Palestine and Syria.

1916*

Western Frontier—Senussi Operations.

23 January ... ... **Halazin** [A Bty. H.A.C., Notts. Bty., Comp. Yeo. Bde., 6/R.S., 2/8/Mddx., 1/N.Z. Rif. Bde., 2/S. Afr. Inf., 15/Sikhs].

26 February .. .. **Agagiya** " Lukin's Force " **:—Dorset. Yeo., 1 Sqdn. Bucks. Yeo., Notts. Bty., 6/R. Scots, 1st and 3rd S. Afr. Inf.].

20 March ... ... On this day the Mediterranean Expeditionary Force and the Force in Egypt were amalgamated and became the Egyptian Expeditionary Force. This Force was placed under the supreme command of General Sir A. J. Murray.***

DEFENCE OF EGYPT.

22 April ... ... **Dueidar** [4/R. Scots, 5/R. Scots (155th Bde., 52nd Div.)].

23 April ... ... **Qatia** [5th Mtd. Bde., 2/Aus. L. H. Bde., Bikanir Camel Corps, 4/R. Scots, and 5/R. Scots].

Sudan—Darfur Operations.

22 and 23 May ... ... **Beringia and Occupation of el Fasher** [" Kelly's Force "† (Egyptian Army) :—8 Mtn. guns (Egyptian Arty.), 14 Maxims, 4 Cos. Camel Corps, 8 Cos. 13/ and 14/ Sudanese Inf., and Arab. Bn.].

DEFENCE OF EGYPT.

4 and 5 August ... **Battle of Romani** [R.F.C., 5th Mtd. Bde., A. and N.Z. Mtd. Bde., 3rd A. L. H. Bde., Impl. Camel Corps, Bikanir Camel Corps, 1st Dismtd. Bde., 42nd Div., 52nd Div., and 158th Bde. (53rd Div.) under 52nd Div. on 4 and 5/8/16].

---

* On the 9th January, Lieut.-General Sir A. J. Murray became G.O.C.-in-C. of the Mediterranean Expeditionary Force, and Lieut.-General Sir J. Maxwell then became responsible for the security of the Nile Delta, except in respect of an attack from the east.
** Br.-Gen. H. T. Lukin.
*** Lieut.-General Sir John G. Maxwell left Cairo for England on 21/3/16, and on 27/4/16 became G.O.C. Irish Command (App. 2).
† Lieut.-Col. P. V. Kelly.

1916 (*Contd.*)

Hejaz*

22 September ... ... **Capture of Taif** [Arab Forces, with Egyptian Army Arty. Detnt. (4, 5″ Hows., 6 Mtn. guns), and 1 Maxim Bty.].

Western Frontier—Senussi Operations.

17–22 October ... ... **Dakla Oasis** [Impl. Camel Corps and Light Armoured Cars].

Sudan—Darfur Operations.

6 November ... ... **Giuba** [1 Mtn. gun, 4 Maxims, and 150 rifles, 13/Sudanese Inf.].

Defence of Aden.

7 December ... ... **Jabir** [26/Cavalry, 4/D.C.L.I., 75/Carnatic Inf., and 109/Inf.].

DEFENCE OF EGYPT.

23 December ... ... **Magdhaba** [R.F.C., A. and N.Z. Mtd. Div. (less 2/A.L.H. Bde.) Impl. Camel Bde., Inverness and Somerset. Bties., and Hong Kong and Singapore Mtn. Bty.].

1917

DEFENCE OF EGYPT.

9 January ... ... **Rafa** [R.F.C., 5th Mtd. Bde., A. and N.Z. Mtd. Div. (less 2/A.L.H. Bde.), Impl. Camel Bde., No. 7 Light Car Patrol, B. Bty. H.A.C., Leicester, Inverness, and Somerset Bties., and Hong Kong and Singapore Mtn. Bty.].

Hejaz**

24 January ... ... **Capture of Er Wejh** [Arab Forces, assisted by R.F.C. and Naval Landing Party].

---

* In the Attack on Medina (6/6/16) and the Captures of Mecca (13/6/16), Jidda (16/6/16), and Yambo (27/7/16) only Arab Forces were engaged.
   The attacks to put the Hejaz Railway out of action were begun in October, 1916, and were continued until the end of the war.
   ** Only Arab Forces under the Emir Feisal were engaged in the Fight at Abu el Lissan (15 miles S.S.W. of Ma'an) on the evening of 2/7/17, and in the Occupation of Aqaba (6/7/17.) The Turkish attack on Petra (21/10/17) was met by Arab Forces under Gaafer Pasha.

1917 *(Contd.)*

Western Frontier—Senussi Operations.

3–5 February ... ... **Siwa Oasis** ["Hodgson's Column"*: Light Armoured Cars and Light Car Patrols].

INVASION OF PALESTINE.

26 and 27 March .. **FIRST BATTLE OF GAZA** [*Eastern Force***: 5th Wing R.F.C.; 53rd and 54th Divs., 52nd Div. (in reserve); *Desert Column*—A. & N.Z. Mtd. Div., Impl. Mtd. Div., and Impl. Camel Bde.; with R. Secs. 10th, 15th, 91st Hy. Bties. (60-pdrs.), 11/ and 12/L.A. Motor Bties., and 7/Light Car Patrol].

17–19 April ... ... **SECOND BATTLE OF GAZA** [*Eastern Force***: 5th Wing R.F.C.; 52nd, 53rd, and 54th Divs., and 74th Div. (in reserve); *Desert Column*—A. & N.Z. Mtd. Div., Impl. Mtd. Div., and Impl. Camel Bde.; and 10th, 15th, 91st Hy. Bties. (60-pdrs.), 201st Siege Bty. (6" and 8" Hows.); E Tank Company (8 Tanks)***, 11 and 12 L.A. Motor Bties., 17 M.M.G. Bty., and 7 Lt. Car Patrol].

---

* Br.-Gen. H. W. Hodgson.

** *Eastern Force* was formed on 18/10/16 and placed under Lt.-Gen. Sir C. M. Dobell; *Desert Column* was formed on 7/12/16 and was commanded by Lt.-Gen. Sir P. W. Chetwode, Bt. On 21/4/17 Lt.-Gen. Sir P. W. Chetwode took over the command of Eastern Force from Lt.-Gen. Sir C. M. Dobell, and Maj.-Gen. Sir H. G. Chauvel then took over Desert Column. On the reorganisation of the E.E.F., in August, 1917, both Eastern Force and Desert Column disappeared, and E.E.F. was reorganized in three Corps—XX, XXI, and Desert Mounted Corps.

*** On 9/1/17 E Tank Coy, M.G. Corps (Heavy Branch)—Major N. H. Nutt with 14 officers, 123 other ranks, and 8 tanks (all but 3 being the already obsolete Mk. I type)—disembarked at Alexandria from H.M.T. *Euripedes* and went to A Camp at Gabbari. On 27/1/17 E Tank Coy. concentrated at Gilban (10 miles W.S.W. of Romani), moved from there on 30/3/17 by train to Khan Yunis, reached Deir el Balah (4 miles S. of mouth of Wadi el Ghazze) on 5/4/17, and on 14/4/17 the 8 tanks moved forward into the Wadi el Ghazze.

The tanks co-operated in the Second Battle of Gaza: 2 tanks with 163rd Bde. (54th Div.) on 17/4/17; and on 19/4/17 1 tank attacked with 163rd Bde. (54th Div.), 4 tanks with 155th Bde. (52nd Div.), and 2 tanks with 160th Bde. (53rd Div.). After the Battle E Tank Coy. concentrated at Deir el Balah.

On 1/8/17 E Tank Coy. became Detachment Tank Corps E.E.F. (on 27/7/17 M.G.C. Heavy Branch had become Tank Corps).

1917 *(Contd.)*

INVASION OF PALESTINE *(Contd.)*

27 Oct.–16 Nov. ...	**THIRD BATTLE OF GAZA** [Palestine Bde. R.F.C.,* D.M.C.,** XX,*** and XXI*** Corps].
31 October	**Capture of Beersheba** [XX Corps (53rd, 60th, 74th Divs.), D.M.C. (Aus. Mtd. Div., A. & N.Z. Mtd. Div., 7th Mtd. Bde.), and Impl. Camel Bde. ; with Berks. Bty., 10th Mtn. Bty., and XCVI H.A.G.].
1–3 November	**Attack on the Gaza Defences** [XXI Corps (54th Div. and 156th Bde., 52nd Div.) ; with Detnt. Tank Corps (8 tanks), and XCVII, C, and CII H.A.G.s].
3–7 November	**Capture of Tell Khuweilfe** [53rd Div. (XX), and A. & N.Z. Mtd. Div.].
6 November	**Capture of the Sheria Position** [XX Corps (10th, 60th, and 74th Divs.), and Yeo. Mtd. Div., and Aus. Mtd. Div.].
8 November	**Huj** (10 miles E. of Gaza) [1/War. Yeo. and 1/Worc. Yeo. (5th Mtd. Bde.—Aus. Mtd. Div.)].
8 November	**Capture of the Wadi el Hesi Defences** [52nd Div. (XXI)].
12 November	**Burqa** (18 miles N.N.E. of Gaza) [156th Bde. (52nd Div.—XXI)].
13 November	**El Maghar** and
14 November	**Occupation of Junction Station** [XXI Corps (52nd and 75th Divs.), and D.M.C. (Yeo. Mtd. Div., Aus. Mtd. Div., A. & N.Z. Mtd. Div., 7th Mtd. Bde., Impl. Camel Bde.), and 12/L.A.M. Bty.].

---

* 5th (Corps) Wing—14th and 113th Sqdns. and 21st Balloon Coy. ; and 40th (Army) Wing—67th and 111th Sqdns.
** D.M.C. was formed at Abasan (3 miles E. of Khan Yunis) on 12/8/17. D.M.C. was commanded by Lt.-Gen. Sir H. G. Chauvel and consisted of : Yeomanry, Australian and A. and N.Z. Mounted Divisions, and Imperial Camel Corps Brigade.
*** XX Corps was formed at Deir el Balah (Palestine) on 2/8/17 (pp. 247, 249).
XXI Corps was formed at Deir el Balah (Palestine) on 12/8/17 (pp. 251, 253).

1917 *(Contd.)*

JERUSALEM OPERATIONS.

17–24 November ... ... **Battle of Nabi Samweil** [Palestine Bde. R.F.C., and XXI Corps (52nd, 60th, 75th Divs.), Yeo. Mtd. Div., 5th Mtd. Bde.].

27 Nov.–3 Dec. ... ... **Turkish Counter-Attacks in Defence of Jerusalem** [XXI Corps (52nd, 54th, 75th Divs.) until *noon 28/11*; then XX Corps (52nd, 60th, 74th Divs., Yeo. Mtd. Div., and 7th Mtd. Bde.), and D.M.C. (54th Div., Aus. Mtd. Div., A. & N.Z. Mtd. Div., and Impl. Camel Bde.)].

27 November ... ... **Defence of Wilhelma** (5 miles N.N.E. of Lydda) [4/North'n. (162nd Bde., 54th Div., attd. to D.M.C.)].

7–9 December ... ... **Capture of Jerusalem*** [Palestine Bde. R.F.C., XX Corps (60th and 74th Divs., and Mott's. Detnt.—53rd Div.) and XX Corps Cav.].

20–22 December ... **BATTLE OF JAFFA** [XXI Corps (52nd and 54th Divs.); and 1st A.L.H. Bde., and Auckland Mtd. Rif. (A. & N.Z. Mtd. Div.)].

8 p.m. 20–21 December **Passage of the Nahr el'Auja** [52nd Div. (XXI)].

26–30 December ... **Defence of Jerusalem** [XX Corps—10th, 53rd, 60th, and 74th Divs. and XX Corps Cav.].

1918**

OPERATIONS IN THE JORDAN VALLEY

19–21 February ... ... **Capture of Jericho** [XX Corps—60th Div. and 1st A.L.H. Bde. and N.Z. Mtd. Rif. Bde. (A. & N.Z. Mtd. Div.)].

---

* Jerusalem surrendered on 9/12/17 ; and on 11/12/17 General Sir E. H. H. Allenby made his official entry, through the Jaffa Gate, into the Holy City.

** In 1918 the Arab Forces in the Hejaz fought the following actions : *Fight at et Tafile* (25/1/18—Arab Forces under Emir Zeid) ; *Capture of Turkish Dead Sea Flotilla,* at el Mezra'a (27/1/18—Arab Camelry) ; *Shahim Stn.,* on Hejaz Rly. (20/4/18—Arab Regulars, with R.F.C. and Hejaz A.C. Bty.) ; *Mudawara Stn.,* on Hejaz Rly. (6/8/18—2 Cos. Impl. Camel Corps from E.E.F.) ; and *Reoccupation of Ma'an* (23/9/18—Arab Regular Army).

The *Arab Northern Army* (Emir Feisal) included : (1) *Arab Regular Army* (Ja'far Pasha el Askeri)— 1 Bde. Inf., 1 Bn. mule-mtd. Inf., 1 Bn. Camel Corps, and 8 guns ; with Lt.-Col. T. E. Lawrence's Arab Tribesmen ; and Section Indian machine-gunners ; (2) *British Section* (Lt.-Col. P. C. Joyce)— Hejaz A.C. Bty. (2, 10-pdrs. and m. guns), 1 Flight of Aeroplanes R.F.C., 1 Coy. Egyptian Camel Corps (Capt. F. G. Peake) ; with Tpt. and Labour Corps, and Wireless Stn. at Aqaba ; and (3) *French Section* (Capt. Pisani)—2 Mtn. Guns, 4 M.G.s, and 10 auto-rifles.

In March and April, 1918, the Arab Northern Army operated in the Mountains of Moab.

1918 (*Contd.*)

8–12 March	**Tell 'Asur** (9 miles N. of Jerusalem) [XX Corps—10th, 53rd, and 74th Divs., and 181st Bde. (60th Div.), and 1st A.L.H. Bde. and Auckland Mtd. Rif. (A. & N.Z. Mtd. Div.); and XXI Corps—54th and 75th Divs.].
12 March	**Fight at Ras el 'Ain** [162nd Bde. (54th Div.)—XXI Corps].

OPERATIONS IN AND BEYOND THE JORDAN VALLEY.

21 March–2 April ...	**First Trans-Jordan Raid** [" Shea's Force ":* A. & N.Z. Mtd. Div., Impl. Camel Bde., L.A.C. Bde., and 60th Div.].
27–30 March	**Attack on 'Amman** [" Chaytor's Force ": 2nd A.L.H. Bde. and N.Z. Mtd. Rif. Bde. (A. & N.Z. Div.), Impl. Camel Bde., 181st Inf. Bde., 2/17 and 2/18/Lond. of 180th Bde. (60th Div.)].
11 April	**Turkish Attack on the Jordan Bridgeheads** [A. & N.Z. Mtd. Div., and Impl. Camel Bde.].

9–11 April	**Berukin** (20 miles E. of Jaffa) [XXI Corps—7th Ind.,** 54th, and 75th Divs., and Aus. Mtd. Div.].

OPERATIONS BEYOND THE JORDAN VALLEY.

30 April–4 May	**Second Trans-Jordan Raid** [D.M.C. (Chauvel)—Aus. Mtd. Div., A. & N.Z. Mtd. Div., 6th Mtd. Bde., Impl. Service Cav. Bde., 60th Div., and 20th Ind. Bde.].
30 April–4 May	**Occupation of Es Salt** [Aus. Mtd. Div. (Hodgson)—3rd A.L.H. Bde., 5th Mtd. Bde.; and 1st A.L.H. and 2nd A.L.H. Bdes. (A. & N.Z. Mtd. Div.); with Hong Kong and Singapore Mtn. Bty., and 12th L.A.M. Bty.].

---

14 July	**Abu Tulul (Jordan Valley)** (7 miles N.W. of Ghoraniye Br.) [D.M.C.—A. & N.Z. Mtd. Div., 2nd Mtd. Div., and Alwar and Patiala Inf. Bns.].

---

* Under Maj.-Gen. J. S. M. Shea, commanding 60th Division.
** 7th (Meerut) Div.—Maj.-Gen. Sir V. B. Fane—arrived in Egypt in January, 1918; and 3rd (Lahore) Div.—Maj.-Gen. A. R. Hoskins—in April, 1918.

1918 *(Contd.)*

THE FINAL OFFENSIVE.

19–25 September ... **BATTLES OF MEGIDDO** [Palestine Bde. R.A.F.,* D.M.C.,** XX and XXI Corps, and " Chaytor's Force "***].

19–21 September ... **BATTLE OF NABLUS** [XX Corps].

19–21 September ... **BATTLE OF SHARON** [XXI Corps and D.M.C.].

20 September ... ... **Capture of Nazareth** [13th Cav. Bde. (5th Cav. Div.†)—D.M.C.]•

23 September ... ... **Capture of Haifa** [15th Cav. Bde. and 1 Sqdn. 1/Sherwood Rgrs. of 14th Cav. Bde. (5th Cav. Div.), and B. Bty., H.A.C.—D.M.C.].

24 September ... ... **Makhadet el Mas'udi** (Jordan ford—11 miles S.S.E. of Beisan) [11th Cav. Bde. (4th Cav. Div.†), and Hants. Bty. and 21/M.G. Sqdn.—D.M.C.].

25 September ... ... **Capture of Samakh** (E. of Jordan—on S. shore of Sea of Galilee) [4th A.L.H. Bde. (less 4/A.L.H. and 5 Trps. 12/A.L.H.) of Aus. Mtd. Div.—D.M.C.].

OPERATIONS BEYOND JORDAN.

25 September†† ... **Capture of 'Amman** [A. & N.Z. Mtd. Div.—" Chaytor's Force "].

---

* *R. Air Force (Middle East)*—Maj.-Gen. W. G. H. Salmond—Palestine Bde. R.A.F. (Br.-Gen. A. E. Borton) : 5th (Corps) Wing—14th, 113th, 142nd Sqdns ; 40th (Army) Wing—111th, 144th, 145th Sqdns. ; No. 1 Sqdn. Aus. F.C. ; and No. 21 Balloon Coy.
(On 1/4/18 R.F.C. and R.N.A.S. amalgamated and formed a separate Service, designated Royal Air Force.)
** For these operations D.M.C. (Lt.-Gen. Sir H. G. Chauvel) consisted of : 4th Cav. and 5th Cav. Divs., Aus. Mtd. Div., with *Régiment Mixte de Marche de Cavalerie*, and XIX R.H.A. (A and B Bties. H.A.C.).
*** Maj.-Gen. Sir E. W. C. Chaytor's Force (in Jordan Valley) consisted of : A. & N.Z. Mtd. Div. (with XVIII R.H.A.—Inverness., Ayr., and Somerset. Bties), 20th Ind. Inf. Bde., 38/R.F., 39/R.F., 1/B.W.I., 2/B.W.I., and 75th Bty. R.F.A., 195th Hy. Bty. R.G.A., and 29th and 32nd Ind. Mtn. Bties.
† *Yeomanry Mtd. Div.* (Indianized) on 24/4/18 became 1*st Mtd. Div.* (6th, 8th, and 22nd Mtd. Bdes.) ; and on 27/7/18 became 4*th Cavalry Div.* (10th, 11th, and 12th Cav. Bdes.) under Maj.-Gen. G. de S. Barrow (from 20/6/17—with XX R.H.A. (Berks., Hants., and Leicester Bties.).
2*nd Mtd. Div.*, formed in Palestine in May and June, 1918 (5th and 7th Mtd. Bdes., both Indianized, and Impl. Service Cav. Bde.—Jodhpore, Mysore, and 1/Hyderabad I.S. Lancers) under Maj.-Gen. H. J. M. Macandrew (31/5/18), became 5*th Cav. Div.* (13th, 14th, and 15th Cav. Bdes.), with Essex Bty. R.H.A. For these operations Notts. Bty., of XIX R.H.A., was attached to 5th Cav. Div.
†† On 23/9/18 Es Salt was occupied by N.Z. Mtd. Rifles Bde. (A. & N.Z. Mtd. Div.).

1918 *(Contd.)*

PURSUIT THROUGH SYRIA.

26 September	**Attack on Irbid** (E. of Jordan—19 miles W.S.W. of Der'a) [10th Cav. Bde. (4th Cav. Div.)—D.M.C.].
27 September	**Capture of Der'a** [Taken by Anazeh Tribesmen (Arab Northern Army) ; and R.A.F., Egyptian Camel Corps, Gurkhas on Camels, 450 Arab Regular Camelry, and Hejaz A.C. Bty. co-operated].
1 October	**Capture of Damascus*** [D.M.C.: 4th Cav. Div., 5th Cav. Div., Aus. Mtd. Div., *R.M.M.C.* (French), 11 and 12/L.A.M. Bties., and 7/Lt. Car Patrol].
26 October**	**Haritan** (9 miles N.W. of Citadel, Aleppo) [15th Cav. Bde., with M.G. Sqdn. and 12/L.A.M. Bty. (5th Cav. Div.)].
10 a.m. 26 October ...	**Occupation of Aleppo***** [5th Cav. Div. H.Q. and Armoured Cars].

Noon 31 October—Turkey signs Armistice.

---

* Arab Irregulars had entered Damascus by Mn. 30/9/18. On 3/10/18 Gen. Sir E. H. H. Allenby and the Emir Feisal made their official entries into Damascus. The advance since Zero on 19/9/18 was more than 160 miles.

** After the fall of Damascus the 5th Cav. Div. (Maj.-General Macandrew) opened the pursuit northward on 5/10: occupied Riyaq on 6/10, Baalbek on 11/10, and the leading column (Gen. Macandrew, with Divnl. H.Q., 15th Cav. Bde., and Armoured Cars) reached el Qa'aon on 14/10, and Homs on 16/10. On 20/10, Nos. 2, 11, and 12 L.A.M. Bties. and Nos. 1, 2, and 7 L.C. Patrols joined the leading column, which entered Hama on 21/10, Ma'arret en Numan on 23/10, and Khan Tuman on 25/10. Farther eastward the Arab Northern Army advanced as swiftly.

Whilst this energetic and bold pursuit was being undertaken, a final flare-up occurred on 22/10 near Aden, at Imad. In this fighting R.A.F., 26/Cav., 7/Hants. (of 43rd Div.), 75/Carnatic Inf., 1105 (H.) Bty. R.F.A. (of 45th Div.), Field Group (15-pdrs.), Malay States Guides Bty., 10-pdr. Section, Mobile Group Hy. Arty., and Aden M.G. Coy. were engaged.

*** Aleppo had surrendered to Sherifian Troops before Gen. Macandrew with 5th Cav. Div. H.Q. and Armoured Cars entered the City. At 8.30 p.m. on 26/10/18 the 14th Cav. Bde. reached Aleppo. From Damascus to Aleppo is over 200 miles, Gen. Macandrew's force had covered it in 22 days.

1918 *(Contd.)*

When the Armistice with Turkey came into force the general situation of the E.E.F. in Syria was broadly as follows : the 5th Cavalry Division occupied Aleppo and two of its cavalry brigades covered the city to the N.W. and N.E. At the same time the 7th Indian Division had secured the Syrian coast and held Tripoli, whilst the 54th Division had begun to arrive in Beirut.

Owing to sickness, the 4th Cavalry Division halted on reaching Baalbek, and its strongest brigade was drawn back to guard Damascus. The Australian Mtd. Division was then ordered to reinforce the 5th Cavalry Division at Aleppo, and it marched north on the 27th October, but it was still south of Homs (at Hasi) when the news reached it that Turkey was out of the war. The A. & N.Z. Mtd. Division, having captured 'Amman, was drawn back to Jerusalem ; it suffered severely from malaria and influenza, and it was resting near er Ramle at the time of the Armistice.*

All Turkish resistance collapsed in the face of that tireless pursuit : opened in the hour of victory on the 19th September it was sustained for forty-eight days. In this time both Damascus and Aleppo had fallen. This resistless advance over nearly 400 miles of enemy territory brought to a fitting end the Campaign in the Holy Land.

---

* Despite the Armistice concluded by Turkey, the Turkish commandant at Medina (General Fakhri Pasha) refused to surrender the Holy City, and the Arabs settled down to blockade it. In January, 1919, the garrison and city were faced with famine ; and, Fakhri becoming ill, his officers surrendered the place to the investing force.

MEDITERRANEAN EXPEDITIONARY FORCE

(GALLIPOLI)

G.H.Q.

COMMANDER-IN-CHIEF.

11 March, 1915	General Sir I. S. M. HAMILTON.
17 October, 1915	Lieut.-General Sir W. R. BIRDWOOD (tempy.).
27 October, 1915	General Sir C. C. MONRO.*
23 November, 1915	Lieut.-General Sir W. R. BIRDWOOD.*

C.G.S.

11 March, 1915...Maj.-Gen. W. P.
BRAITHWAITE.
27 Oct., 1915...Maj.-Gen. A. L. LYNDEN-
BELL.
23 Nov., 1915...Br.-Gen. C. F. ASPINALL
(B.-G.G.S.).

G.S.O. 1 (O).

13 March, 1915...Lt.-Col. W. de L.
WILLIAMS.
26 April, 1915...Lt.-Col. C. F. ASPINALL.
23 Nov., 1915...Lt.-Col. G. P. DAWNAY.

A. & Q.

D.-A.-G.

20 March, 1915...Br.-Gen. E. M.
WOODWARD.

D.-Q.-M.-G.

17 March, 1915...Br.-Gen. S. H. WINTER.
8 Aug., 1915...Br.-Gen. G. F. ELLISON.
23 Oct., 1915...Maj.-Gen. W. CAMPBELL.
23 Nov., 1915...Br.-Gen. G. F. MACMUNN
(D.-A. and Q.-M.-G.).

B.-G.R.A.

20 March, 1915...Br.-Gen. R. W. FULLER
(invalided).
10 Oct., 1915...Br.-Gen. S. C. U. SMITH.
23 Nov., 1915...Br.-Gen. C. CUNLIFFE
OWEN.

B.-G.R.E.

20 March, 1915...Br.-Gen. A. W. ROPER.
7 Sept., 1915...Maj.-Gen. G. WILLIAMS.
23 Nov., 1915...Br.-Gen. A. C. de L.
JOLY DE LOTBINIÈRE.

D. Army Signals.

20 March, 1915	Lt.-Col. M. G. E. BOWMAN-MANIFOLD.
23 November, 1915	Major H. L. MACKWORTH (i/c Army Signals).

---

* On 23/11/15 General Monro was transferred to command all forces in the Eastern Mediterranean, and was in general command both in Gallipoli and Salonika, with G.H.Q. at Mudros.
The Force on the Gallipoli Peninsula was renamed Dardanelles Army, and General Birdwood commanded the Gallipoli Force with G.H.Q. at Imbros. Early in 1916 the Dardanelles Army was broken up at Imbros and in Egypt.

D. S. and T.

22 Feb., 1915...Br.-Gen. F. W. B. KOE.
23 Nov., 1915...Col. W. K. TARVER
(D.-D.S. & T.).

D.O.S.

22 Feb., 1915...Br.-Gen. R. W. M. JACKSON.
2 Nov., 1915...Br.-Gen. H. W. PERRY.
23 Nov., 1915...Col. P. A. BAINBRIDGE
(D.-D.O.S.).

D. Works.

20 March, 1915 ... ... Br.-Gen. G. S. McD. ELLIOTT.
1 July, 1915 ... ... Br.-Gen. A. C. DE L. JOLY DE LOTBINIÈRE.
23 November, 1915 ... ... Col. J. P. BLAKEWAY (D.-D. Works).

D.M.S.

1 March, 1915...Maj. Gen. W. G. BIRRELL.
Oct., 1915...Maj.-Gen. W. G. A. BEDFORD.
23 Nov., 1915...Col. C. C. REILLY
(D.-D.M.S.)

D.V.S.

March, 1915...Lt.-Col. E. TAYLOR.

A.-D. Remounts.

22 February, 1915 ... ...⎫
— October, 1915 ... ...⎭Lt.-Col. V. R. HINE-HAYCOCK.

I.-G. Communications.

14 July, 1915...Lt.-Gen. E. A. ALTHAM.
23 Nov., 1915...Br.-Gen. C. R. R. McGRIGOR.

Deputy-I.-G. Communications.

14 July, 1915⎫
–7 Aug., 1915⎭Br.-Gen. G. F. ELLISON.

Base Commandant.

22 February, 1915 ... ... Br.-Gen. C. R. R. McGRIGOR.
22 September, 1915 ... ... Maj.-Gen. G. G. A. EGERTON.

Liaison Officer with French E.F.*

1 April, 1915...Lt.-Col. H. D. FARQUHARSON.
17 June, 1915...Capt. C. DE PUTRON.
31 July, 1915...Major C. DE PUTRON.

French Liaison Officer at G.H.Q., M.E.F.

April, 1915...Cdt. de Cav. DE BERTIER DE SAUVIGNY.

---

* *Corps Expéditionnaire d'Orient.*

LOCATION OF G.H.Q.

1915.

11 March	C.-in-C. appointed.
Friday, 13 March ...	G.H.Q. (14 officers) left London.
13 March	Dover (H.M.S. *Foresight*).
14 March	Marseilles (H.M.S. *Phaeton*).
3 p.m., 17 March ...	Tenedos.
18 March	Lemnos.
26 March	Port Said.
27 March	Alexandria.
28 March	Cairo.
29 March	Alexandria.
8 April	Embarked on s.s. *Arcadian*.
6 a.m., 10 April ...	Off Mudros (Lemnos).
8–24 April	*Arcadian*.
1 p.m. 24 April ...	H.M.S. *Queen Elizabeth* (remdr. of G.H.Q. on *Arcadian*).
30 April	*Arcadian*.
31 May	Mudros (*Arcadian*).
31 May	Imbros.

1916.

1 January	Imbros.
12 January	Imbros—G.H.Q. Dardanelles Army* ceased to exist.

---

* On 23/11/15 the Force on the Gallipoli Peninsula was renamed Dardanelles Army.

MEDITERRANEAN EXPEDITIONARY FORCE

(GALLIPOLI)

FORMATION.

On the 11th March, 1915, both the Commander-in-Chief and the Chief of the General Staff were appointed to the M.E.F. (Gallipoli), and the 29th Division was ordered to prepare to embark for service in the Eastern Mediterranean. On the 13th March the C.-in-C. and the officers of the General Staff left London ; but, at such short notice, it had not been possible to assemble the A. and Q. staffs.

H.M.S: *Phaeton* took the advanced party of 14 officers on board at Marseilles and reached Tenedos on the 17th March. On arrival at Tenedos General Sir Ian Hamilton held a conference on H.M.S. *Queen Elizabeth**, and the next day proceeded to Lemnos. Between 26th March and 8th April Sir Ian Hamilton visited Egypt, and, on the later date, G.H.Q. embarked on the Transport *Arcadian*, and remained on her until the day before the assault was made on the Gallipoli Peninsula, when the C.-in-C. and General Staff transferred to H.M.S. *Queen Elizabeth*.

By the 22nd March the 29th Division had left England and it began to arrive at Alexandria on the 28th. On the 7th April re-embarkation began for Mudros, and at 10 p.m. on the 24th April the division left the anchorage at Mudros to carry out the landings at Helles.

The Royal Naval Division** sailed from England on the 1st March, it waited at Port Said from the 29th March until the 5th April, and on the 8th its transports began to leave for Mudros. On the 25th April the Royal Naval Division carried out a demonstration in the Gulf of Saros (off the Bulair Peninsula).

With reference to the Australian & New Zealand Corps (Anzac Corps) : the 1st Australian Division and one brigade of New Zealand infantry had assembled in Egypt before the end of 1914, and these troops completed their war-training after arrival. Early in 1915 the remainder of the Australian and New Zealand Division reached Egypt, and in April the two divisions from the southern hemisphere were combined for the Gallipoli operations to form the Anzac Corps. On the 24th April the Anzac Corps began embarkation at Mudros for the assault next morning at Anzac.***

---

* General d'Amade with 1st Div. of the *Corps Expéditionnaire d'Orient* had reached Lemnos on 15/3/15, and he met General Hamilton and Admiral de Robecq at this conference. The French 2nd Div. did not arrive until the 6th May. The French command of the C.E.O. (later C.E.D.) was held as follows : 24/2/15—General d'Amade ; 15/5/15—General Gouraud (wounded, 30/6/15) ; 1/7/15—General Bailloud† (acting) ; and 4/10/15—General Brulard.

† Commanding 2nd Div. (C.E.O.).

** Later numbered " 63rd " on 19/7/16 (in France).

*** The area on the western seaboard of the Gallipoli Peninsula enclosed between Gaba Tepe—Anderson's Knoll—Scrubby Knoll—Battleship Hill—Fisherman's Hut, was known as Anzac. It was 3 miles from Gaba Tepe to Fisherman's Hut and 1¼ miles from Scrubby Knoll to the beach at Ari Burnu ; but from the Anzac front line at Quinn's and Courtney's Posts to Ari Burnu was only three-quarters of a mile.

BATTLES AND ENGAGEMENTS.

1915

BATTLES OF HELLES [29th Div. ; and 42nd and R.N. Divs., and 29th Ind. Inf. Bde., 2nd Aus., and N.Z. Inf. Bdes., and *C.E.O.*].

25 and 26 April ... **Landing at Kum Kale** (In Asia Minor—E. side of Dardanelles) [6th Col. Regt., 1 Fd. Bty., 1/2 Coy Engrs., 1st Div., *C.E.O.**].

25 and 26 April ... **THE LANDING AT CAPE HELLES**** [29th Div.].

25 and 26 April ... **The Landing at S Beach** (On E. side—In Morto Bay, near Eski Hissarlik) [2/S.W.B. (less 1 Coy.), party R.E., party R.A.M.C., and party from *Cornwallis*].

25 and 26 April ... **The Landing at V Beach** (On S. Side—Near Sedd el Bahr) [2/Hants., 1/R.M.F., 1/R.D.F., with *River Clyde*].

26 April ... ... **Capture of Sedd el Bahr** [2/Hants., 1/R.M.F., 1/R.D.F.].

25 and 26 April ... **The Landing at W. Beach** (On·S.W. Side—Near Tekke Burnu) [1/L.F., 4/Worc., 1/Essex].

25 and 26 April ... **The Landing at X Beach** (On W. Side—North of Tekke Burnu) [2/R.F., 1/R. Innis.F., 1/Border].

25 and 26 April ... **The Landing at Y Beach***** (On W. Side—Near Ghurkha Bluff) [1/K.O.S.B., Plymouth Bn. (R.M.L.I.), and 1 Coy. 2/S.W.B.].

---

* *Corps Expéditionnaire d'Orient* (C.E.O.) was formed between 22/2—4/3/15 ; it became *Corps Expéditionnaire des Dardanelles* (*C.E.D.*) on 4/10/15.

The last French troops left Helles between 1–4/1/16 ; and on 6/1/16 *C.E.D.* was broken up. 1st Div. became 17th Colonial Inf. Div. on 6/1/16.

2nd Div. became Serbia Div. on 28/9/15, evacuated Helles on 1/10/15, landed at Salonika early in October, 1915, and was then styled 1st Inf. Div. of the *Armée d'Orient.* On 15/10/15 the Division became again 156th Inf. Div. (a title it had held from its formation on 17/3/15 until it became 2nd Div., *C.E.O.*, on 29/4/15).

** Br.-Gen. S. W. Hare (Comdg. 86th Inf. Bde.) was G.O.C. Covering Force, which landed at V, W, and X Beaches. The local commanders at Y and S Beaches were under the direct orders of 29th Div. H.Q.

Anson Bn. (R.N. Div.) provided beach-parties at V, W, and X Beaches.

*** Y Beach was 10 miles south of Z Beach (Anzac).

G.H.Q., M.E.F. (GALLIPOLI)

1915 *(Contd.)*

BATTLES OF ANZAC.

25 and 26 April ... **THE LANDING AT ANZAC*** [1st Aus. Div., N.Z. & A. Div.**
—with 7 guns (6 were Mtn. Guns of 21 and 26 Ind. Mtn. Bties.) on 25/4 ; and 25 guns on 26/4 : Anzac Corps].

25 and 26 April ... **Demonstration in the Gulf of Saros** [R.N. Div.—less Plymouth Bn. (R.M.L.I.), Anson, and Drake Bns.].

2 May ... ... **Attack on the Chessboard** [N.Z. and A. Div., with Nelson Bn., and 3rd R.M.Bde. (less 1 Bn.), of R.N. Div. ; supported by 17 guns (out of 38 landed)—Anzac Corps].

10 May ... ... **Quinn's Post (I)** [Part of N.Z. and A. Div. : Anzac Corps].

BATTLES OF HELLES *(Contd.)*.

28 April ... ... **First Battle of Krithia** [29th Div., and Plymouth, Anson, and Drake Bns. (R.N. Div.), and *C.E.O.*—with 28 guns].

1 and 2 May ... ... **Eski Hissarlik** [29th Div., 2nd R.N.Bde., and Plymouth and Drake Bns. (R.N. Div.) ; and 29th Ind. Inf. Bde.***].

6–8 May ... ... **Second Battle of Krithia**†† [29th Div. and 29th Ind. Inf. Bde. ; 2nd R.N. Bde., and Plymouth and Drake Bns. (R.N. Div.) ; 42nd Div.† (125th and 127th Bdes.) ; 2nd Aus. Inf. Bde. ; N.Z. Inf. Bde. *C.E.O.* (1st Div. and part 2nd Div.)—with 72 guns].

6–8 May ... ... **First Action of Kereves Dere** [1st Div. and part 2nd Div., *C.E.O.* ; with 2nd R.N. Bde.].

12 May ... ... **Gurkha Bluff** [29th Ind. Inf. Bde. (under 29th Div.)].

---

* The intended landing place, Z Beach, was 1½ miles north of Gaba Tepe ; but the landing was made another ¾-mile north of Z Beach—at Ari Burnu (1 mile S. of Fisherman's Hut).
** Up to 12/5/15 N.Z. & A. Div. consisted of N.Z. Inf. Bde. and 4th Aus. Inf. Bde. The N.Z. Mtd. Rif. Bde. and 1/Aus. L. H. Bde. landed (from Egypt) on 12 and 13/5/15.
*** Arrived on 1/5/15, but kept in Reserve in this action.
† Completed disembarkation (from Egypt) on 9/5/15 at Helles.
†† For 2nd Battle of Krithia (6–8/5/15) the British Forces at Helles were organized in two divisions :

29th Division { 87th and 88th Inf. Bdes., 125th (Lanc. Fus.) Bde. (transferred on 7/5 to Comp. Div.), 29th Ind. Bde., and 86th Inf. Bde. (less 1/Lanc. Fus.) split up among 29th Div. ;

Composite Division. { 2nd Aus. Inf. Bde. (with 29th Div. on 8/5), N.Z. Inf. Bde. (transferred to 29th Div. on 7/5), Comp. Naval Bde.—1/L.F. with Plymouth and Drake Bns.—127th (Manchester) Inf. Bde. (from 7/5), and 125th (Lanc. Fus.) Bde. (from 7/5).

NOTE—The 2nd R.N. Bde. was attached to *C.E.O.* for this Battle ; it joined Composite Division at 8 a.m. on 10/5/15.

50

1915 *(Contd.)*

BATTLES OF ANZAC *(Concld.)*.

19–21 May	**Defence of Anzac** [1st Aus. Div. and N.Z. and A. Div.—with 40 guns : Anzac Corps].
29 May	**Quinn's Post (II)** [Part of N.Z. and A. Div.].
28 June	**Holly Ridge** [2nd L.H. Bde.,* and part 3rd Aus. Bde.].
30 June	**Defence of Walker's Ridge** [3rd L.H. Bde.*].

BATTLES OF HELLES *(Concld.)*.

4 June	**Third Battle of Krithia** [VIII Corps,** and 29th Ind. Inf. Bde., with 8 Armoured Cars, R.N.A.S. ; and 1st and 2nd Divs., *C.E.O.*—with 78 British guns (20 lent by Anzac Corps), and 24 French guns].
4 June	**Second Action of Kereves Dere** [1st and 2nd Divs., *C.E.O.*].

---

21 June	**Third Action of Kereves Dere** [1st and 2nd Divs., *C.E.O.*].
28 June–2 July	**Gully Ravine** [29th Div., with 156th Bde. (52nd Div.),*** and 29th Ind. Inf. Bde. : VIII Corps].
30 June	**Fourth Action of Kereves Dere** [1st and 2nd Divs., *C.E.O.*].
12–13 July	**Achi Baba Nullah** [52nd Div. : VIII Corps ; and *C.E.O.*].
6–13 August	**Krithia Vineyard** [29th and 42nd Divs. : VIII Corps].

---

* 2nd L. H. Bde. landed on 20/5/15 and joined Corps Troops.
  3rd L. H. Bde. landed on 21/5/15 and joined Corps Troops.
** VIII Corps (including 29th, 42nd, and Royal Naval Divisions) was formed at Helles on 24/5/15 and was at first styled " British Army Corps " ; it became VIII Corps on 5/6/15 (pp. 179, 180, 181).
*** 52nd Division (less II Lowland Bde. R.F.A., D.A.C., and Tpt. Sec. of Train) landed on Gallipoli between 6/6–7/7/15.

1915 *(Contd.)*

BATTLES OF SUVLA* [Anzac and IX** Corps].

6–10 August ... ... **Battle of Sari Bair** [1st Aus. Div. and "Godley's Force"†— N.Z. and A. Div. (N.Z. Inf. Bde., 4th Aus. Bde., 1st and 3rd L.H. Bdes., N.Z. Mtd. Rif. Bde.) 13th Div. (38th, 39th, 40th Bdes.), 29th Bde. (10th Div.), 29th Ind. Inf. Bde., and Ind. Mtn. Arty. Bde.: Anzac Corps].

6–10 August ... ... **Capture of Lone Pine** [1st Aus. Bde. and 7th and 12th Aus. Bns. ; 1st Aus. Div. : Anzac Corps.].

7 August ... ... **Attack at Russell's Top** [3rd L.H. Bde. and 8/Ches. and 8/R.W.F. (40th Bde., 13th Div.) : "Godley's Force"].

6–15 August ... ... **THE LANDING AT SUVLA*** [IX Corps**: 10th and 11th Divs. ; and 53rd Div. (landed 9/8), and 54th Div. (landed 10/8)].

7 August ... ... **Capture of Karakol Dagh** [34th Bde. (11th Div.) : IX Corps].

Night 7/8 August ... **Capture of Chocolate Hill** ["Hill's Force"†—31st Inf. Bde. and 7/R.D.F. of 30th Bde. (10th Div.) : IX Corps].

21 August ... ... **Battle of Scimitar Hill** [11th and 29th Divs., with 2nd Mtd. Div. : IX Corps].

21 August ... ... **Attack on Hill 60** ["Cox's Force"†—4th Aus. Bde., 2 Regts. N.Z.M.R. Bde., 5/Conn. Rgrs., 10/Hants. (10th Div.), and 29th Ind. Inf. Bde. :†† Anzac Corps].

21 August ... ... **Attack on "W" Hills** [11th Div. and 2nd Mtd. Div. : IX Corps].

---

* On 6 and 7/8/15 350 Irregulars under 2 French Officers carried out a Demonstration in the Gulf of Saros.
** IX Corps Headquarters began to form in London on 16/6/15 and reached Mudros at 10 a.m., on 9/7/15 (pp. 185, 186, 187).
*** The first 2 echelons ashore numbered 13,300 all ranks. A. Bty./LIX R.F.A. (11th Div.) and 2 Batteries IV Highland Mtn. Bde. R.A. had landed by 8 a.m. on 7/8/15.
† Maj.-Gen. Sir A. J. Godley, Comdg. A. & N.Z. Div. ; Br.-Gen. F. F. Hill, Comdg. 31st Inf. Bde. (10th Div.) ; Maj.-Gen. H. V. Cox, Comdg. 29th Ind. Inf. Bde.
†† During all these operations and since 1/5/15, the 29th Indian Inf. Brigade was commanded by Maj.-Gen. H. V. Cox and consisted of :
14/Sikhs, 4/Gurkha Rifles (arrived Oct. 1915), 5/Gurkha Rifles, 6/Gurkha Rifles, and 2/10/Gurkha Rifles.

1915 *(Contd.)*

27 and 28 August ... **Attacks on Hill 60** [" Cox's Force "—4th Aus. Bde. ; 2 Regts. N.Z.M.R. Bde. ; 5/Conn. Rgrs., 10/Hants., (10th Div.), 29th Ind. Inf. Bde.—with 4/S.W.B. (13th Div.), 18/Aus. Bn., and 10/A.L.H. : Anzac Corps].

The Last Night, 19/20 December. **EVACUATION OF ANZAC AND SUVLA** [*Anzac*—2nd A.L.H. Bde., 1st Aus. Div., 2nd Aus. Div., N.Z. & A. Div., 29th Ind. Inf. Bde. (less 4/Gurkhas)—10,040 men and 8 guns and hows. : Anzac Corps ; *Suvla*—4/Gurkhas, 2nd Mtd. Div., 11th Div., 13th Div., 88th Bde. (29th Div.)—10,612 men and 21 guns and hows. : IX Corps].

HELLES.

29 December ... ... **Krithia Nullahs** [52nd Div. : VIII Corps].

1916

7 January ... ... **The Last Turkish Attacks** [13th Div. : VIII Corps].

The Last Night, 8/9 January. **EVACUATION OF HELLES** [13th, 29th, 52nd, and R.N. Divs.—16,918 men and 37 guns and hows. (out of 54) ; VIII Corps].

On the 7th December, 1915, the Cabinet decided to withdraw the troops from Anzac and Suvla. But it was not until the 28th December a telegram from the C.I.G.S. announced that the Government had decided the troops at Helles could also be withdrawn.

After Evacuation the troops were taken first of all to Imbros and Lemnos, and from these islands the majority went on to Egypt.

General Monro was transferred, from the command of M.E.F. (Gallipoli) on the 23rd November, 1915, to the command of all forces in the Eastern Mediterranean ; and for a time he was in general command both in Gallipoli and Salonika, with his G.H.Q. at Mudros (on Lemnos). The Force on the Gallipoli Peninsula was then renamed the Dardanelles Army and had its headquarters on Imbros, with Lieut.-General Sir W. R. Birdwood as G.O.C.

The Evacuations having been carried out, the Dardanelles Army was broken up on Imbros and in Egypt.

BRITISH SALONIKA ARMY

G.H.Q.*

COMMANDER-IN-CHIEF.*

4 November, 1915	General Sir C. C. MONRO.**
15 November, 1915	Lieut.-General Sir B. T. MAHON.
9 May, 1916	Lieut.-General G. F. MILNE.
3 January, 1917	Lieut.-General Sir H. F. M. WILSON (tempy.).
11 January, 1917	Lieut.-General G. F. MILNE.
25 June, 1918	General G. F. MILNE.

C.G.S.

15 Nov., 1915...Br.-Gen. P. HOWELL.
6 June, 1916...Br.-Gen. W. GILLMAN.
25 June, 1916...Maj.-Gen. W. GILLMAN.
25 Aug., 1917...Maj.-Gen. G. N. CORY.

G.S.O. 1.

O.

15 Nov., 1915...Maj. F. H. G. STANTON (tempy.).
19 Nov., 1915...Lt.-Col. F. H. G. STANTON.
19 Mar., 1916...Lt.-Col. R. E. SOLLY FLOOD.
29 Oct., 1916...Lt.-Col. P. L. HANBURY.

I.

15 Nov., 1915...Lt.-Col. F. CUNLIFFE OWEN.
27 May, 1917...Lt.-Col. Sir E. I. B. GROGAN, BART.
28 May, 1918...Lt.-Col. T. G. G. HEYWOOD.

A. and Q.

D.-A.-G.

9 Nov., 1915 ⎱
–28 Nov., 1915 ⎰ Br.-Gen. R. C. BOYLE.***

D.-Q.-M.-G.

15 Nov., 1915...Br.-Gen. TRAVERS E. CLARKE.

D.-A. and Q.-M.-G.

22 December, 1915 ... ... Br.-Gen. TRAVERS E. CLARKE.
25 June, 1916 ... ... Maj.-Gen. TRAVERS E. CLARKE.

D.-A.-G.

20 Feb., 1917...Maj.-Gen. W. H. RYCROFT.
1 Aug., 1917...Maj.-Gen. H. J. EVERETT.

D.-Q.-M.-G.

20 Feb., 1917...Maj.-Gen. TRAVERS E. CLARKE.
1 Aug., 1917...Maj.-Gen. W. H. RYCROFT.

---

* The Headquarters was known as Army Headquarters, and the Commander as G.O.C. until January, 1917, when they became respectively G.H.Q. and C.-in-C.
** General Monro became C.-in-C. Eastern Mediterranean Forces (23/11/15–9/1/16) ; he then returned to France to command First Army, B.E.F. (4/2/16).
*** Left to join H.Q., M.E.F. at Mudros.

B.-G.R.A.
15 Nov., 1915...Br.-Gen. W. H. ONSLOW.

M.-G.R.A.
11 April, 1917...Maj.-Gen. W. H. ONSLOW.

C.E.
26 Jan., 1916...Maj.-Gen. S. R. RICE.
5 Mar., 1916...Br.-Gen. A. R. REYNOLDS.
5 July, 1916...Br.-Gen. H. L. PRITCHARD (tempy.).
12 Aug., 1916...Br.-Gen. H. A. A. LIVINGSTONE.

E.-in-C.
17 Jan., 1917...Maj.-Gen. H. A. A. LIVINGSTONE.

L.-G. Communications.
6 Nov., 1915
-12 Feb., 1916 } Maj.-Gen. J. ADYE.
22 July, 1916
-22 Feb., 1917 } Maj.-Gen. F. W. B. KOE.

D. Supplies and Transport.
4 Nov., 1915...Br.-Gen. R. FORD.
7 Jan., 1916...Br.-Gen. A. LONG.

D. Railways.
Nov., 1915...Lt.-Col. M. E. SOWERBY (A.-D.).
Mar., 1916...Lt.-Col. F. D. HAMMOND (A.-D.).
25 Nov., 1916...Col. F. D. HAMMOND.

C.H.A.
....

4 Oct., 1917...Br.-Gen. P. L. HOLBROOKE.

Offr. i/c Army Signals.
9 Jan., 1916...Lt.-Col. A. H. W. GRUBB.

D. Signals.
19 April, 1917...Col. A. H. W. GRUBB.

Base Commandant.
25 Nov., 1915...Br.-Gen. J. H. POETT.
21 Oct., 1916...Col. D. K. E. HALL.
6 April, 1918...Br.-Gen. D. K. E. HALL.

D. Ordnance Services.
Nov., 1915...Br.-Gen. R. W. M. JACKSON.
31 Dec., 1915...Br.-Gen. C. M. MATHEW.
20 Aug., 1917...Br.-Gen. W. H. U. SMITH.

D.-D. Works.
19 Nov., 1915...Col. A. R. REYNOLDS.
9 Mar., 1916...Col. J. P. BLAKEWAY.
19 April, 1917...Br.-Gen. J. P. BLAKEWAY.
8 Sept., 1917...Col. H. E. WEBB-BOWEN.

D.M.S.

25 Nov., 1915...Maj.-Gen. W. G. MACPHERSON.
27 Mar., 1916...Maj.-Gen. H. R. WHITEHEAD.
1 June, 1917...Col. M. P. C. HOLT (A.-D.).
20 Dec., 1917...Maj.-Gen. Sir M. P. C. HOLT.

D.-D.V.S.

1 Dec., 1915...Col. F. EASSIE.

D. Remounts.

1 December, 1915 ... ... Maj. G. W. DOWELL (D.-A.-D.).
March, 1916 ... ... Lt.-Col. G. W. DOWELL (A.-D.).
23 January, 1917 ... ... Br.-Gen. G. W. DOWELL.

Liaison Officers.

with:

War Office.	French.	Serbians.	Italians.
11/15 -3/16 } Col. W. E. FAIRHOLME.	11/15...Lt.-Col. Sir E. I. B. GROGAN, Bt.		
	5/16...Capt. D. J. MONTAGU-DOUGLAS-SCOTT (acting).	7/16...Maj. H. J. SOLOMON.	
8/16...Lt.-Col. C. C. M. MAYNARD.	10/16...Lt.-Col. E. L. STRUTT.		10/16...Capt. R. G. JEBB.
		11/16...Capt. R. B. GOODDEN.	11/16...2/Lieut. H. E. GOAD (acting).
12/16...Lt.-Col. E. A. PLUNKETT.			2/17...Capt. H. E. GOAD.
		8/17...Capt. E. L. PHARAZYN.	
6/18...Lt.-Col. K. BARGE.			

LOCATION OF G.H.Q.

8 October, 1915	...	**Salonika.***
24 September, 1918	...	**Yanesh** (25 miles N.N.W. of Salonika).
30 September, 1918	...	**Armistice with Bulgaria came into force.**
11 October, 1918	...	**Salonika.**
Noon, 31 October, 1918		**Armistice with Turkey came into force.**
16 December, 1918	...	**Constantinople.**

---

* Lieut.-General Sir B. T. Mahon, on reaching Macedonia (from Mudros) with the 10th (Irish) Division, established his headquarters at Salonika.

G.H.Q. was formally opened at Salonika from 15th November 1915, when General Mahon became G.O.C. British Salonika Army. (Headquarters was known as Army Headquarters until January, 1917, when it became G.H.Q.)

BRITISH SALONIKA ARMY

FORMATION.

The 29th Infantry Brigade (10th Division) disembarked at Salonika between the 5th and 10th October, 1915, and by the 24th the remainder of the 10th Division had landed. On the 29th October a mobile force left by train for the interior and it detrained to the west of Lake Dojran.

Lord Kitchener (on his way from Salonika to Athens) on the 4th November placed General Sir C. C. Monro in command of all forces in the Eastern Mediterranean. The War Office, however, did not recognize this arrangement and continued to deal directly with Lieut.-General Sir B. T. Mahon (G.O.C. 10th Division) ; and on the 15th November, 1915, General Mahon formed a new Headquarters for Macedonia—chiefly taken from the Staff of XII Corps, which had landed three days previously at Salonika from France.

Lieut.-General Sir B. T. Mahon held the command of the British Salonika Army until the 9th May, 1916 ; then he was transferred to Egypt to command against the Senussi, and Lieut.-General G. F. Milne was appointed to take over the command of the British Salonika Army.

BATTLES AND ENGAGEMENTS.

1915

3–12 December ... ... **RETREAT FROM SERBIA** [10th Div. ; and from 8/12/15 part of 22nd Div.].

7 and 8 December ... **Kosturino** [10th Division].

1916

DOJRAN OPERATIONS.

10–18 August ... ... **Horseshoe Hill** (2¼ miles S.W. of Dojran) [22nd and 26th Divs. : XII Corps.].

13 and 14 September **Machukovo** [22nd Div. : XII Corps].

1916 *(Contd.)*

OPERATIONS IN THE STRUMA VALLEY.

30 September–2 October	**Capture of the Karajaköis** [10th and 27th Divs. : XVI Corps].*
2 October	**Occupation of the Mazirko** [84th Bde. (28th Div.) : XVI Corps].
3 and 4 October ...	**Capture of Yeniköi** [10th and 27th Divs. : XVI Corps].
31 October	**Capture of Bairakli Jum'a** (14 miles W.N.W. of Seres) [28th Div. : XVI Corps].
17 November, and 6 and 7 December }	**Tumbitza Farm** (6 miles S.S.E. of Seres) [82nd Bde. (27th Div.) : XVI Corps].

1917

24 and 25 April, and 8 and 9 May }	**BATTLE OF DOJRAN** [22nd, 26th, and 60th Divs. : XII Corps].
15 May	**Capture of Ferdie and Essex Trenches** (Near Bairakli Jum'a) [28th Div. : XVI Corps].
14 October	**Capture of Homondos** (5 miles S.W. of Seres) [27th Div. : XVI Corps].
16 October	**Capture of Bairakli and Kumli** [28th Div. : XVI Corps].

1918

THE OFFENSIVE.

1 and 2 September ...	**Capture of the Roche Noire Salient** (4 miles W. of the R. Vardar) [27th Div. : XII Corps].

---

* XVI Corps Headquarters was formed at Avestokhorion (4 miles east of Salonika) in the latter half of January, 1916 (pp. 229, 230).

1918 *(Contd.)*

THE OFFENSIVE *(Contd.)*.

18 and 19 September   **BATTLE OF DOJRAN** [22nd and 26th Divs., and 83rd Bde. (less 2 Bns.) of 28th Div. ; and Greek Seres Div., and 2ᵉbis Régt. de Zouaves : XII Corps ; and 28th Div.* and 228th Inf. Bde.;** and Greek Crete Div.: XVI Corps***].

22–30 September   ...   **Pursuit to the Strumica Valley** [22nd and 28th Divs. : XII Corps ;† and 26th Div. and 27th Div. (from 27/9), and Greek 14th Div. : XVI Corps].

In the Pursuit the Serbia-Bulgaria boundary was crossed on the 25th September. On the next day the 26th Division occupied Strumica, thus securing the bridge over the river.

At noon on the 30th September the Armistice with Bulgaria brought hostilities to a close in this theatre of war, the 26th Division (the leading British Division) was then occupying a line from Hamzali to Grandosor, some five miles to the northward of the River Strumica ; in touch on the right with the Greek 14th Division, whose front ran northwards from the Strumica, round the town of Yeniköi to Barbarevo, and then swung westward to meet the right of the 26th Division.

The 22nd Division still occupied the crest of the Belašica Planina ; the 28th Division was on its left (near Dorlobos), and the Greek Crete Division continued the line to the eastward along the Belašica Planina (6 miles south of Strumica). Advanced Headquarters of XVI Corps had been established at Kosturino since the 26th September ; and at this time the 27th Division was in the area Kosturino—Rabrovo—Cestovo.

On the 6th October the 26th Division advanced towards Sofia, and it had reached Radomir (20 miles S.W. of the capital) when the Division, on the 19th, received orders to entrain for Jisr Mustafa Pasha. By the 24th the division had concentrated there and was ready to seize Adrianople (15 miles away), when the Armistice with Turkey came into force at noon on the 31st October.

Meanwhile on the 11th October the 22nd Division began to move southward to Stavros ; it then embarked and, on the 28th, landed at Dede Agach and was ready to operate against Turkey, but any further activity was prevented by the Armistice.

---

   * 83rd Inf. Bde. (less 2/E. York. and 1/York. and Lanc.) was with XII Corps (on W. side of Lake Dojran).

   ** The *228th Inf. Bde.* (Br.-Gen. W. C. Ross) was formed in Macedonia on 1/3/17, and served with the 28th Div. It was composed of : 2/Garr. Bn., King's ; 2/5 Garr. Bn. D.L.I. ; 1/Garr. Bn. Sea. H. ; 22/R.B. ; 2/Garr. Bn. R. Ir. Fus. ; 277/M.G. Coy. ; 228/T.M. Bty. ; 228/Bde. Sig. Sec. ; 143/Fd. Amb. ; and 228/Bde. Train (1,061 Coy.). 228th Inf. Bde. was broken up on 6/1/1919.

   *** 11 Heavy Batteries, and 9 Siege Batteries—40, 60-pdrs. ; 4, 6″ Mk. VII guns ; 4, 8″ hows. ; 32, 6″ hows. ; and 6 Mountain Batteries—co-operated in this Battle of Dojran with the British Salonika Army. Headquarters, Heavy Artillery, was attached to XII Corps for the Battle.

   † XII Corps halted on 26/9, after occupying the crest of the Belašica Planina.

NOTE—For the Offensive, the Greek I Corps (1st, 2nd, and 13th Divs.) in the Struma Valley was placed under General Milne until 25/9/18 ; it was then transferred and came under the Greek C.-in-C. (General Danglis).

1918 *(Contd.)*

The 27th Division continued to advance on Sofia until the end of October, and reached Krupnik, some 60 miles south of the capital. On the other hand, after the surrender of Bulgaria, the 28th Division drew back to Güvezne, preparatory to being sent to seize the forts securing the Dardanelles.

On the 11th November the situation in the Eastern Section of the Balkans (under General Milne) was as follows :—

The 22nd Division was at Dede Agach with a detachment at Ipsala (near the mouth of the Maritsa) ; the 26th Division* was at Jisr Mustafa Pasha, with a detachment at Rusčuk (on the Danube) ; the 27th Division was between Seres and Salonika, in the Lake Tahinos district ; and the 28th Division was in occupation of both shores of the Dardanelles Narrows, from Chanaq to Gallipoli. This was the situation in the Balkans when the capitulation of Germany brought the Great War to a close.**

---

* On the 2nd November the 26th Division was transferred from XVI Corps to the Army of the Danube (General Berthelot), and it would have moved to Tirnovo, but at 3 p.m. on the 4th November the Armistice with Austria came into force.
** On this date in the Eastern Section of the Balkans, i.e., east of the River Vardar, there were the French 122nd Div., Italian Sicilia Bde., and Greek 1st, 2nd, 13th, 14th, Archipelago, Crete, and Seres Divisions.

BRITISH FORCE IN ITALY, 1917-1918
G.H.Q.

COMMANDER-IN-CHIEF.

6 November, 1917	Lieut.-General EARL OF CAVAN (tempy.).
13 November, 1917	General Sir H. C. O. PLUMER.
Noon 10 March, 1918	Lieut.-General EARL OF CAVAN.
25 June, 1918	General EARL OF CAVAN.

G.S.

6 Nov., 1917...Br.-Gen. Hon. J. F.
GATHORNE-HARDY (tempy.).
13 Nov., 1917...Maj.-Gen. C. H.
HARINGTON.
13 Mar., 1918...Br.-Gen. Hon. J. F.
GATHORNE-HARDY.
14 Oct., 1918...Maj.-Gen. Hon. J. F.
GATHORNE-HARDY.

G.S.O. 1.

....

10 Mar., 1918...Lt.-Col. J. E. TURNER.

A. and Q.

D.-A.-G.

6 Dec., 1917 } Maj.-Gen. W. G. B.
–10 Mar., 1918 }   WESTERN.

D.-Q.-M.-G.

6 Dec., 1917 } Maj.-Gen. A. A.
–10 Mar., 1918 }   CHICHESTER.

D.-A. and Q.-M.-G.

10 March, 1918	Br.-Gen. H. L. ALEXANDER.
14 October, 1918	Maj.-Gen. H. L. ALEXANDER.

M.-G.R.A.

13 Nov., 1917 } Maj.-Gen. C. R. BUCKLE.
–10 Mar., 1918 }

C.H.A.

....

B.-G.R.A.

10 Mar., 1918...Br.-Gen. A. E. WARDROP.
5 Aug., 1918...Br.-Gen. W. H. KAY.

10 Mar., 1918...Br.-Gen. T. R. C.
    HUDSON.

M.-G.R.A.

14 Oct., 1918...Maj.-Gen. W. H. KAY.

G.H.Q. BRITISH FORCE IN ITALY

E.-in-C.

14 Nov., 1917...Maj.-Gen. F. M. GLUBB.
18 Mar., 1918...Br.-Gen. C. S. WILSON.
14 Oct., 1918...Maj.-Gen. C. S. WILSON.

A.-D. Signals.

21 Nov., 1917...Col. A. B. R.
HILDEBRAND.
10 Mar., 1918...Lt.-Col. O. C. MORDAUNT.
14 Oct., 1918...Col. O. C. MORDAUNT
(D.-D.).

D.-G. Transportation.

13 Nov., 1917...Maj.-Gen. W. H. GREY.
25 Mar., 1918...Br.-Gen. G. L. COLVIN.

I.-G. Communications.

21 Nov., 1917...Lt.-Gen. H. M. LAWSON
(Cdr. L. of C. Area).
10 Mar., 1918...Lt.-Gen. H. M. LAWSON.
4 July, 1918...Maj.-Gen. J. A. STRICK.

D. Supplies and Transport.

9 April, 1918 ... ... Br.-Gen. W. S. SWABEY.

D. Supplies.

19 Nov., 1917...Br.-Gen. W. S. SWABEY.
9 April, 1918...Lt.-Col. C. BURTON
(A.-D. Supplies).

D. Transport.

17 Nov., 1917...Br.-Gen. J. M. YOUNG.
9 April, 1918...Lt.-Col. R. SHELTON
(A.-D. Transport).

D. Ordnance Services.

17 November, 1917 ... ... Br.-Gen. T. W. HALE.

D. Medical Services.

17 Nov., 1917...Maj.-Gen. F. R. NEWLAND.

D.-D. Veterinary Services.

4 Dec., 1917...Col. F. W. WILSON.
26 May, 1918...Lt.-Col. H. S. MOSLEY
(A.-D.).

British Mission with Italian G.H.Q.

6 Nov., 1917...Br.-Gen. C. DELME-
RADCLIFFE (Chief of Mission.
since 1915).

British Mission with French G.H.Q.

14 Mar., 1918...Lt.-Col. G. J. P.
GEIGER (G.S.O. 1).
18 April, 1918...Maj. G. R. MITCHISON
(G.S.O. 2).

Liaison Officer from War Office.

November, 1917 ... ... Br.-Gen. J. H. V. CROWE.
11 March, 1918 ... ... Lt.-Col. A. F. C. WILLIAMS (tempy.).
19 April, 1918 ... ... Maj.-Gen. L. A. E. PRICE-DAVIES, V.C.

LOCATION OF G.H.Q.

1917.

6 November	**Pavia.**
8 November	**Mantua.**
13 November*	**Padua.**
20 November	**Legnago.**
30 November	**Padua.**

1918

16 January	**Noventa** (3 miles E. of Padua).
10 March**	**Fanzolo** (15 miles W.N.W. of Treviso).
18 March	**Noventa.**
29 March	**Lonedo** (4 miles N.E. of Thiene).
11 October	**Villa Marcello** (4½ miles S. of Treviso).
3 p.m. 4 November	**Armistice with Austria came into force.**

---

* General Sir H. C. O. Plumer arrived and assumed command.
** General Sir H. C. O. Plumer handed over command to Lieut.-General Earl of Cavan, and returned to the Western Front.

BRITISH FORCE IN ITALY

FORMATION.

On the 24th October, 1917, the Austro-German offensive opened against the left of the Italian Army, then in the Julian Alps. Gorizia' and Udine fell and the Austro-German Forces crossed the Tagliamento.

British and French reinforcements were immediately promised to Italy. On the 6th November XIV Corps H.Q. reached Pavia from France ; and until the 13th November XIV Corps H.Q. acted temporarily as G.H.Q. British Force in Italy.*

On the 7th November, 1917, Second Army Headquarters (then at Cassel) was warned that it would move to Italy ;** and on the 10th November the Army Commander with certain of his Staff Officers left Cassel, and on the 13th detrained at Mantua. General Sir H. C. O. Plumer then assumed command of the British Force in Italy ;*** and on the 4th December General Plumer took over the Montello Sector of the Piave front with XIV Corps (7th, 23rd, and 41st Divisions).

BATTLES AND ENGAGEMENTS.

1918

On the 27th January the British Force in Italy took over the Arcade Sector of the Piave front with XI Corps* (5th and 48th Divisions). Then, on the 18th February, British G.H.Q. in Italy was warned that it would move back to the Western Front and on the 24th February XI Corps H.Q. and the 7th† and 41st Divisions also received orders to return to France. On the 1st March the 41st Division began to entrain, and it was followed on the 10th March by G.H.Q. and XI Corps H.Q. ; but it was not until the 1st April that the 5th† Division started to entrain.

Meanwhile in Italy, Lieut.-General the Earl of Cavan assumed command of the British Force from noon on the 10th March, and on the 29th took over the Asiago Sector on the Piave with the XIV Corps.††

---

* XI Corps Headquarters reached Mantua on 1/12/17.
** At this time the Second Army was engaged in fighting the Second Battle of Passchendaele (Battles of Ypres, 1917).
*** General Plumer, whilst he was in Italy, held the rank and position of an Army Commander, directly under G.H.Q. Italy (*Comando Supremo*).
The five British Divisions sent to Italy and their dates of concentration were as follows :
23rd Div. (16/11) ; 41st Div. (18/11) ; 7th Div. (28/11) ; 48th Div. (1/12) ; and 5th Div. (20/12/17).
† On 24/3/18 the 5th Division was substituted for the 7th Division.
†† XIV Corps included 7th, 23rd, and 48th Divs. On the 18th April XIV Corps H.Q. finally merged in and became G.H.Q. British Force in Italy.

1918 *(Contd.)*

BATTLES AND ENGAGEMENTS.

BATTLE OF THE PIAVE.

15 and 16 June ... **Fighting on the Asiago Plateau** [23rd and 48th Divs., with 7th Div. in Reserve—under Sixth (It.) Army: General Montuori].

At the beginning of October the 7th and 23rd Divisions left the mountain front, leaving the 48th Division there under the Italian XII Corps (Sixth Army).

On the 9th October the XIV Corps was re-formed with the 7th and 23rd Divisions, and was transferred to the Piave front. The XIV Corps and the Italian XI Corps were then placed under General the Earl of Cavan as the new Italian Tenth Army.*

The British Force then took part in the following operations :**

24 October–4 November **BATTLE OF VITTORIO VENETO** [XIV Corps—Tenth (It.) Army : under General Lord Cavan].

23–26 October ... ... **Capture of the Grave di Papadopoli** [7th Div. : XIV Corps].

Night 26/27–28 October **Passage of the Piave** [23rd Div. : XIV Corps].

29 October ... ... **Passage of the Monticano** [23rd Div. : XIV Corps].

3 November ... ... **Crossing of the Tagliamento** [7th Div. : XIV Corps].

---

    * From this date (9/10) the Staff of the British Force in Italy again had the Status of an Army Staff.
    ** The 48th Division was engaged as follows :
24 October–4 November **BATTLE OF VITTORIO VENETO** [48th Div., in XII (It.) Corps, under Sixth (It.) Army].
  1–4 November ... ... **Fighting in the Val d'Assa** [48th Div., in XII (It.) Corps].

G.H.Q. BRITISH FORCE IN ITALY

1918 (*Contd.*)

The Armistice with Austria brought hostilities to a close on the Italian front at 3 p.m. on the 4th November.   At this time the right of the British Force in Italy (XIV Corps) was north of the Tagliamento and its advanced troops had covered one-third of the way to Udine, whilst the left of the XIV Corps was already midway between the Rivers Livenza and Meduna.   Farther to the westward, the 48th Division (operating in the Sixth Italian Army) had pushed forward into the Trentino, and by Armistice its leading troops were some eight miles to the north-westward of Levico.

ARMIES

B.E.F.

FIRST ARMY

G.O.C.

26 December, 1914	General Sir D. HAIG.*
22 December, 1915	General Sir H. S. RAWLINSON, Bt.**
4 February, 1916	General Sir C. C. MONRO.***
7 August, 1916	Lieut.-General Sir R. C. B. HAKING (tempy.).
30 September, 1916	General Sir H. S. HORNE.

M.-G.G.S.

26 Dec., 1914...Maj.-Gen. J. E. GOUGH, V.C. (killed, 21/2/15).
21 Feb., 1915...Maj.-Gen. R. H. K. BUTLER.
26 Dec., 1915...Maj.-Gen. G. de S. BARROW.
4 Feb., 1917...Maj.-Gen. W. H. ANDERSON

D.-A. and Q.-M.-G.

26 Dec., 1914...Maj.-Gen. P. E. F. HOBBS.
3 Mar., 1917...Maj.-Gen. P. G. TWINING.
15 Feb., 1918...Maj.-Gen. A. W. PECK.

M.-G.R.A.

16 Feb., 1915...Maj.-Gen. H. F. MERCER.
8 July, 1915...Maj.-Gen. E. A. FANSHAWE.
23 Aug., 1915...Maj.-Gen. H. F. MERCER.
9 April, 1918...Maj.-Gen. E. W. ALEXANDER, V.C.

C.E.

4 Feb., 1915...Maj.-Gen. S. R. RICE.
6 Nov., 1915...Maj.-Gen. G. M. HEATH.
1 Nov., 1917...Maj.-Gen. E. H. de V. ATKINSON.

A.-A. Defence Cdr.†

16 Nov., 1916...Lt.-Col. D. H. GILL

D.-D. Signals.

26 Dec., 1914...Col. S. H. POWELL.
15 Nov., 1915...Maj. A. H. W. GRUBB (i/c Army Signals).
30 Nov., 1915...Maj. E. G. GODFREY-FAUSSETT (i/c Army Signals).
6 Feb., 1916...Col. E. G. GODFREY-FAUSSETT.
19 June, 1916...Col. H. T. G. MOORE.

---

* Became C.-in-C. B.E.F. (France) at Noon, 19/12/15.
** Became G.O.C. Fourth Army on 5/2/16.
*** Became C.-in-C. Army in India on 1/10/16.
† First Army A.-A. Group (A, B, C, and D A.-A. Batteries, each 2 Sections of 13-pdrs.—16, 13-pdrs.) was formed in November, 1916. In November, 1918, C, E(Cdn.), K, and Y A.-A. Bties., with the First Army, had **38**, 13-pdrs. and **6, 3″** A.-A. guns.

FIRST ARMY

D.-D. S. and T.

1 Feb., 1915...Col. A. LONG.
14 July, 1915...Col. St. J. W. T. PARKER.
16 Oct., 1917...Br.-Gen. St. J. W. T.
                           PARKER.

D.-D.O.S.

1 Feb., 1915...Col. W. H. U. SMITH.
3 Aug., 1917...Col. A. FORBES.
29 May, 1918...Br.-Gen. R. K. SCOTT.

D.M.S.

29 December, 1914 ... ... Maj.-Gen. W. G. MACPHERSON.
1 November, 1915 ... ... Maj.-Gen. W. W. PIKE.
21 July, 1917 ... ... Maj.-Gen. H. N. THOMPSON.

D.-D.V.S.

6 Feb., 1915...Lt.-Col. W. D. SMITH.
20 Aug., 1915...Lt.-Col. A. C. NEWSOM.
    Mar., 1916...Lt.-Col. E. E. MARTIN.
14 Feb., 1918...Col. E. W. LARNDER.
15 Oct., 1918...Lt.-Col. W. H. NICOL
                      (acting).
17 Oct., 1918...Col. T. W. RUDD.

D.-D. Remounts.

4 Feb., 1915...Col. C. L. BATES.
6 Nov., 1915...Col. F. J. RYDER.
17 June, 1917...Lt.-Col. F. S. K. SHAW.

LOCATION OF ARMY HEADQUARTERS.

(INCLUDING ADVD. A.H.Q.).

	26 December, 1914	**Hinges** (2 miles N. of Bethune).
	27 December, 1914	**Lillers.**
2 p.m.	1 February, 1915	**Aire.**
3 p.m.	7 May, 1915	**Merville.**
3 p.m.	3 June, 1915	**Chocques** (3 miles W. of Bethune).
3 p.m.	26 June, 1915	**Aire.**
3 p.m.	5 August, 1915	**Hinges.**
3 p.m.	5 February, 1916	**Aire.**
3 p.m.	26 June, 1916	**Chocques.**
3 p.m.	16 August, 1916	**Lillers.**
Noon	4 April, 1917	**Ranchicourt** (3 miles S. of Bruay).
	29 March, 1918	**Ranchicourt.** *
Noon	17 October, 1918	**Duisans** (4 miles W. of Arras).
4 p.m.	26 October, 1918	**Auberchicourt** (7 miles S.S.E. of Douai).
11 a.m.	11 November, 1918	**Armistice with Germany.**
	13 November, 1918	**Valenciennes** (advd. A.H.Q.).
	19 November, 1918	**Valenciennes** (A.H.Q. concentrated).

---

* 29/3/1918. 2nd Echelon of First Army H.Q. moved to Matringhem (12 miles S.W. of Aire).
9/5/1918. D.M.S., D.-D.V.S., etc., closed at Matringhem and opened at Heuchin (8 miles N.N.W. of St. Pol).

FIRST ARMY

FORMATION.

First Army Headquarters began to form at Hinges on the 26th December, 1914, and moved on the next day to Lillers. First Army held the right (southern) half of the B.E.F. front from La Bassée Canal—Bois Grenier, some 10 miles in extent. With this front the First Army took over the I and IV Corps in the line ; and the Indian Corps and the Indian Cavalry Corps formed the Army Reserve*. Until the 1st February, 1915, First Army Headquarters remained at Lillers, and on that day it moved to Aire on the R. Lys.

BATTLES AND ENGAGEMENTS.

1914

1915

25 January	**1st Action of Givenchy** [1st Div. : I Corps].
29 January	**Cuinchy** [1st Div. : I Corps].
1 and 6 February ...	**Cuinchy** [2nd Div. : I Corps].
10–13 March	**Battle of Neuve Chapelle** [IV and Indian Corps ; with 5th Cav. Bde. in Army Reserve].
9 May	**Battle of Aubers Ridge :** [I, IV, and Indian Corps]. { **Attack at Fromelles** [IV Corps]. { **Attack at Rue du Bois** [I and Indian Corps].
15–25 May	**Battle of Festubert** [I and Indian Corps].**
15 and 16 June ...	**2nd Action of Givenchy** [7th, 51st, and 1st Cdn. Divs. : IV Corps].
25 Sept.–8 Oct.	**Battle of Loos** [I, IV, and XI Corps ; with 3rd Cav. Div. (26–28/9) ; and from 29/9 Indian Corps].

---

* On 26/12/14 the First Army consisted of : I Corps (1st and 2nd Divs.), IV Corps (7th and 8th Divs.) ; and in Army Reserve : Indian Corps (3rd Lahore, and 7th Meerut, Divs.), part 27th Div., 1st Indian Cav. Div., and Secunderabad Cav. Bde. (of 2nd Ind. Cav. Div.)—the remainder of 2nd Ind. Cav. Div. was at Orléans.

** From 19/5—1 p.m. 22/5/15 "Alderson's Force " (51st Div. and 1st Cdn. Div.) was interpolated between I and Indian Corps.

1915 *(Contd.)*

25 September	**Piètre** [19th and Meerut Divs. : Indian Corps].
25 September	**Bois Grenier** [8th Div. : III Corps].
13–19 October	**Hohenzollern Redoubt and The Quarries, Hulluch** [IV, XI, and (part) I Corps].

1916

2–18 March	**Hohenzollern Craters** [12th Div. : I Corps].
27–29 April	**German Gas Attacks, Hulluch** [15th and 16th Divs. : I Corps].
11 May	**The Loss of the Kink** [15th Div. : I Corps].
21 May	**German Attack on Vimy Ridge** [47th Div. : IV Corps].*
19 July	**Attack at Fromelles** [61st and 5th Aus. Divs. : XI Corps].

1917

	BATTLES OF ARRAS [I, XIII, and Cdn. Corps ; with (part) 1st Tank Bde.].
9–14 April	**Battle of Vimy Ridge** [I and Cdn. Corps ; with 12 Coy., D Bn., 1st Tank Bde. with Cdn. Corps ; and, from 12/4, XIII Corps].
23 and 24 April ...	**Second Battle of the Scarpe** [XIII Corps].
23 April	**Capture of Gavrelle** [63rd Div. : XIII Corps].
23 April	**Attack on la Coulotte** [5th Div., 2nd Cdn., and 3rd Cdn. Divs. : Cdn. Corps].
28 and 29 April ...	**Battle of Arleux** [XIII and Cdn. Corps].
3 and 4 May	**Third Battle of the Scarpe** [XIII and Cdn. Corps].
3 May	**Capture of Fresnoy** [1st Cdn. Div. : Cdn. Corps].

---

* Also see XVII Corps and Third Army.

1917 (Contd.)

3–25 June ... ...   **South of the Souchez River** [3rd Cdn. and 4th Cdn. Divs.: Cdn. Corps].

26–29 June ... ...   **Capture of Avion** [3rd Cdn. and 4th Cdn. Divs.: Cdn. Corps].

28 June ... ...   **Capture of Oppy Wood** [5th and 31st Divs.: XIII Corps].

1 July ... ...   **Attack on Liévin** [46th Div.: I Corps].

15–25 August ... ...   **Battle of Hill 70, Lens** [6th and 46th Divs., I Corps, and 1st Cdn., 2nd Cdn., 3rd Cdn., and 4th Cdn. Divs.: Cdn. Corps].

1918

FIRST BATTLES OF THE SOMME [XIII Corps].

28 March ... ...   **First Battle of Arras** [XIII Corps].

BATTLES OF THE LYS [I, XI, and XV Corps].

9–11 April ... ...   **Battle of Estaires** [XI and XV Corps].

9–17 April ... ...   **First Defence of Givenchy** [55th Div.: in XI Corps until 12/4, then in I Corps].

12–15 April ... ...   **Battle of Hazebrouck** [I and XI Corps; and XV Corps until Noon 12/4*].

12–15 April ... ...   **Defence of Hinges Ridge** [I and XI Corps].

12–15 April ... ...   **Defence of Nieppe Forest** [5th Div.: XI Corps].

18 April ... ...   **Battle of Béthune** [I (part) and XI Corps].

18 and 19 April ...   **Second Defence of Givenchy** [1st Div.: I Corps].

---

28 June ... ...   **La Becque** [5th and 31st** Divs.: XI Corps].

---

* At Noon on 12/4 XV was transferred to Second Army.
** 31st Div. (of XV Corps, Second Army) was placed under XI Corps, First Army, for this operation.

1918 (*Contd.*)

THE ADVANCE TO VICTORY.

On the 18th August the First Army, in the centre of the B.E.F.,* held a 22-mile front from S.E. of Arras to north of Givenchy with XVII,** XXII, VIII, and I Corps.

18 August–18 September **ADVANCE IN FLANDERS** [I Corps].

24 August ... ... **Capture of Givenchy Craters** [55th Div. : I Corps].

17 September ... ... **Capture of Canteleux Trench** [55th Div. : I Corps***].

SECOND BATTLES OF ARRAS [VIII (part), XXII, and Cdn.** Corps ; with 3rd Tank Bde.].

26–30 August ... ... **Battle of the Scarpe** [VIII (part) and Cdn.** Corps ; with 3rd Tank Bde. ; and, from *29/8* XXII Corps].

26 August ... ... **Capture of Monchy le Preux** [3rd Cdn. Div. : Cdn. Corps ; with 2 tanks, 11th Bn., 3rd Tank Bde.].

2 and 3 September ... **Battle of the Drocourt-Quéant Line** [XXII and Cdn. Corps ; with 9th, 11th, and 14th Bns., 3rd Tank Bde.].

BATTLES OF THE HINDENBURG LINE [XXII and Cdn. Corps ; with 7th Bn., 1st Tank Bde.].

27 September–1 October **Battle of the Canal du Nord** [XXII and Cdn. Corps ; with 7th Bn., 1st Tank Bde.].

27 September ... ... **Capture of Bourlon and Wood** [4th Cdn. Div. : Cdn. Corps ; with 2 tanks A. Coy. 7th Bn., 1st Tank Bde.].

8 and 9 October ... **Battle of Cambrai** [XXII and Cdn. Corps].

9 October ... ... **Capture of Cambrai** [3rd Cdn. Div. : Cdn. Corps.]†

9–12 October ... ... **Pursuit to the Selle** [XXII and Cdn. Corps ;†† with 3rd Cav. Cav. Bde. (2nd Cav. Div.)].

---

* On 18/8/18 the B.E.F. front measured about 86 miles.
** At Noon on 6/4/18 XVII Corps had been transferred (in the line) from Third to First Army. XVII Corps was transferred back (in the line) to the Third Army at Noon on 23/8/18 ; and at Noon on 23/8/18 Canadian Corps (from Fourth Army) joined the First Army and took over part of the battle-front.
*** At Noon on 19/9/18 I Corps was transferred (in the line) from First Army to Fifth Army.
† Also see Third Army and XVII Corps.
†† From 5 p.m. on 11/10/18 XXII Corps and Cdn. Corps exchanged fronts.

1918 *(Contd.)*

THE FINAL ADVANCE.

17 Oct.–11 Nov. ...	**IN PICARDY** [XXII and Cdn. Corps].
17–25 October	**Battle of the Selle** [XXII Corps].
1 and 2 November ...	**Battle of Valenciennes** [XXII and Cdn. Corps].
1 November	**Capture of Mont Houy** [4th Cdn. Div. : Cdn. Corps].
4 November	**Battle of the Sambre** [XXII and Cdn. Corps].
5–7 November	**Passage of the Grande Honnelle** [XXII and Cdn. Corps].

---

2 October–11 November	**IN ARTOIS** [VIII Corps ; with 3rd Cav. Bde., (2nd Cav. Div.)].
7 and 8 October ...	**Forcing the Rouvroy-Fresnes Line** [8th Div. : VIII Corps].
17 October	**Capture of Douai** [8th Div. : VIII Corps].
11 November	**Capture of Mons** [5/Lcrs. and 1 Sec. D. R.H.A. (2nd Cav. Div.) and 3rd Cdn. Div. : Cdn. Corps].

When hostilities ceased at 11 a.m. on the 11th November the First Army front line was already 5 miles beyond Mons, standing astride the Mons–Condé canal in the centre of the 55-mile front of the B.E.F. The 14-mile Army front was occupied by XXII, Canadian, and VIII Corps. Between the 18th August and the 11th November—86 days—the First Army had fought in seven battles and advanced 55 miles.

On the 15th November the Commander of the First Army made his official entry into Mons, and in the *Grande Place* he took the salute of representative detachments from each Corps in the First Army.

SECOND ARMY*

G.O.C.

26 December, 1914	General Sir H. L. SMITH-DORRIEN.
7 May, 1915	General Sir H. C. O. PLUMER.**
9 November, 1917	}General Sir H. S. RAWLINSON, Bt.
-19 December, 1917* ...	

---

13 March, 1918**	General Sir H. C. O. PLUMER.

M.-G.G.S.

26 Dec., 1914...Maj.-Gen. G. T. FORESTIER-WALKER.
23 Feb., 1915...Maj.-Gen. G. F. MILNE.
15 July, 1915...Maj.-Gen. H. B. WILLIAMS.
5 June, 1916...Maj.-Gen. C. H. HARINGTON.
29 April, 1918...Maj.-Gen. J. S. J. PERCY.

D.-A. and Q.M.G.

26 Dec., 1914...Maj.-Gen. W. H. RYCROFT.
30 June, 1915...Maj.-Gen. F. WINTOUR.
9 Nov., 1915...Maj.-Gen. A. A. CHICHESTER.

M.-G.R.A.

25 Feb., 1915...Maj.-Gen. J. E. W. HEADLAM.
18 Dec., 1915...Maj.-Gen. G. McK. FRANKS.
7 July, 1917...Maj.-Gen. C. R. BUCKLE.

C.E.

26 Feb., 1915...Maj.-Gen. A. E. SANDBACH.
12 May, 1915...Maj.-Gen. F. M. GLUBB.***
18 Mar., 1918...Maj.-Gen. Sir F. M. GLUBB.

A.-A. Defence Cdr.†

16 Nov., 1916...Lt.-Col. R. R. CURLING.
20 Dec., 1917...Lt.-Col. H. W. HILL.††

D.-D. Signals.

26 Dec., 1914...Maj. A. B. R. HILDE-BRAND (i/c Army Signals).
18 Feb., 1915...Lt.-Col. A. B. R. HILDEBRAND.
6 Feb., 1916...Col. A. B. R. HILDEBRAND.
Oct., 1918...Col. H. C. SMITH.

---

* On 20/12/17 Second Army was designated Fourth Army ; and on 17/3/18 Fourth Army was renamed Second Army.
** C.-in-C. British Force in Italy, 13/11/17—Noon 10/3/18.
*** E.-in-C. British Force, in Italy, 14/11/17—17/3/18.
† Second Army A.-A. Group (F., G., H., and J., A.-A. Batteries, each 2 Secs of 13-pdrs.--16, 13-pdrs.) was formed in November, 1916. In November, 1918, H., J., R., T., U. A.-A. Bties., and 2 Secs. (171 and 177) of 13-pdrs., with Second Army, had altogether 42, 13-pdrs. and 12, 3″ A.-A. guns.
†† Came up with Fourth Army Staff, when H.Q. Second Army went to Italy, and remained with Second Army after Army H.Q. returned from Italy in March, 1918.

SECOND ARMY

D.-D.S. and T.

1 Feb., 1915...Col. E. R. O. LUDLOW.
27 May, 1915...Col. A. PHELPS.
16 Oct., 1917 }
–17 Nov., 1917 } Br.-Gen. A. PHELPS.

———————

20 Dec., 1917...Br.-Gen. F. M. WILSON.*

D.-D.O.S.

1 Feb., 1915...Col. T. W. HALE.
20 Dec., 1917...Col. H. S. BUSH.*

D.M.S.

1 February, 1915   ...   ...   Maj.-Gen. R. PORTER.
8 April, 1918   ...   .   Maj.-Gen. S. G. MOORES.

D.-D.V.S.

4 Feb., 1915...Lt.-Col. F. W. WILSON.
20 Dec., 1917...Col. F. W. HUNT.*

D.-D. Remounts.

4 Feb., 1915...Lt.-Col. H. I. E. PALMER.
20 Dec., 1917...Col. W. E. MATCHAM.*

———————————————————————

* From Fourth Army.

LOCATION OF ARMY HEADQUARTERS
(INCLUDING ADVD. A.H.Q.).

26 December, 1914 ... ...   **Bailleul.**

Noon 2 January, 1915 ... ...   **Hazebrouck.**

5 p.m. 6 May, 1915 ... ...   **Château de Jardin, Oxelaere** (S. of Cassel).

2 p.m. 23 October, 1915 ... ...⎫
  –9 November, 1917 ... ...⎭**Cassel.**

10/11/1917...Second Army H.Q. move to Italy; and G.O.C. and Staff Fourth Army took over Second Army Front in Flanders on the previous day.

20/12/1917...Second Army was designated Fourth Army.

[9/11/1917–13/3/1918..A.H.Q. at Cassel.]

10/3/1918...General Plumer and Staff returned from Italy to Flanders.

13/3/1918...Second Army was reconstituted.

17/3/1918...The present Fourth Army was renamed Second Army.

13 March, 1918 ... ...   **Cassel.**

14 April, 1918 ... ...   **Blendecques** (2½ miles S. by E. of St. Omer).

1 September, 1918 ... ...   **Cassel.**

23 October, 1918 ... ...   **Château Ternynck, Roubaix.**

11 a.m. 11 November, 1918 ... ...   **Armistice with Germany.**

24 November, 1918 ... ...   **Namur** (Advd. A.H.Q.).*

1 December, 1918 ... ...   **Spa** (Advd. A.H.Q.).

9 December, 1918 ... ...   **Düren** (Advd. A.H.Q.).**

19 December, 1918 ... ...   **Cologne** (Advd. A.H.Q.).

21 December, 1918 ... ...   **Cologne** (A.H.Q. concentrated).

* All Directorates were left at Roubaix until 21/12/1918.
** 22 miles W.S.W. of Cologne.

SECOND ARMY

FORMATION.

Second Army Headquarters began to form at Bailleul on the 26th December, 1914, and moved to Hazebrouck on the 2nd January, 1915. Second Army held the left (northern) half of the B.E.F. front from Bois Grenier—opposite Wytschaete, some 10 miles in length. With this front the Second Army took over the II and III Corps in the line and the Cavalry Corps formed the Army Reserve.*

Second Army Headquarters remained at Hazebrouck until the 6th May ; it was then established at Oxelaere for five and a half months, before it began its long tenure of Cassel, that elevated eyrie on the Flanders Plain with which it is generally associated.**

BATTLES AND ENGAGEMENTS.

1914

1915

14 and 15 March	...	**St. Eloi** [27th Div. : V Corps].
17–22 April	... ...	**Capture of Hill 60** [5th Div. : II Corps].

		BATTLES OF YPRES [II, V, and Cav. Corps].***
22 and 23 April	...	**Battle of Gravenstafel Ridge** [V and (part) II Corps].
22 April	.. .. ..	**The Gas Attack** [1st Cdn. Div. and B Coy., 2/Buffs : V Corps].
24 April–4 May ...	...	**Battle of St. Julien***** [V and (part) II Corps].
8–13 May	...	**Battle of Frezenburg Ridge** [V and Cav. Corps].
24 and 25 May ...	...	**Battle of Bellewaarde Ridge** [V and Cav. Corps].

---

* Second Army on 26/12/14 consisted of : II Corps (3rd and 5th Divs.), III Corps (4th and 6th Divs.) ; and, in Army Reserve : Cavalry Corps (1st Cav., 2nd Cav., and 3rd Cav. Divs.) and part 27th Div.

** Second Army H.Q. was in Italy from 13/11/17—10/3/18 (see p. 81).

*** Between 7.50 a.m. 28/4–6 a.m. 7/5/1915 the Second Army on the Ypres battlefront was replaced by *PLUMER'S FORCE :* V Corps (2nd Cav. Div., 27th, 28th, 1st Cdn., and Lahore Divs.) ; together with 10th and 11th Inf. Bdes. (4th Div.) ; 149th, 150th, and 151st Inf. Bdes. (50th Div.); 13th Inf. Bde. (5th Div.) ; and 54th and 55th Fd. Cos. R.E. (7th Div.).

1915 *(Contd.)*

16 June	**First Attack on Bellewaarde** [3rd Div. : V Corps].
19 July	**Hooge** [3rd Div. : V Corps].
30 and 31 July	**Hooge** (German Liquid-Fire Attack) [139th Bde. (46th Div.) : V Corps ; and 14th Div. : VI Corps].
9 August	**Hooge** [6th Div. : VI Corps].
25 September	**Second Attack on Bellewaarde** [3rd Div. : V Corps ; and 14th Div. : VI Corps].
19 December	**First Phosgene Gas Attack** (German) [49th Div. : VI Corps].

1916

14 February	**Loss of the Bluff** [17th Div. : V Corps].
2 March	**Recapture of the Bluff** [17th Div. : V Corps].
27 March–16 April ...	**St. Eloi Craters** [3rd Div. : V Corps—until 4/4 ; then 2nd Cdn. Div. : Cdn. Corps].
30 April	**Wulverghem** (German Gas Attack) [3rd and 24th Divs. : V Corps].
2–13 June	**Battle of Mount Sorrel*** [1st, 2nd, and 3rd Cdn. Divs. : Cdn. Corps ; and 20th Div. : XIV Corps].

---

* 1¾ miles S. of Hooge.

SECOND ARMY

1917

7–14 June ... ... **Battle of Messines** [IX, X, and II Anzac Corps ; with 2nd Tank Bde. (A Bn.—36 tanks, and B. Bn.—36 tanks)].

7 June ... ... **Capture of Messines** [N.Z. Div. : II Anzac Corps ; with part of 2nd Tank Bde.].

7 June ... ... **Capture of Wytschaete** [16th and 36th Divs. : IX Corps ; with part of 2nd Tank Bde.].

BATTLES OF YPRES [II, IX, X, I Anzac, II Anzac, and Cdn. Corps ; with E Bn., 1st Tank Bde.].

31 July–2 August ... **Battle of Pilckem Ridge** [IX (part) and X Corps].

16–18 August ... ... **Battle of Langemarck** [Part of X Corps].

20–25 September ... **Battle of Menin Road Ridge** [IX, X, and I Anzac Corps].

26 September–3 October **Battle of Polygon Wood** [IX, X, I Anzac, and II Anzac* Corps ; 15 tanks, E Bn., 1st Tank Bde. with II Anzac Corps on *28/9*].

4 October ... ... **Battle of Broodseinde** [IX, X, I Anzac, and II Anzac Corps].

9 October ... ... **Battle of Poelcappelle** [IX, X, I Anzac, and II Anzac Corps].

12 October ... ... **First Battle of Passchendaele** [IX, X (part), I Anzac, and II Anzac Corps].

26 Oct.–10 Nov. ... **Second Battle of Passchendaele** [II,** IX (part), X, I Anzac, and Cdn.** Corps].

---

* II Anzac Corps entered the Battle on 28/9/17, taking over from V Corps, Fifth Army.
** II Corps entered the Battle on 2/11/17 (relieving XVIII Corps of Fifth Army) ; and between 14–21/10/17 Cdn. Corps took over the II Anzac Corps front in Second Army.

1917 *(Contd.)*

On 9/11/17 Second Army Headquarters moved to Italy, and on 13/11/17 the Second Army Commander became C.-in-C. British Force in Italy. The Second Army Front in Flanders was taken over by General Sir H. S. Rawlinson, Bt., and on 20/12/17 the Second Army was designated Fourth Army.

1918

On 10/3/18 General Sir H. C. O. Plumer handed over the command of the British Force in Italy to Lieut.-General Earl of Cavan and returned to the Western Front. On 13/3/18 the Second Army was reconstituted. General Plumer took over again the command of the Ypres Front ; and on 17/3/18 the Fourth Army was renamed Second Army.

	BATTLES OF THE LYS [IX, XV, and XXII Corps; with 4th, 5th, and 13th Tank Bns. (Lewis Guns); and (Fr.) XXXVI and (Fr.) II Cav. Corps].
10 and 11 April	**Battle of Messines** [IX Corps].
11 April	**Loss of Hill 63** [25th Div. : IX Corps].
12–15 April	**Battle of Hazebrouck** [XV,* and (part) IX Corps; with 2nd Cav. Div. in Reserve to XV Corps].
12–15 April	**Defence of Nieppe Forest** [29th, 31st, and 1st Aus. Divs. : XV Corps].
13–15 April	**Battle of Bailleul** [IX and XXII Corps; with Lewis Guns 5th Tank Bn., 4th Tank Bde.].
13 and 14 April ...	**Defence of Neuve Église** [148th Bde. (49th Div.) and 100th Bde. (33rd Div.) : IX Corps].
17–19 April	**First Battle of Kemmel Ridge** [IX and XXII Corps; with 4th, 5th, and 13th Tank Bns. (Lewis Guns), 4th Tank Bde. and (Fr.) II Cav. Corps].**
25 and 26 April ...	**Second Battle of Kemmel Ridge** [XXII Corps; with 4th, 5th, and 13th Tank Bns. (Lewis Guns), 4th Tank Bde. ; and (Fr.) XXXVI Corps and (Fr.) II Cav. Corps— D.A.N.**].

---

* Transferred from First Army at Noon on 12/4/18.
** On 25/4/18 the French II Cav. Corps held the line on the east of Kemmel Hill. After the Hill had been lost, the British 25th Div. reinforced the Fr. II Cav. Corps on 25/4. Next day the 25th Div. was transferred to XXII Corps. The Fr. XXXVI Corps also co-operated in this Battle under Second Army. II Cav. Corps took part in the operations from 16/4–5/5/18 on this front ; and XXXVI Corps from 21/4–31/5/18. The *Détachement d'Armée du Nord (Général de Mitry)* functioned between 19/4–5/7/18.

1918 *(Contd.)*

BATTLES OF THE LYS *(Contd.)*

29 April ... ... **Battle of the Scherpenberg** [XXII Corps; with 4th, 5th, and 13th Tank Bns. (Lewis Guns), 4th Tank Bde.; and Fr. XXXVI and Fr. II Cav. Corps*].

---

19 July ... ... **Capture of Meteren** [9th Div.: XV Corps].

THE ADVANCE TO VICTORY.

18 Aug.**–6 Sept. ... **THE ADVANCE IN FLANDERS** [II, X, XV, and XIX Corps***].

18 August ... ... **Capture of Outtersteene Ridge** [87th Bde. (29th Div.): XV Corps].

18 August ... ... **Capture of Hoegenacker Ridge** [9th Div.: XV Corps].

1 September ... ... **Capture of Neuve Eglise** [89th Bde. (30th Div.): X Corps].

2 September ... ... **Capture of Wulverghem** [21st Bde. (30th Div.): X Corps].

4 September ... ... **Capture of Ploegsteert and Hill 63** [86th and 88th Bdes. (29th Div.): XV Corps].

---

28 Sept.–11 Nov. ... **THE FINAL ADVANCE IN FLANDERS** [II, X, XV, and XIX Corps].†

28 September–2 October **Battle of Ypres** [II, X, XV, and XIX Corps].

14–19 October ... ... **Battle of Courtrai** [II, X, XV, and XIX Corps].

25 October ... ... **Ooteghem** [II, X, and XIX Corps].

31 October ... ... **Tieghem** [II and XIX Corps].

On the 9th November the 3rd Cavalry Division joined the Second Army and co-operated with this Army during the last phase of the Final Advance.

When hostilities ceased at 11 a.m. on the 11th November the leading troops of the 3rd Cavalry Division had secured the line of the River Dendre at Leuze and at Lessines, and the general line of the Second Army, which was on the left of the B.E.F., ran from

---

* After the Battles of the Lys had concluded, on 5/5/18 Fr. XVI Corps relieved Fr. II Cav. Corps; and on 12/5/18 Fr. XIV Corps took over the front in the Second Army to the N. of Fr. XVI Corps. On 28/5/18 orders were received to withdraw Fr. XXXVI Corps from the Flanders Front, and at Noon on 31/5/18 XXXVI Corps was withdrawn and Fr. XVI Corps extended to its right (S.) and took over the sector previously held by XXXVI Corps. On 30/6/18 British XIX Corps relieved Fr. XIV Corps, and on 8/7/18 British X Corps relieved Fr. XVI Corps. On 6/7/18 *D.A.N.* had become Fr. Ninth Army, with Army H.Q. at Fère Champenoise.

** On 18/8/18 Second Army (on the left of the B.E.F.) held a 19-mile front, from S. of Vieux Berquin to N.E. of Ypres—with XV, X, XIX, and II Corps.

*** 27th Am. Div. was included in XIX Corps, and 30th Am. Div. in II Corps.

† For this advance the Second Army was placed under King Albert of Belgium.

1918 *(Contd.)*

Lessines to Voorde. The 10-mile front of the Army was occupied by the X and XIX Corps. Since the Advance began on the 18th August the Second Army had fought two battles and advanced across Belgium 53 miles in 86 days.

It was now a question of occupying Germany to enforce the Armistice Terms. To carry out the first stage of this manœuvre, two British Armies (Second and Fourth) and the Cavalry Corps were ordered to advance from the Armistice Line to the German frontier, preparatory to the second stage : the further advance to secure the Rhine bridgeheads.

In the first stage each Army was composed of 4 Corps, and each Corps of 4 divisions. In accordance with this order the Second Army was reorganized as follows :

II Corps (9th, 29th, 34th, and 41st Divisions) ; III Corps (8th, 15th, 55th, and 74th Divisions) ; XXII Corps (4th, 51st, 52nd, and 56th Divisions) ; and Canadian Corps (1st, 2nd, 3rd, and 4th Canadian Divisions).

On the 17th November the advance began : the Second Army, covered by the 1st and 3rd Cavalry Divisions, crossed the Armistice Line and opened the march towards the German frontier. The leading infantry divisions started on the following morning. On the 29th November the cavalry reached the German frontier, and the infantry closed up behind the mounted troops so as to be ready to enter Germany.

It now became necessary to make a further reorganization of the Army of Occupation owing to the comparatively narrow front on the Rhine which had been allotted to the B.E.F. For this task the Second Army (General Sir H. C. O. Plumer) was selected, and its advance across Germany to the Rhine was covered by the 1st Cavalry Division and the 17th (Armoured-Car) Battalion of the Tank Corps. The composition of the Second Army was altered and it was reorganized as follows :

II Corps (9th, 29th, and New Zealand Divisions) ; VI Corps (Guards, 2nd and 3rd Divisions) ; IX Corps (1st, 6th, and 62nd Divisions) ; and Canadian Corps (1st Canadian and 2nd Canadian Divisions).

The 1st Cavalry Division entered Germany on the 1st December ; on the 6th the 2nd Cavalry Brigade reached Cologne, and the 17th (A.-C.) Battalion at once piqueted the Rhine bridges. On the next day the 28th Brigade (9th Division, II Corps) arrived by train in Cologne, and the 1st and 9th Cavalry Brigades also reached the Rhine to the south and north of Cologne. On the 12th December the 1st Cavalry Division crossed the Rhine by the Hohenzollern Bridge, and at Bonn the 1st Cavalry Brigade also crossed the river.

On the 2nd April, 1919, the Second Army became the British Army of the Rhine ; and on the 21st April General Sir Herbert Plumer relinquished the command and was succeeded by General Sir W. R. Robertson.

THIRD ARMY

G.O.C.

13 July, 1915 ... ... General Sir C. C. MONRO.*
23 October, 1915 ... ... General Sir E. H. H. ALLENBY.**
9 June, 1917 ... ... General Hon. Sir J. H. G. BYNG.

M.-G.G.S.

13 July, 1915...Maj.-Gen. A. L. LYNDEN-BELL.
21 Oct., 1915...Maj.-Gen. L. J. BOLS.
21 May, 1917...Maj.-Gen. L. R. VAUGHAN.

D.-A. and Q.-M.-G.

13 July, 1915...Maj.-Gen. W. CAMPBELL.
25 Oct., 1915...Maj.-Gen. H. A. L. TAGART.
1 Mar., 1916...Maj.-Gen. A. F. SILLEM.

M.-G.R.A.

19 July, 1915...Maj.-Gen. R. A. K. MONTGOMERY.
7 Sept., 1915...Br.-Gen. A. B. SCOTT (tempy.).
9 Oct., 1915...Maj.-Gen. F. E. JOHNSON.
12 June, 1916...Maj.-Gen. A. E. A HOLLAND.
19 Feb., 1917...Maj.-Gen. R. St. C. LECKY.
3 Aug., 1918...Maj.-Gen. A. E. WARDROP.

C.E.

26 July, 1915...Maj.-Gen. J. E. CAPPER.
3 Oct., 1915...Maj.-Gen. W. HUSKISSON.
16 July, 1916...Maj.-Gen. E. R. KENYON (wounded 2/5/17).
3 May, 1917...Maj.-Gen. H. C. NANTON (tempy.).
1 June, 1917...Maj.-Gen. E. R. KENYON.
18 Dec., 1917...Maj.-Gen. W. A. LIDDELL.

A.-A. Defence Cdr.***

16 Nov., 1916...Lt.-Col. W. H. LEWIS.

D.-D. Signals†

23 July, 1915...Lt.-Col. W. P. E. NEWBIGGING.
6 Feb., 1916...Col. W. P. E. NEWBIGGING.

---

* Became C.-in-C. E.E.F. on 27/10/15.
** Became C.-in-C. E.E.F. at Midnight, 28/6/17.
*** Third Army A.-A. Group (K., L., and M. A.-A. Batteries, each two sections of 13-pdrs.—12 13-pdrs.) was formed in November, 1916. In November, 1918, L., M., N., O. A.-A. Bties., with Third Army, had 38, 13-pdrs. and 2, 3″ A.-A. guns.
† Third Army Signal Coy. (Lt.-Col. W. P. E. Newbigging) mobilized at Houghton Regis on 15/4/15, and disembarked at Le Havre on 20/7/15.

THIRD ARMY

D.-D.S. and T.

14 July, 1915...Col. A. Long.
16 Jan., 1916...Col. W. S. Swabey.
16 Oct., 1917...Br.-Gen. W. S. Swabey.
18 Nov., 1917...Br.-Gen. A. Phelps.
 5 April, 1918...Br.-Gen. A. K. Seccombe.

D.-D.O.S.

18 July, 1915...Col. E. A. Moulton-
                        Barrett.
20 Dec., 1917...Col. C. D. R. Watts.
23 May, 1918...Col. L. C. G. Tufnell.

D.M.S.

13 July, 1915 ... ... Maj.-Gen. F. H. Treherne.
 1 April, 1916 ... ... Maj.-Gen. J. M. Irwin.

D.-D.V.S.

July, 1915...Lt.-Col. H. J. Axe.
25 May, 1917...Col. W. A. Pallin.

D.-D. Remounts.

2 Aug., 1915...Lt.-Col. S. R. A.
                        Hankey.
11 Dec., 1917...Col. S. R. A. Hankey.

LOCATION OF ARMY HEADQUARTERS
(INCLUDING ADVD. A.H.Q.).

13 July, 1915 ... ... **St. Omer.**

19 July, 1915 ... ... **Beauquesne** (5 miles S.S.E. of Doullens).

20 March, 1916 ... **St. Pol.**

1 May, 1917 ... ... **Noyelle Vion** (11 miles S.E. of St. Pol).

1 July, 1917 ... ... **Albert.**

23 March, 1918 ... ... **Beauquesne** (5 miles S.S.E. of Doullens).

8 April, 1918 ... ... **Hesdin** (20 miles N.W. of Doullens).

30 July, 1918 ... ... **Villers l'Hôpital** (7 miles N.W. of Doullens).

21 October, 1918 ... **Masnières** (4 miles S. of Cambrai).

11 a.m., 11 November, 1918 **Armistice with Germany.**

5 December, 1918 ... **Flixécourt** (15 miles S.W. of Doullens).

THIRD ARMY

FORMATION.

Third Army Headquarters began to form at St. Omer on the 13th July, 1915, and six days later moved to Beauquesne. At first the Third Army was composed of the VII* and X* Corps and the Indian Cavalry Corps.** The Third Army took over part of the front line from the French Second Army (held in July by the French XI and XIV Corps), a fifteen-mile stretch running from Curlu on the Somme to Hébuterne, with the French Tenth Army to the northward between the left of the Third Army and the right of the British First Army, which was opposite Lens (20 miles from Hébuterne). It was not until March, 1916, when the Fourth Army came into being, that the Third Army moved northward, relieved the French Tenth Army, and at last the British line ran unbroken from opposite Lens, through Hébuterne, to Curlu. At this time the 70-mile British Front extended from Bœsinghe (north of Ypres) to Curlu on the Somme.

BATTLES AND ENGAGEMENTS.

1915

19 July–31 December.

1916

21 May ... ... **German Attack on Vimy Ridge** [25th Div. : XVII Corps].***

BATTLES OF THE SOMME [VII Corps].

1 July ... ... **Attack on the Gommecourt Salient** [46th and 56th Divs. : VII Corps].

1917

14 March–5 April ... **German Retreat to the Hindenburg Line** [VII Corps ; and, until 19/3, part of XVIII Corps].

---

* In July, 1915, VII Corps had 4th, 37th, and 48th Divs., and X Corps had 5th, 18th, and 51st Divs.
** 1st and 2nd Indian Cavalry Divisions. (In March, 1916, the Indian Cavalry Corps H.Q. disappeared, and was not re-formed in France ; and on 26/11/16 the 1st and 2nd Indian Cavalry Divisions became the 4th and 5th Cavalry Divisions.)
*** Also see IV Corps and First Army.

1917 *(Contd.)*

BATTLES OF ARRAS [VI, VII, XVII, and Cav. Corps; with 1st Tank Bde.].

9–14 April ... ... **First Battle of the Scarpe** [VI, VII, and XVII Corps, and Cav. Corps; with C. Bn. and 10 Coy. D. Bn., 1st Tank Bde.].

10 and 11 April ... **Attack and capture of Monchy le Preux** [3rd Cav. Div. (Cav. Corps), and 37th Div. (VI Corps); with 7 tanks, C. Bn.].

11 April ... ... **Capture of Wancourt** [14th Div. (VII Corps); with 4 tanks D. Bn., 1st Tank Bde.].

13–15 April ... ... **Attack and capture of Wancourt Ridge** [50th Div. : VII Corps].

23 and 24 April ... **Second Battle of the Scarpe** [VI, VII, and XVII Corps; with 20 tanks, 1st Tank Bde.].

23 April ... ... **Capture of Guémappe** [15th Div. : VI Corps].

28 and 29 April ... **Battle of Arleux** [VI and XVII Corps].

3 and 4 May ... ... **Third Battle of the Scarpe** [VI, VII, and XVII Corps; with 4 Tanks, 1st Tank Bde (with VII)].

---

12 May ... ... **Attack on Devil's Trench** [12th Div. : VI Corps].

13–16 May ... ... **Capture and defence of Rœux** [3rd Div. (VI Corps), and 17th and 51st Divs. (XVII Corps)].

20 May—16 June ... **Actions on the Hindenburg Line** [21st and 33rd Divs. (VII Corps); and from *10 ‹.m. 31/5,* 20th Div. (IV Corps), and 58th and 62nd Divs. (V Corps)—from Fifth Army].

1917 *(Contd.)*

20 November ... ... **Attack at Bullecourt*** [3rd and 16th Divs.: VI Corps].

                       BATTLE OF CAMBRAI [III, IV, V, VI, VII, and Cav. Corps; with 1st, 2nd, and 3rd Tank Bdes.].

20 and 21 November   **The Tank Attack** [III, IV, VII (part), and Cav. Corps; with 1st Tank Bde. (with IV), and 2nd and 3rd Tank Bdes. (with III)**]

21 November ... ... **Recapture of Noyelles** [6th Div. (III); with 2 tanks B Bn., 2nd Tank Bde.].

21 November ... ... **Capture of Cantaing** [51st Div. (IV); with 12 Tanks B Bn., 2nd Tank Bde.].

21 November ... ... **Capture of Tadpole Copse** [56th Div.: IV Corps].

23–28 November ... **Capture of Bourlon Wood** [III, IV, VI (part), and Cav. Corps; with 1st and 3rd Tank Bdes. (with IV), and 2nd Tank Bde. (with III and IV)].

30 Nov –3 Dec. ... ... **The German Counter-Attacks** [III, IV, V,*** VI (part), VII, and Cav. Corps; with 1st and 2nd Tank Bdes. (with III), and 3rd Tank Bde. (with IV)].

30 November ... ... **Attack on Gouzeaucourt** [Gds. Div.: III Corps; with 22 tanks, 2nd Tank Bde.].

1 December ... ... **Attack on Villers Guislain and Gauche Wood** [Gds. and 12th Divs., and 4th (Ind.) and 5th (Ind.) Cav. Divs.: III Corps; with 19 tanks, 2nd Tank Bde.].

---

30 and 31 December   **Welch Ridge** [63rd Div.: V Corps].†

---

* Subsidiary attack on northern flank of the Battle of Cambrai.
** 204 tanks with III Corps, and 120 tanks with IV Corps on 20/11/17.
*** On 1/12/17 V Corps relieved IV Corps in the line.
† Also see Fifth Army.

1918

FIRST BATTLES OF THE SOMME [IV, V, VI, VII, and XVII Corps ; with 2nd, 3rd, 4th, and 5th Tank Bdes.].

21–23 March ... ... **Battle of St. Quentin** [IV, V, and VI Corps ; with 2nd Tank Bde. in Army Res., less 1 Coy. 8th Bn. with IV Corps ; and 6th Bn., 3rd Tank Bde. with VI Corps].

22 March ... ... **Counter-Attack at Beugny** [19th Div. (IV) ; with 25 tanks, 2nd Bn., 2nd Tank Bde.].

24 and 25 March ... **First Battle of Bapaume** [IV, V, VI, VII,* and XVII (part) Corps, and 1st Cav. Bde. ; with 8th Bn. (V), 10th Bn. (IV), 2nd Tank Bde. ; and 4th Tank Bde. and 1 Coy. (Lewis Guns) 13th Bn. Also, in Defence of the Ancre and of the Camp : 3rd Tank Bde., and 9th Comp. Bn., 4th Bn., and 13th Bn. (part), with details and tanks].

28 March ... ... **First Battle of Arras** [IV, V, VI, and XVII Corps ; with Detnts. 2nd Tank Bde., and 1 Sec. 3rd Bn., and B Coy. 9th Bn. (Lewis Guns), 3rd Tank Bde., and 2nd, 8th and 13th Bns., 5th Tank Bde.].

5 April ... ... **Battle of the Ancre** [IV, V, VI (part), and VII with 18 teams of Lewis Guns of 4th Bn., 4th Tank Bde., with VII Corps, and 1 tank 10th Bn. with IV].

Night, 22/23 June ... **Bucquoy**** [5 Pltns., 5/K.O.Y.L.I. (D Coy. and 1 Pltn. B.), 62nd Div. : IV Corps ; with party Tank Engr. Bn., and 5 female tanks of C Coy. 10th Bn., 4th Tank Bde.].

---

* VII Corps was transferred from Fifth Army to Third Army at 4 a.m. on 25/3/18.
** First night raid on which tanks were engaged.

1918 (*Contd.*)

THE ADVANCE TO VICTORY.

On the 21st August the Third Army, in the right centre of the B.E.F., held a 17-mile front from Albert to Neuville Vitasse (S.S.E. of Arras) with the IV, V, and VI Corps.

SECOND BATTLES OF THE SOMME [IV, V, and VI Corps ; with 1st, 2nd, and 3rd Tank Bdes.].

21–23 August ... ... **Battle of Albert** [IV, V, and VI Corps, and 1st Cav. and 2nd Cav. Divs. ; with 3rd (Whippets), 7th, 10th, and 17th (A.-C.) Bns., 1st Tank Bde. (with IV) ; and 6th (Whippets), 12th, and 15th Bns., 2nd Tank Bde., and 9th and 11th Bns., 3rd Tank Bde. (with VI)].

24 August ... ... **Capture of Mory Copse** [99th Bde., 2nd Div. : VI Corps].

25 August ... ... **Capture of Behagnies and Sapignies** [5th Bde., 2nd Div. : VI Corps].

31 Aug –3 Sept. ... **Second Battle of Bapaume** [IV, V, and VI Corps, and 2nd Cav. Div. ; with 3rd (Whippets), 7th, 10th, and 17th (A.-C.) Bns., 1st Tank Bde. (with IV), and 6th (Whippets), 12th, and 15th Bns., 2nd Tank Bde. (with VI)].

SECOND BATTLES OF ARRAS [VI and XVII* Corps].

26–30 August ... ... **Battle of the Scarpe** [VI and XVII* Corps].

2 and 3 September ... **Battle of the Drocourt-Quéant Line** [VI (part) and XVII Corps].

---

* At Noon on 6/4/18 XVII Corps had been transferred (in the line) from Third Army to First Army ; and at Noon on 23/8/18 XVII Corps was transferred back (in the line) from First Army to Third Army. Its place in the First Army was filled by Canadian Corps.

1918 (*Contd.*)

BATTLES OF THE HINDENBURG LINE [IV, V, VI, and XVII Corps; with 1st and 2nd Tank Bdes.].

12 September	**Battle of Havrincourt** [IV, V (part), and VI Corps].
18 September	**Battle of Epéhy** [IV (part) and V Corps].
27 Sept.–1 Oct.	**Battle of the Canal du Nord** [IV, VI, and XVII Corps, and 3rd and 4th Cav. Bdes. (2nd Cav. Div.); with 11th Tank Bn. (IV and V), 12th Tank Bn. (Army Reserve), 1st Tank Bde.; and 15th Tank Bn. (XVII), 2nd Tank Bde.].
1 October	**Capture of Mont sur l'Œuvre** [2nd Div.: VI Corps].
29 Sept.–2 Oct.	**Battle of the St. Quentin Canal** [V Corps; with part 11th Bn., 1st Tank Bde.].
3–5 October	**Battle of the Beaurevoir Line** [V Corps; and 5th Cav. Bde. (2nd Cav. Div.)].
8 and 9 October ...	**Battle of Cambrai** [IV, V, VI, and XVII Corps, and 2nd Cav Div. (less 5th Cav. Bde.); with 2 Comp. Cos. 11th Tank Bn. (V), and 12th Tank Bn. (IV, VI, and XVII), 1st Tank Bde.].
8 October	**Capture of Villers Outréaux** [38th Div.: V Corps; with tank[S] of 11th Bn., 1st Tank Bde.].
8 October	**Capture of Forenville** [2nd Div.: VI Corps].
8 October	**Capture of Niergnies** [63rd Div.: XVII Corps].
9 October	**Capture of Cambrai** [57th Div.: XVII Corps*].

9–12 October ...	**Pursuit to the Selle** [IV, V, VI (part), and XVII Corps, and 4th Cav. Bde. (2nd Cav. Div.) and 3rd Cav. Div.].

---

* Also see First Army.

1918 *(Contd.)*

THE FINAL ADVANCE IN PICARDY [IV, V, VI, and XVII Corps; with 1st and 2nd Tank Bdes.].

17–25 October	**Battle of the Selle** [IV, V, VI, and XVII Corps; with, on 20/10, 11th Tank Bn. (V), and, on 23/10, 11th and 12th Tank Bns. (IV and V), 1st Tank Bde.].
20 October	**Crossing of the Selle** [17th and 38th Divs.: V Corps; with 4 tanks 11th Bn., 1st Tank Bde.].
20 October	**Capture of Solesmes** [62nd Div.: VI Corps].
23 October	**Attack on Forest and Ovillers** [21st and 33rd Divs.: V Corps; with 6 tanks 11th Bn., 1st Tank Bde.].
23 October	**Capture of Grand Champ Ridge** [5th Div.: IV Corps; with 2 tanks 12th Bn., 1st Tank Bde.].
1 and 2 November ...	**Battle of Valenciennes** [Part of XVII Corps].
4 November	**Battle of the Sambre** [IV, V, VI, and XVII Corps, and 4th Cav. Bde. (2nd Cav. Div.); with 11 tanks of 10th and 301st (Am.) Tank Bns. (IV and V), 2nd Tank Bd. .
4 November	**Capture of Le Quesnoy** [N.Z. Div.: IV Corps].
5–7 November	**Passage of the Grande Honnelle** [VI and XVII Corps; with 6th (Whippets) Tank Bn. (with VI), 2nd Tank Bde.].
9 November	**Occupation of Maubeuge** [Gds. Div.: VI Corps].

When hostilities ceased at 11 a.m. on the 11th November the leading troops, the 4th Cavalry Brigade (2nd Cavalry Division), were at Erquelinnes (on the Sambre, 7 miles S.W. of Thuin); and the general line of the Third Army, which was in the right-centre of the 55-mile front of the B.E.F., stood astride the Sambre midway between Maubeuge and Thuin. The 11-mile front of the Army was occupied by the V, IV, VI, and XVII Corps. In the 83 days which had elapsed since the 21st August the Third Army had fought in 7 battles, and had advanced over 60 miles in the face of continuous opposition.

FOURTH ARMY

G.O.C.

5 February, 1916	... ...	General Sir H. S. RAWLINSON, Bt.*
21 February, 1918	... ...	General Sir W. R. BIRDWOOD (tempy.).
28 March, 1918 ...	... ...	General Sir H. S. RAWLINSON, Bt.

M.-G.G.S.

5 Feb., 1916...Maj.-Gen. A. A.
MONTGOMERY.**

D.-A. and Q.-M.-G.

5 Feb., 1916...Maj.-Gen. H. C. SUTTON.
13 Nov., 1916...Maj.-Gen. H. C.
HOLMAN.

M.-G.R.A.

5 Feb., 1916...Maj.-Gen. J. F. N. BIRCH.
28 May, 1916...Maj.-Gen. C. E. D.
BUDWORTH.

C.E.

13 Feb., 1916...Maj.-Gen. R. U. H.
BUCKLAND.

A.-A. Defence Cdr.***

27 Nov., 1916...Lt.-Col. H. W. HILL.†
1 May, 1918...Lt.-Col. R. B. HAY.

D.-D. Signals.

6 Feb., 1916...Col. R. G. EARLE.

---

* General Sir H. S. Rawlinson was British Representative, Supreme War Council, at Versailles.
** In 1926 this surname was changed to Montgomery-Massingberd.
*** Fourth Army A.-A. Group (N, O, and P A.-A. Batteries, each two sections of 13-pdrs.—
12 13-pdrs.) was formed in November, 1916. In November, 1918, F, G, P, Q, Z, A-A. Bties., with
Fourth Army, had 30, 13-pdrs. and 6, 3″ A.-A. guns.
† Came up in November, 1917, when H.Q. Fourth Army relieved H.Q. Second Army; and
remained with Second Army after Army H.Q. returned from Italy in March, 1918.

D.-D.S. and T.

25 Feb., 1916...Col. F. M. WILSON.
16 Oct., 1917...Br.-Gen. F. M. WILSON.*
2 April, 1918...Br.-Gen. E. C. F.
GILLESPIE.**

D.-D.O.S.

26 Feb., 1916...Col. J. A. STEWART.
21 May, 1916...Col. H. S. BUSH.*
2 April, 1918...Col. R. S. HAMILTON.**

D.M.S.

26 February, 1916 ... ... Maj.-Gen. M. W. O'KEEFFE.

D.-D.V.S.

27 Feb., 1916...Lt.-Col. F. W. HUNT.*
2 April, 1918...Col. W. J. TATAM.**

D.-D. Remounts.

5 Feb., 1916...Lt.-Col. W. E.
MATCHAM.*
2 April, 1918...Col. J. W. YARDLEY.**

---

* To Second Army, when it was designated Fourth Army on 20/12/17 ; and these officers remained with Second Army (q.v.).
** From Fifth Army—when Fifth Army was designated Fourth Army (on 2/4/18).

LOCATION OF ARMY HEADQUARTERS.
(INCLUDING ADVD. A.H.Q.).

5 February, 1916 ...	**Tilques** (3 miles N.W. of St. Omer).
24 February, 1916 ...	**Querrieu** (6 miles N.E. of Amiens).
15 April, 1917	**Villers Carbonnel** '(4 miles S.S.W. of Péronne).
5 July, 1917	**Malo les Bains** (1 mile N.E. of Dunkirk).
25 October, 1917 ...	**Rosendael** (1 mile E. of Dunkirk).
5 November, 1917 ... –9 November, 1917 ... }	**Dury** (3 miles S. of Amiens).

9/11/1917...Second Army Front in Flanders was taken over by G.O.C. and Staff of Fourth Army.

20/12/1917...Second Army was designated Fourth Army.

9 November, 1917 ... –13 March, 1918 ... }	**Cassel.**

13/3/1918...All units under Fourth Army came under Second Army.

17/3/1918...The present Fourth Army was renamed Second Army.

22 March, 1918	**Querrieu** (6 miles N.E. of Amiens).
25 March, 1918	**Picquigny sur Somme.**
27 March, 1918	**Abbeville.**

4.30 p.m., 28/3/1918...Fourth Army took over command of Fifth Army.

30 March, 1918	**Auxi le Château** (29 miles W. by S. of Arras).
31 March, 1918 ... ... –4 April, 1918 ... ... }	**Flixécourt** (15 miles S.W. of Doullens).

2/4/1918...The present Fifth Army was redesignated Fourth Army, under G.O.C. Fourth Army, and the Fifth Army ceased to exist.

2 April, 1918	**Dury** (Advd. A.H.Q.).
5 April, 1918	**Flixécourt** (A.H.Q. concentrated).
30 August, 1918	**Bertangles** (5 miles N. of Amiens).
25 September, 1918	**Éterpigny** ($2\frac{1}{2}$ miles S. of Péronne).
14 October, 1918	**Montigny Farm,** near Roisel (in Railway Train).
3 November, 1918	**In train for Honnéchy** (4 miles S.S.W. of le Cateau).

11 a.m., 11/11/1918...**Armistice with Germany.**

12 November, 1918	**Honnéchy.**
16 November, 1918	**Avesnes.**
30 November, 1918	**Ham sur Heure** (6 miles S.S.W. of Charleroi).
10 December, 1918	**Namur.**

FOURTH ARMY

FORMATION.

Fourth Army Headquarters began to form at Tilques on the 5th February, 1916, and nineteen days later Army Headquarters moved to Querrieu. A week later the Fourth Army took over the right sector of the B.E.F. front, a 15-mile stretch from Curlu on the Somme to Hébuterne. The Fourth Army was in touch on the south with the French Sixth Army and to the north with the right of the British Third Army. Fourth Army took over this front with the XIII and X Corps, in the line, and the VIII Corps in Army Reserve.*

BATTLES AND ENGAGEMENTS.

1916

BATTLES OF THE SOMME [III, VIII, X, XIII, XIV, XV, and Cav. Corps; with C and D Tank Cos.].

1–13 July	**Battle of Albert** [III, VIII,** X,** XIII, and XV Corps].
1 July	**Capture of Montauban** [30th Div.: XIII Corps].
1 July	**Capture of Mametz** [7th Div.: XV Corps].
2 July	**Capture of Fricourt** [17th Div.: XV Corps].
2–4 July	**Capture of La Boisselle** [19th Div.: III Corps].
3 July	**Capture of Bernafay Wood** [9th Div.: XIII Corps].
7–11 July	**Mametz Wood** [38th Div.: XV Corps].
10 July	**Capture of Contalmaison** [23rd Div.: III Corps].
7–13 July	**Fighting in Trônes Wood** [30th Div.: XIII Corps].
14–17 July	**Battle of Bazentin Ridge** [III, XIII, and XV Corps].
14 July	**Capture of Trônes Wood** [54th Bde. (18th Div.): XIII Corps].

* X Corps had 32nd, 36th, 48th, and 49th Divs., and XIII Corps had 7th, 18th, and 30th Divs., VIII Corps (at that time in Army Reserve) had only the 31st Div.
** On 4/7/16 the Reserve (later Fifth) Army took over (in the line) VIII Corps (4th, 29th, 31st, and 48th Divs.) and X Corps (25th, 32nd, 36th, and 49th Divs.) from the Fourth Army.

1916 *(Contd.)*

BATTLES OF THE SOMME (Contd.).

14–18 ; and 29 July ...   **Capture of Longueval** [*14–18/7*—3rd and 9th Divs. : XIII Corps ; and on *29/7*—5th Div. : XV Corps].

15 July–3 September   **Battle of Delville Wood** [XIII Corps, until *Mn. 16/8/16* ; then XIV Corps ; also from *31/8/16*, XV Corps].

20–30 July ... ...   **Attacks on High Wood*** [19th Div. : III Corps ; and 5th, 7th, 33rd, and 51st Divs. : XV Corps].

27 and 28 July ... ...   **Capture and consolidation of Delville Wood** [2nd Div. : XIII Corps].

8 and 9 August   ...   **Attack of Waterlôt Farm—Guillemont** [2nd Div. : XIII Corps].

23 July–3 September   **Battle of Pozières Ridge** [III Corps].

3–6 September ... ...   **Battle of Guillemont** [XIV and XV Corps].

9 September   ... ...   **Battle of Ginchy** [XIV and (part) XV Corps].

15–22 September   ...   **Battle of Flers-Courcelette** [III, XIV, and XV Corps, and 1st Cav. and 5th (Ind.) Cav. Divs. (Cav. Corps) ; with 42 tanks (C Coy.—17 tanks, and D Coy.—25 tanks). 17 tanks C Coy. with XIV ; 17 tanks D Coy. with XV ; and 8 tanks D Coy. with III].

15 September   ... ...   **Capture of Flers** [41st and N.Z. Divs., with 1 tank : XV Corps].

15 September   ... ...   **Capture of Martinpuich** [15th Div., with 4 tanks : III Corps].

25–28 September   ...   **Battle of Morval** [III, XIV, and XV Corps, and Cav. Corps ; with, on *25/9*, 2 tanks D Coy. with III ; and, on *26/9*, 2 tanks C Coy. with XIV, and 1 tank D Coy. with XV].

25 September   ... ...   **Capture of Lesbœufs** [Gds. and 6th Divs. : XIV Corps].

---

* High Wood was finally captured by 47th Div., III Corps, on 15/9/16.

1916 *(Contd.)*

BATTLES OF THE SOMME (Contd.).

26 September	**Capture of Combles** [56th Div., with 2 tanks C Coy. : XIV Corps.]
26 September	**Capture of Gird Trench* and Gueudecourt** [21st Div., with 1 tank D Coy. : XV Corps].
1–18 October	**Battle of the Transloy Ridges** [III, XIV, and XV Corps ; with 5 tanks C and D Cos.—3 with XIV and 2 with XV].
1–3 October	**Capture of Eaucourt l'Abbaye** [47th Div. : III Corps].
7 October	**Capture of Le Sars** [23rd Div. : III Corps].
7 October–5 November	**Attacks on the Butte de Warlencourt** [9th, 23rd, 47th, 48th, and 50th Divs. : III Corps].
3–11 November	**Battle of the Ancre Heights** [Part of III Corps].
13–18 November ...	**Battle of the Ancre** [Part of III Corps].

1917

4 March	**Bouchavesnes** [8th Div. : XV Corps].
14 March–5 April ...	**German Retreat to the Hindenburg Line** [III, IV, XIV, and XV Corps, and 5th (2nd Ind.) Cav. Div.].
18 March	**Occupation of Péronne** [48th Div. : III Corps].
21 ; 24 and 25 April ; and 5 May.	**Capture of Fifteen Ravine ; Villers Plouich ; Beaucamp ; and La Vacquerie** [40th Div. : XV Corps].
21 June–18 November	**Operations on the Flanders Coast** [1st, 9th, 32nd, 33rd, 41st, 42nd, 49th, and 66th Divs. : XV Corps].
10 and 11 July	**Defence of Nieuport** [1st and 32nd Divs. : XV Corps].

On 9/11/17 Second Army H.Q. moved to Italy, and the Second Army Front in Flanders was then taken over by General Sir H. S. Rawlinson and the Fourth Army Staff.

On 20/12/17 Second Army (in Flanders) was designated Fourth Army.

---

* The first instance of the co-operation of tank and aeroplane in the field.

1918

In February, 1918, General Sir H. Rawlinson went to Versailles as British Representative on the Supreme War Council. During his absence, on 13/3/18, General Sir H. Plumer and Staff returned to Flanders from Italy and once more took over the Ypres front. All units at that time under the Fourth Army forthwith came under Second Army H.Q.; and on 17/3/18 the designation of Fourth Army was changed, and it was renamed Second Army.

General Sir H. Rawlinson returned from Versailles on 28/3/18, and at 4.30 p.m. officially took over command of the Fifth Army (now reduced to the XIX Corps*) which was holding the right of the B.E.F. front from the R. Luce to the R. Somme, between the left of the French First Army and the right of the British Third Army.

On 2/4/18 the Fifth Army was renamed Fourth Army; and before the Great War came to an end in France the Fourth Army took part in the following battles and engagements:

2–5 April ... ... **FIRST BATTLES OF THE SOMME** [XIX Corps and 3rd Cav. Div.].

4 April ... ... **Battle of the Avre** [XIX Corps and 3rd Cav. Div.].

24 and 25 April ... **Villers Bretonneux** [8th, 18th, and 58th Divs.: III Corps, and 4th Aus. and 5th Aus. Divs.: Aus. Corps; with 1st and 3rd Tank Bns., 3rd Tank Bde.].

4 July ... ... **Capture of Hamel** [2nd Aus. (part), 3rd Aus. (part), and 4th Aus. Divs.; Aus. Corps; and Detnts. 131st and 132nd Regts., 33rd Am. Div.; with 62 tanks of 8th and 13th Bns., 5th Tank Bde.].

On the 8th August the Fourth Army, on the right of the B.E.F., held from south of the R. Luce to the north-west of Albert. The 16-mile Army front was held by the Canadian, Australian, and III Corps, with the Cavalry Corps in reserve to the Army.

---

* III Corps was in the Army Reserve area.

1918 *(Contd.)*

8 Aug.–11 Nov. ... ... **THE ADVANCE TO VICTORY.**

8–11 August ... ... **Battle of Amiens** [III, Cdn., and Aus. Corps, and 1st, 2nd, and 3rd Cav. Divs. (Cav. Corps) ; with 430 tanks (96 Whippets) : 3rd (Wh.), 6th (Wh.), and 17th (A.-C.) Bns., 3rd Tank Bde., with Cav. Corps ; 1st, 4th, 5th, and 14th Bns., 4th Tank Bde., with Cdn. Corps ; and 2nd, 8th, 10th, 13th, and 15th Bns., 5th Tank Bde., with Aus. Corps].*

15–17 August ... ... **Actions round Damery** [1st, 2nd, 3rd, and 4th Cdn. Divs. : Cdn. Corps].

SECOND BATTLES OF THE SOMME [III and Aus. Corps ; with 4th and 5th Tank Bdes.].

21–23 August ... ... **Battle of Albert** [III and Aus. Corps ; with 1st, 4th, and 5th Bns., 4th Tank Bde. (with III) ; and 2nd, 8th, and 13th Bns., 5th Tank Bde. (with Aus.)].

23 August ... ... **Capture of Chuignes** [1st Aus. Div. : Aus. Corps].

31 Aug.–3 Sept. ... **Second Battle of Bapaume** [III and Aus. Corps].

1 September ... ... **Capture of Mont St. Quentin** [2nd Aus. Div. : Aus. Corps].

1 and 2 September ... **Occupation of Péronne** [5th Aus. Div. : Aus. Corps].

BATTLES OF THE HINDENBURG LINE [III, IX, XIII, Aus., and II Am. Corps ; with 3rd, 4th, and 5th Tank Bdes.].

18 September ... ... **Battle of Epéhy** [III, IX,** and Aus. Corps ; with 2nd Bn., 5th Tank Bde. with III (8), IX (4), and Aus. (9 tanks)].

21 September ... ... **Attack on the Knoll, Ronssoy** [12th and 18th Divs. : III Corps ; with 9 tanks, 2nd Bn., 5th Tank Bde.].

24 September ... ... **Attack on Quadrilateral and Fresnoy** [1st and 6th Divs. : IX Corps ; with 20 tanks, 13th Bn., 5th Tank Bde.].

---

* 130th Inf. Regt., 33rd Am. Div., operated with III Corps (8–11/8) ; and 131st Inf. Regt., 33rd Am. Div., with III Corps on 8 and 9/8 ; and on 10 and 11/8 with Aus. Corps.
** IX Corps took over (in the line) on 11/9/18.

1918 (Contd.)

BATTLES OF THE HINDENBURG LINE (Contd.).

29 Sept.–2 Oct. ... ... **Battle of the St. Quentin Canal** [III*, IX, XIII,* Aus.,** and II Am.** Corps, and 5th Cav. Bde. (2nd Cav. Div.) ; with 5th, 6th (Wh.), and 9th Bns., 3rd Tank Bde., with IX ; 1st, 4th, and 301st (Am.) Bns., 5th Tank Bde., with Aus. and II Am. Corps (on 29/9) ; and 3rd (Wh.), 8th, 13th, 16th, and 17th (A.-C.) Bns., 5th Tank Bde., with Aus. Corps].

29 September ... ... **Passage at Bellenglise** [46th Div. : IX Corps ; with 2 Cos. 9th Bn., 3rd Tank Bde.].

29 September ... ... **Capture of Bellicourt Tunnel Defences** [5th Aus. and 30th Am. Divs. : Aus. Corps ; with 1st, 4th, and 301st (Am.) Tank Bns., with Aus. Corps.].

3–5 October ... ... **Battle of the Beaurevoir Line** [IX, XIII, Aus. and II Am. Corps, and 5th Cav. Bde. (2nd Cav. Div.) ; with 5th Bn., and detnt. 6th (Wh.) Bn., 3rd Tank Bde., with IX ; and 3rd (Wh.), 8th, 13th, and 16th Bns., 5th Tank Bde., with Aus. Corps].

5 October ... ... **Capture of Beaurevoir** [25th Div. : XIII Corps ; with 6 tanks 4th Bn., 4th Tank Bde.].

8 and 9 October ... **Battle of Cambrai** [IX, XIII, and II Am.** Corps, and 1st Cav. Div., 5th Cav. Bde. (2nd Cav. Div.), and 3rd Cav. Div. ; with 5th Bn., 3rd Tank Bde., with IX ; and 1st, 3rd (Wh.), 4th, 6th (Wh.), 10th, 16th, and 301st (Am.) Bns., 4th Tank Bde., with XIII and II Am. Corps].

9–12 October ... ... **Pursuit to the Selle** [IX, XIII, and II Am. Corps, and 1st Cav. Div. and 5th Cav. Bde. (2nd Cav. Div.) ; with 17th (A.-C.) Bn., with Cav. ; and 5th Bn. and detnt. 6th (Wh.) Bn., 3rd Tank Bde., with IX Corps].

---

* III Corps handed over (in the line) to XIII Corps at Noon on 1/10/18 ; III Corps then moved to Fifth Army.

** II American Corps (27th and 30th American Divisions) was placed under Fourth Army on 22/9/18, and it was combined with the Australian Corps (under the command of the latter) on 29/9/18. At 9 a.m. on 6/10/18 II Am. Corps took over the front from Aus. Corps.

1918 (*Contd.*)

THE FINAL ADVANCE IN PICARDY [IX, XIII, and II Am. Corps, and Bethell's Force (from 9/11) ; with 2nd and 4th Tank Bdes., and 17th (A.-C.) Bn.].

17–25 October ... ... **Battle of the Selle** [IX, XIII, and II Am.* Corps, and 1st Cav. Div. and 5th Cav. Bde. (2nd Cav. Div.) ; with, from *17–19/10*, 6th (Whs.–12), 16th Bn. (12 tanks) with IX ; and 301st Am. Bn. (25 tanks), with II Am. ; 1st Bn. (12 tanks) with XIII ; and 10th Bn. (23 tanks) in Army Reserve, 4th Tank Bde. On *19/10* 4th Tank Bde. handed over to 2nd Tank Bde.—6th (Wh.), 10th, and 301st (Am.) Bns. ; and, on *23/10*, 2nd Tank Bde. co-operated with IX and XIII].

23 October ... ... **Capture of Bousies** [18th Div.: XIII Corps ; with 6 tanks 10th Bn., 2nd Tank Bde.].

2 November ... ... **Attack S.W. of Landrecies** (Happegarbes Spur) [96th Bde., 32nd Div.: IX Corps ; with 3 tanks 10th Bn., 2nd Tank Bde.].

4 November ... ... **Battle of the Sambre** [IX and XIII Corps, and 5th Cav. Bde. (2nd Cav. Div.) ; with 21 tanks 9th and 14th Bns. with XIII ; 5 tanks 10th Bn. with IX. ; and 6 cars 17th (A.-C.) Bn. with XIII—2nd Tank Bde.].

4 November ... ... **Passage of the Sambre—Oise Canal** [1st and 32nd Divs.: IX Corps ; and 25th Div.: XIII Corps ; with tanks of 9th, 10th, and 14th Bns. ; and 6 cars of 17th (A.-C.) Bn.—2nd Tank Bde.].

5 Nov.–11 a.m. 11 Nov. **Final Operations** [IX and XIII Corps. From *5–7/11*, 9th and 14th Bns. and 17th (A.-C.) Bn. with IX and XIII—2nd Tank Bde. On *8/11*, 5 cars 17th (A.-C.) Bn. with XIII. From *9/11—Armistice* 5 cars 17th (A.-C.) Bn. with " Maj.-Gen. H. K. Bethell's Force "** and 5th Cav. Bde. (2nd Cav. Div.)].

---

* II American Corps (27th Am. and 30th Am. Divs.) was withdrawn to rest on 20/10/18.
** *Bethell's Force* was formed on 9/11/18 and was broken up after Armistice (for its composition see p. 213).

1918 (*Contd.*)

On the 9th November the G.O.C. Fourth Army decided that the main bodies of the IX and XIII Corps should be distributed in depth on and west of the north—south La Capelle—Avesnes—Maubeuge highway, and covered by an outpost line to the east of this road. The German forces on this front were in full retreat and a comparatively small force would suffice to keep in touch with them. For this purpose a mobile force was now organized, and Major-General H. K. Bethell (of the 66th Division) was selected to command it.

On the morning of the 10th November, " Bethell's Force " advanced and established contact with the Germans about Hestrud and Sivry. Slow, but steady, progress was made ; and when the Armistice brought hostilities to a close, at 11 a.m. on the 11th November, the leading troops of " Bethell's Force " had reached a line (along the Army front) from Pont de la République—eastern outskirts of Grandrieu—east of Sivry—Montbliart. On its right (south) " Bethell's Force " was in touch with troops of the French First Army at Eppé Sauvage.

At the cessation of hostilities, the Fourth Army held a 9-mile front on the right of the B.E.F. Since the opening of the Battle of Amiens on the 8th August the Army had fought in 9 battles, and had advanced in the face of continued opposition 72 miles in 96 days.

The Fourth Army with the Cavalry Corps and Second Army were now ordered to move forward from the Armistice Line to the German Frontier, preparatory to a further advance, which would secure the Rhine bridgeheads on the front allotted to the B.E.F. For the first stage each Army would consist of 4 corps and each corps of 4 divisions ; and the composition of the Fourth Army would be :—IV Corps (5th, 37th, 42nd, and New Zealand Divisions), VI Corps (Guards, 2nd, 3rd, and 62nd Divisions), IX Corps (1st, 6th, 32nd, and 66th Divisions), and Australian Corps (1st, 2nd, 3rd, 4th Australian Divisions).

On the 18th November the Fourth Army, preceded on the 17th by the 2nd Cavalry Division, crossed the Armistice Line. On the night of the 28th/29th November the leading cavalry patrols reached the German Frontier to the southward of Malmedy, and the infantry closed up behind the mounted troops.

Owing, however, to the narrow front on the Rhine allotted to the B.E.F. some re-organization of the Army of Occupation became necessary before Germany was entered ; and a reconstituted Second Army was now ordered to take over the whole front of the British advance.

In consequence of this change the Fourth Army did not cross the German frontier. Its four reorganized corps then carried out a gradual withdrawal to the area about Namur, and on the 10th December Fourth Army Headquarters was established in this ancient fortress on the junction of the Meuse and Sambre.

FIFTH ARMY*

G.O.C.

22 May, 1916	Lieut.-General Sir H. DE LA P. GOUGH.
7 July, 1916	General Sir H. DE LA P. GOUGH.
4.30 p.m. 28 March, 1918	}General Sir H. S. RAWLINSON, Bt.**
–2 April, 1918	

---

8 April, 1918	Lieut.-General Sir W. E. PEYTON.**
23 May, 1918	General Sir W. R. BIRDWOOD.

M.-G.G.S.

22 May, 1916...Br.-Gen. N. MALCOLM.
7 July, 1916...Maj.-Gen. N. MALCOLM.
23 Dec., 1917...Maj.-Gen. J. S. J. PERCY.
1 June, 1918...Maj.-Gen. C. B. B. WHITE.

D.-A. and Q.-M.-G.

28 May, 1916...Br.-Gen H. N. SARGENT.
7 July, 1916...Maj.-Gen. H. N. SARGENT.
20 Dec., 1917...Maj.-Gen. P. O. HAMBRO.

M.-G.R.A.

22 May, 1916...Br.-Gen. W. STRONG (tempy.).
27 July, 1916...Maj.-Gen. H. C. C. UNIACKE.
9 July, 1918...Maj.-Gen. C. C. VAN STRAUBENZEE.

C.E.

24 May, 1916...Br.-Gen. R. P. LEE.
7 July, 1916...Maj.-Gen. R. P. LEE.
15 Jan., 1917...Maj.-Gen. P. G. GRANT.

A.-A. Defence Cdr.***

4 Dec., 1916 }Lt.-Col. T. C. NEWTON.
–30 April, 1918

D.-D. Signals.

22 May, 1916...Maj. L. W. DE V. SADLIER-JACKSON.
19 June, 1916...Col. E. G. GODFREY-FAUSSETT.

---

26 May, 1918...Lt.-Col. G. P. R. MACMAHON.

23 May, 1918...Col. F. A. ILES.

---

* Called Reserve Army until 30/10/16.
** Fifth Army was designated Fourth Army on 2/4/18.
   A.H.Q. Reserve Army was opened on 3/4/18 ; and on 23/5/18 the Fifth Army was reconstituted.
*** Fifth Army A.-A. Group (Q, R, and S A.-A. Batteries, each of 2 sections of 13-pdrs.—12, 13-pdrs.) was formed on 26 and 27/11/16. In November, 1918, A, B, and D A.-A. Bties., with Fifth Army, had 32, 13-pdrs. and 6, 3″ A.-A. guns.

D.-D.S. and T.

3 July, 1916...Col E. C. F. GILLESPIE.
16 Oct., 1917 ⎫ Br.-Gen. E. C. F.
–2 April, 1918 ⎭   GILLESPIE.*

9 April, 1918...Lt.-Col. H. A. JOHNSON
                 (A.-D.S. and T.).
23 May, 1918...Br.-Gen. C. S. DODGSON.

D.-D.O.S.

30 June, 1916 ⎫ Col. R. S. HAMILTON.*
–2 April, 1918 ⎭

15 April, 1918...Lt.-Col. H. B. WARWICK
                 (A.-D.O.S.).
23 May, 1918...Col. H. C. FERNYHOUGH.

D.M.S.

22 May, 1916 ... ... Capt. A. J. A. MENZIES (D.-A.-D. M.S.).
28 June, 1916 ... ... Maj.-Gen. C. E. NICHOL.
1 November, 1916 ... ... ⎫ Maj.-General B. M. SKINNER.
–2 April, 1918 ... ... ⎭

23 April, 1918 ... ... Col. J. D. ALEXANDER (D.-D.M.S.).
7 June, 1918 ... ... Lt.-Col. S. B. SMITH (A.-D.M.S.).
22 July, 1918 ... ... Maj.-Gen. J. J. GERRARD.

D.-D.V.S.

4 July, 1916...Lt.-Col. H. M. LENOX-
                 CONYNGHAM.
2 June, 1917 ⎫ Col. W. J. TATAM.*
–2 April, 1918 ⎭

3 April, 1918...Lt.-Col. J. A. B.
                 McGOWAN (acting).
17 April, 1918...Lt.-Col. G. CONDER
                 (acting).
26 May, 1918...Col. R. L. CRANFORD.

D.-D. Remounts.

22 May, 1916 ⎫ Lt.-Col. J. W. YARDLEY.*
–2 April, 1918 ⎭

10 April, 1918...Maj. H. S. BRITTEN
               (D.-A.-D. ; died 18/8/18).
21 Aug., 1918...Maj. H. H. ROBERTSON-
                AIKMAN (D.-A.-D.).
11 Oct., 1918...Col. C. D. MILLER.

---

* To Fourth Army on 2/4/18—when Fifth Army was designated Fourth Army.

LOCATION OF ARMY HEADQUARTERS
(INCLUDING ADVD. A.H.Q.).

22 May, 1916 ... ...   **Regnière Écluse** (5 miles W.N.W. of Crécy).

12 June, 1916 ... ...   **Daours** (6 miles E. of Amiens).

2 July, 1916 ... ...   **Toutencourt** (10 miles S.E. of Doullens).

30/10/1916...Reserve Army was renamed Fifth Army.

30 October, 1916 ... ...   **Toutencourt.**

28 March, 1917 ... ...   **Albert.**

2 June, 1917 ... ...   **La Lovie Château** (3 miles N.W. of Poperinghe).

15 November, 1917 ... ...   **Dury** (3 miles S. of Amiens).

13 December, 1917 ... ...   **Villers Bretonneux** (10 miles E. of Amiens).

15 February, 1918 ... ...   **Nesle** (12 miles S. of Péronne).

22 March, 1918 ... ...   **Villers Bretonneux.**

25 March, 1918 ... ...
–2 April, 1918 ... ... } **Dury.**

2/4/1918...Fifth Army was designated Fourth Army, and the Fifth Army ceased to exist and became Reserve Army.

---

3 April, 1918 ... ...   **Crécy en Ponthieu.**

23/5/1918...Fifth Army was reconstituted.

23 May, 1918 ... ...   **Crécy en Ponthieu.**

27 June, 1918 ... ...   **Upen d'Aval** (8 miles S. of St. Omer).

21 October, 1918 ... ...   **Labuissière** (1 mile E. of Bruay).

26 October, 1918 ... ...   **Lille** (Advd. H.Q.).

29 October, 1918 ... ...   **Lille** (Army H.Q. concentrated).

11 a.m., 11/11/1918...**Armistice with Germany.**

FIFTH ARMY*

FORMATION.

Headquarters of the Reserve Corps (then at Regnière Écluse—5 miles W.N.W. of Crécy en Ponthieu) became the Headquarters of the Reserve Army on the 22nd May, 1916 (p. 265). Three weeks later Reserve Army H.Q. moved to Daours (6 miles east of Amiens); and on the 2nd July, 1916, preparatory to taking over the northern part of the Somme battle-front, Reserve Army H.Q. was installed at Toutencourt (10 miles S.E. of Doullens).

Two days later the Reserve Army took over (from the Fourth Army) the left of the Somme battle-front from la Boisselle to Hébuterne (8 miles), and with it the X and VIII Corps.** At the outset of this change of command, the immediate attack of this sector of the German position was postponed and on this part of the front trench-warfare tactics were adopted; though the X Corps fought on to extend the two footings it had already gained to the north and south of Thiepval.

BATTLES AND ENGAGEMENTS.

1916

BATTLES OF THE SOMME [II, V, VIII, X, XIII, Cdn., and I Anzac Corps; with A, C, and D Tank Cos.].

4–13 July ... ... **Battle of Albert** [VIII and X Corps].***

14–17 July ... ... **Battle of Bazentin Ridge** [X Corps].

17 July ... ... **Capture of Ovillers** [48th Div.: X Corps].

23 July–3 September **Battle of Pozières Ridge** [X (until *24/7*); then II Corps; and, from *28/7*, I Anzac Corps].

6 August–3 September **Fighting for Mouquet Farm** [12th, 25th, and 48th Divs.: II Corps; and 1st Aus., 2nd Aus., and 4th Aus. Divs: 1 Anzac Corps].

14 September ... ... **Capture of the Wonder Work** [11th Div.: II Corps].

---

* Reserve Army was renamed Fifth Army on 30/10/1916.
** At this time X Corps comprised the 25th, 32nd, 36th, and 49th Divs., and in VIII Corps were the 4th, 29th, 31st, and 48th Divs.
*** VIII and X Corps were taken over (in the line) from Fourth Army on 4/7/16.

1916 *(Contd.)*

BATTLES OF THE SOMME *(Contd.)*.

15–22 September ... **Battle of Flers–Courcelette** [II and Cdn. Corps ; with 6 tanks C Coy. with 2nd Cdn. Div.].

26–28 September ... **Battle of Thiepval Ridge** [II, V (part), and Cdn. Corps ; with, on *26/9*, 8 tanks C Coy.—6 tanks with II, and 2 tanks with Cdn. Corps].

26 September ... ... **Capture of Mouquet Farm** [11th Div. : II Corps ; with 2 tanks C Coy.].

1–18 October ... ... **Battle of Transloy Ridges** [Cdn. Corps].

1 Oct.–11 Nov. ... ... **Battle of the Ancre Heights** [II, V (part), and Cdn. Corps ; with 4 tanks A Coy. with 18th Div. : II Corps].

9 October ... ... **Capture of Stuff Redoubt** [25th Div. : II Corps].

14 October ... ... **Capture of Schwaben Redoubt** [39th Div. : II Corps].

21 October ... ... **Capture of Regina Trench and Redoubt** [18th and 25th Divs. : II Corps ; with 4 tanks A Coy. with 18th Div.].

21 October ... ... **Capture of Stuff Trench** [39th Div. : II Corps].

On 30/10/1916, Reserve Army was renamed Fifth Army.

13–18 November ... **Battle of the Ancre** [II, V, and XIII* Corps ; with, on *13/11*, 3 tanks A Coy. with 39th Div. (II), and 2 tanks D Coy. with 51st Div. (V) ; on *14/11*, 3 tanks D Coy. with 63rd Div. (V) ; on *16/11*, 2 tanks D Coy. with 2nd Div. (V) ; and, on *18/11*, 5 tanks D Coy. with 32nd (4) and 51st (1) : V Corps ; and 3 tanks A Coy. with 19th Div. (II)].

13 November ... ... **Capture of Beaumont Hamel** [51st Div. : V Corps ; with 2 tanks D Coy.].

14 November ... ... **Capture of Beaucourt** [190th Bde., 63rd Div. : V Corps ; with 2 tanks D Coy.].

---

* On 4/10/16 XIII Corps took over the left of Reserve (later Fifth) Army, from opposite Serre to Hébuterne.

1917

11 Jan.–13 March ...	**Operations on the Ancre** [II, IV, V, and I Anzac Corps].
17 and 18 February ...	**Actions of Miraumont** [2nd, 18th, and 63rd Divs. : II Corps].
25 February–2 March	**Capture of the Thilloys** [2nd Div. : II Corps ; and 1st, 2nd, and 4th Aus. Divs. : I Anzac Corps].
10 March	**Capture of Grévillers Trench and Irles** [2nd and 18th Divs. : II Corps].
12 March	**Attack on Rettemoy Graben** [46th Div. : V Corps].
14 March–5 April ...	**German Retreat to the Hindenburg Line** [II, V, and I Anzac Corps, and 4th (1st Ind.) Cav. Div.].
17th March	**Capture of Bapaume** [2nd Aus. Div. : I Anzac Corps].

---

11 April	**First Attack on Bullecourt** [62nd Div. : V Corps ; and 4th Aus. Div. : 1 Anzac Corps ; 11 tanks of 11 coy., D Bn., 1st Tank Bde., with V Corps].
15 April	**German Attack on Lagnicourt** [62nd Div. ; V Corps ; and 1st and 2nd Aus. Divs. : I Anzac Corps].
3–17 May	**Battle of Bullecourt** [7th, 58th, 62nd Divs. : V Corps ; and 1st, 2nd, and 5th Aus. Divs. : I Anzac Corps ; with 12 tanks, 1st Tank Bde. with V Corps].
20–31 May	**Actions on the Hindenburg Line** [5th Aus. Div. : I Anzac Corps until *10 a.m. 26/5*, then relieved by 20th Div. : IV Corps, and 58th and 62nd Divs. : V Corps, until *10 a.m. 31/5.* transferred to Third Army].
	BATTLES OF YPRES [II, V, XIV, XVIII, and XIX Corps ; with 1st, 2nd, and 3rd Tank Bdes.].
31 July–2 August ...	**Battle of Pilckem Ridge** [II, XIV, XVIII, and XIX Corps ; with G Bn., 1st Tank Bde., with XVIII ; A and B Bns., 2nd Tank Bde., with II ; C and F Bns., 3rd Tank Bde., with XIX ; and D Bn., 1st Tank Bde. in Army Reserve].

116

1917 *(Contd.)*

BATTLES OF YPRES *(Contd.)*.

10 August ... ... **Capture of Inverness Copse** [18th Div. : II Corps].

10 August ... ... **Capture of Westhoek** [25th Div. : II Corps].

16–18 August ... ... **Battle of Langemarck** [II, XIV, XVIII, and XIX Corps ; with 20 Coy. G Bn., 1st Tank Bde.].

19 August ... ... **The Cockcroft** [11th and 48th Divs. : XVIII Corps ; with 12 tanks, 19 and 20 Cos. G Bn., 1st Tank Bde.].

22 August ... ... **Fighting in front of St. Julien** [14th and 47th Divs. : II Corps, with 4 tanks, 2nd Tank Bde. ; and 11th and 48th Divs. : XVIII Corps, with 12 tanks D Bn., 1st Tank Bde.].

22 August ... ... **Fighting south of Fortuin** [15th and 61st Divs. : XIX Corps, with 8 tanks C Bn. and 10 tanks F Bn., 3rd Tank Bde.].

22 and 23 August ... **Fighting on the Menin Road** [14th, 23rd, and 24th Divs. : II Corps, with A Bn., 2nd Tank Bde.].

27 August ... ... **Fighting north of St. Julien** [11th and 48th Divs. : XVIII Corps, with 12 tanks, 11 Coy., D Bn., 1st Tank Bde. ; also 38th Div. : XIV, and 61st Div. : XIX Corps.].

20–25 September ... **Battle of the Menin Road Ridge** [V, XIV, and XVIII Corps ; with 34 tanks D and E Bns., 1st Tank Bde., with XVIII ; and C and F Bns. (18 tanks), 3rd Tank Bde., with V].

26 Sept.–3 Oct. ... ... **Battle of Polygon Wood** [V (until *28/9*) ; and XIV, and XVIII Corps].

4 October ... ... **Battle of Broodseinde** [XIV and XVIII Corps ; with 12 tanks, D Bn., 1st Tank Bde., with XVIII].

9 October ... ... **Battle of Poelcappelle** [XIV and XVIII Corps].

1917 *(Contd.)*

BATTLES OF YPRES *(Contd.)*.

12 October ... ... **First Battle of Passchendaele** [XIV and XVIII Corps].

22 October ... ... **Fighting in Houthulst Forest** [34th and 35th Divs. : XIV Corps, and 18th Div. : XVIII Corps].

26 Oct.–10 Nov. ... **Second Battle of Passchendaele** [XIV, relieved by XIX on *29/10* ; and XVIII, relieved by II (of Second Army) on *2/11*].

30 December ... ... **Welch Ridge*** [Part of 26th Bde., 9th Div. : VII Corps].

1918

FIRST BATTLES OF THE SOMME [III, VII, XVIII, and XIX Corps ; with 4th Tank Bde.].

21–23 March ... ... **Battle of St. Quentin** [III, VII, XVIII and XIX Corps ; and 1st Cav. Div. (with XIX), and 2nd and 3rd Cav. Divs. (with III) ; with 1st, 4th, and 5th Bns., 4th Tank Bde.].

24 and 25 March ... **Actions at the Somme Crossings** [Part of VII Corps (transferred at *4 a.m. on 25/3* to Third Army), and XVIII and XIX Corps, and 1st Cav. Div. (less 1st Cav. Bde.) with XIX on *24/3* ; and 2nd and 3rd Cav. Divs. with XVIII ; with Part of 4th Tank Bde.].

24 and 25 March ... **First Battle of Bapaume** [Part of VII Corps, with 1st Cav. Bde.—transferred to Third Army at *4 a.m. on 25/3*].

26 and 27 March ... **Battle of Rosières** [XVIII and XIX Corps, and 1st Cav. Div., and " Carey's Force ; "** with 5th Bn. and L.-G. Coy. 13th Bn., 4th Tank Bde.].

---

* Also see V Corps, Third Army.
** *Carey's Force* : Fifth Army Infantry School, Musketry School, Sniping School, Signals, and Field Survey Coy. ; together with III Corps School, XIX Corps School, and 144, 213, 216, 217 Army Troops Cos. R.E., 353 Electrical and Mechanical Coy. R.E., 253 Tunnelling Coy. R.E., and 2 Cos. 6th U.S. (Railway) Engineers—a force nearly 3,000 strong. This force was placed in position by Maj.-Gen. P. G. Grant (C.E. of Fifth Army) ; Br.-Gen. H. C. Rees (150th Bde., 50th Div.) then took over temporarily on 26/3, and handed over during that afternoon to Maj.-Gen. G. G. S. Carey (G.O.C. 20th Div.). " Carey's Force " remained in position from 26/3—2/4/18. On 28/3, 400 of the 2nd Bn. Canadian Railway Troops joined the Force, and all stragglers were also systematically collected and added to it.

1918 (*Contd.*)

FIRST BATTLES OF THE SOMME (*Contd.*).

2 April   ... ...   Fifth Army was renamed Fourth Army, and the Fifth Army ceased to exist and became Reserve Army.

---

3 April   ... ...   Army Hd. Qrs. of Reserve Army was opened at Crécy en Ponthieu.

23 May... ... ...   The Fifth Army was reconstituted.

10 a.m., 1 July ... ...   The Fifth Army took over the front-line sectors of XI and XIII Corps (from the northern wing of the First Army).* The Fifth Army Front then stretched astride the Lys from Béthune to Merville, and the Army was interpolated between the left of the First Army and the right of the Second Army.

      Before the Great War came to an end on the Western Front the reconstituted Fifth Army took part in the following operations in France and Flanders :

THE ADVANCE TO VICTORY.

    On the 18th August the Fifth Army held a 12-mile front from Festubert to the Forest of Nieppe, in the left centre of the B.E.F. front.

18 Aug.–6 Sept.   ...   **THE ADVANCE IN ARTOIS AND IN FLANDERS** [XI and XIII** Corps].

    Without engaging in any specific action, the Fifth Army, in this period, advanced 5 miles. By the 2nd October the Army had advanced another 5 miles, and then was in occupation of the line from La Bassée through Neuve Chapelle to Fleurbaix.

2 Oct.–11 Nov.   ...   **THE FINAL ADVANCE IN ARTOIS** [I,** III,** and XI Corps ; and, from *7–11/11*, 1st Cav. Div. with I and III Corps].

17 October ... ...   **Occupation of Lille** [57th Div. : XI Corps].

28 October ... ...   **Official Entry into Lille** [47th Div. : XI Corps].

---

  * XI Corps had 5th, 61st, and 74th Divs. ; and XIII Corps had 3rd, 4th, and 46th Divs.

  ** XIII Corps handed over its front (in the Fifth Army), joined the Fourth Army, and took over part of that Army's front (from III Corps) at Noon on 1/10/18.

  I Corps was transferred in the line from First Army to Fifth Army at Noon on 19/9/18.

  III Corps (from Fourth Army) joined the Fifth Army, and took over the centre of the Army front at 10 a.m. on 8/10/18.

1918 *(Contd.)*

When hostilities ceased at 11 a.m. on the 11th November, the advanced troops of the Fifth Army were already across the River Dendre and the front line was established some 4 miles eastward of Ath. The 11-mile front of the Fifth Army, in the left centre of the B.E.F., was occupied by the I and III Corps and the 1st Cavalry Division. At this time the leading mounted troops had reached a line running from north of Mons to a point about 9 miles east of Ath. For the Fifth Army the War was over.

Although it had taken part in no battle, the Fifth Army in the 86 days between the 18th August and the 11th November had advanced 54 miles across enemy territory.

CORPS

CAVALRY CORPS*

G.O.C.

10 October, 1914	Lieut.-General E. H. H. ALLENBY (sick, 19/4/15).
19 April, 1915	Maj.-General Hon. Sir J. H. G. BYNG (acting).
4 May, 1915	Lieut.-General E. H. H. ALLENBY.
7 May, 1915	Lieut.-General Hon. Sir J. H. G. BYNG.
16 August, 1915	Lieut.-General H. D. FANSHAWE.
23 October, 1915 } -12 March, 1916* }	Lieut.-General Hon. C. E. BINGHAM.
4 September, 1916* ...	Lieut.-General C. T. McM. KAVANAGH.

B.-G.G.S.

10 Oct., 1914...Br.-Gen. G. DE S. BARROW.
7 Jan., 1915...Br.-Gen. J. F. N. BIRCH.
14 Mar., 1915...Br.-Gen. P. HOWELL.
23 Aug., 1915 } -12 Mar., 1916 } Br.-Gen. A. F. HOME.

4 Sept., 1916...Br.-Gen. A. F. HOME.

D.-A. and Q.-M.-G.

10 Oct., 1914...Br.-Gen. H. A. L. TAGART.
25 Oct., 1915 } -12 Mar., 1916 } Br.-Gen. J. C. G. LONGMORE.

4 Sept., 1916...Br.-Gen. J. C. G. LONGMORE.

G.S.O. 1.

10 Oct., 1914 } -6 Jan., 1915 } Lt.-Col. J. F. N. BIRCH.

....

A.-A. and Q.-M.-G.

10 Oct., 1914...Lt.-Col. J. C. G. LONGMORE.
9 Nov., 1915 } -11 Mar., 1916 } Lt.-Col. O. K. CHANCE.

4 Sept., 1916...Lt.-Col. H. E. MEDLICOTT
[2 Dec., 1918...Lt.-Col. G. P. L. COSENS].

B.-G.R.A.

10 Oct., 1914...Br.-Gen. B. F. DRAKE (sick, 19/1/15).
12 Feb., 1915...Br.-Gen. H. D. WHITE-THOMSON.
9 Sept., 1915 } -12 Mar., 1916 } Br.-Gen. G. GILLSON.

6 Sept., 1916...Br.-Gen. H. H. TUDOR.
10 Oct., 1916...Br.-Gen. H. S. SELIGMAN.

C.R.E.

....

11 Sept., 1916...Lt.-Col. W. H. EVANS.

---

* Formed in France on 10/10/14, the Cavalry Corps was broken up in France on 12/3/16. The Corps was re-formed in France : at first temporarily, on 7/9/16, and then permanently on 30/9/16.

CAVALRY CORPS

A.-D. Signals.

....

---

20 Nov., 1916...Lt.-Col. L. W. DE V.
                SADLEIR-JACKSON.
24 May, 1917...Lt.-Col. R. CHEVENIX-
                TRENCH.
1 Mar., 1918...Lt.-Col. J. B. WHEELER.

D.-D.V.S.

6 Feb., 1915...Lt.-Col. E. E. MARTIN.
16 Nov., 1915 ⎱
−12 Mar., 1916 ⎰ Lt.-Col. F. W. HUNT.

---

4 Sept., 1916...Maj. J. A. B. McGOWAN
                (acting).
2 Nov., 1916...Col. P. J. HARRIS.
19 Aug., 1917...Col. D. BOLTON.

D.-D.M.S.

19 Dec., 1914...Col. S. WESTCOTT.
6 Jan., 1915 ⎱
−25 Feb., 1916 ⎰ Col. M. W. O'KEEFFE.

---

6 Sept., 1916...Col. J. M. F. SHINE.
2 Nov., 1916...Col. O. R. A. JULIAN.
4 Feb., 1917...Col. F. J. MORGAN.

D.-D. Remounts.

7 Feb., 1915 ⎱
−12 Mar., 1916 ⎰ Lt.-Col. J. W. YARDLEY.

---

4 Sept., 1916...Lt.-Col. E. G. HARDY.

CAVALRY CORPS

FORMATION.

Cavalry Corps H.Q. began to form at Doullens on the 10th October, 1914, and the Corps at first consisted of the 1st and 2nd Cavalry Divisions.*

On formation the Cavalry Corps received orders to support the left of the II Corps, and secure the high ground about Mont Noir and Mont des Cats (north of Bailleul).). Thereafter the Cavalry Corps would seize and hold the Messines Ridge and thus link the III Corps (fighting the Battle of Armentières) and the IV Corps (engaged in the Battles of Ypres). After securing the Messines Ridge the Cavalry Corps was to push on and seize the line of the Ypres–Comines Canal. In its endeavour to carry out the task which had been assigned to it, the Cavalry Corps became involved in heavy fighting on the Messines Ridge.

BATTLES AND ENGAGEMENTS.

1914

12 Oct.–2 Nov.	**Battle of Messines** [1st Cav. and 2nd Cav. Divs., and Q.O. Oxf. Hussars ; and 7th (Ferozepore) Ind. Inf. Bde. ;** and 1/N.F. and 1/Lincoln (3rd Div.) ; 2/Essex and 2/Innis. F. (4th Div.) ; 2/K.O.S.B. and 2/K.O.Y.L.I. (5th Div.) ; and 14/London (London Scottish)].

1915

BATTLES OF YPRES.

24 April–4 May	**Battle of St. Julien** [2nd Cav. Div. : Second Army until 28/4, then " Plumer's Force "].***
8–13 May	**Battle of Frezenberg Ridge** [1st Cav. and 3rd Cav. Divs. : Second Army].
24 and 25 May	**Battle of Bellewaarde Ridge** [1st Cav. Div. (in Cav. Corps), and 2nd Cav. Div. (with V Corps) : Second Army].

26–28 September ...	**Battle of Loos** [3rd Cav. Div. (with IV Corps) : First Army].

---

* 3rd Cavalry Division began its formaton at Ludgershall in September, 1914, but the third Brigade (the 8th) was only formed in Belgium on 20/11/14. In 1914 the 3rd Cav. Div. served with the IV and I Corps in the Antwerp Operations and the Battles of Ypres.
** Ferozepore Bde. (of Lahore Div.) served in this Battle from 22–27/10/14.
*** In " Plumer's Force " from 7.50 a.m., 28/4–6 a.m., 7/5/15 (see Second Army).

1916

On the 12th March Cavalry Corps Headquarters was broken up in France.

———————

During the Battles of the Somme, Cavalry Corps Headquarters was re-formed on the 7th September, at first as a temporary measure.; but on the 30th September it was placed on a permanent basis. The Cavalry Corps thus formed consisted of the 1st, 2nd, and 3rd Cavalry Divisions, as well as the 4th (1st Indian) and 5th (2nd Indian) Cavalry Divisions.*

For the remainder of the Great War the Cavalry Corps served in France and Belgium and was engaged in the following operations :

BATTLES OF THE SOMME.

15–22 September   ...   **Battle of Flers-Courcelette** [1st Cav. and 5th (Ind.) Cav. Divs. : in Reserve to XIV Corps—Fourth Army].

25–28 September   ...   **Battle of Morval** [1st Cav., 2nd Cav., 3rd Cav., 4th (Ind.) Cav., & 5th (Ind.) Cav. Divs.—Fourth Army].

1917

14 March–5 April   ...   **German Retreat to the Hindenburg Line** [5th (Ind.) Cav. Div.— Fourth Army ; 4th (Ind.) Cav. Div.—Fifth Army].

BATTLES OF ARRAS.

9–14 April ... ... **First Battle of the Scarpe** [**1st Cav., 2nd Cav., and 3rd Cav. Divs.—Third Army].

10 and 11 April   ...   **Attack and capture of Monchy le Preux** [3rd Cav. Div.—Third Army].

———————

* The Indian Cavalry Corps was formed in France on 18/12/14. This Corps H.Q. was broken up in March, 1916, and was not re-formed in France. On 26/11/16 1st Indian and 2nd Indian Cavalry Divisions were numbered 4th and 5th Cavalry Divisions. These two divisions remained in the Cavalry Corps until March, 1918. The 4th Cav. Div. was then disbanded (6/3/18) and the Indian units were sent to Palestine. At the same time, the 5th Cav. Div. was transferred to Palestine (as an organized formation). The two Indian Cavalry Divisions left behind them in France 4 British Cavalry Regts. (8/Hsrs., 7/D.G., 6/Dgns., and 17/Lcrs.), and 2 Brigades R.H.A. (XVI—A. Q. and U ; and XVII—N. and Cdn. Batteries).

NOTE—To save confusion the two Ind. Cav. Divs. are always alluded to as 4th and 5th Cav. Divs.

** 1st Cav. Bde. (1st Cav. Div.) supported the First Army on 10 and 11/4/17, about Fampoux (N. of R. Scarpe).

1917 *(Contd.)*

BATTLE OF CAMBRAI.

20 and 21 November   **The Tank Attack** [1st Cav. Div. with IV Corps ; 2nd and 5th (2nd Ind.) Cav. Divs. under Cavalry Corps—Third Army].

23–28 November   ...   **Capture of Bourlon Wood** [1st Cav. and 2nd Cav. Divs. with IV Corps—Third Army].

30 Nov.–3 Dec. ...   ...   **The German Counter-Attacks** [1st Cav., 2nd Cav., 4th (1st Ind.), and 5th (2nd Ind.) Cav. Divs., under Cavalry Corps—Third Army].

1918

FIRST BATTLES OF THE SOMME.

21–23 March   ...   ...   **Battle of St. Quentin** [1st Cav. Div. with XIX ; and 2nd Cav. and 3rd Cav. Divs. with III Corps—Fifth Army].

24 and 25 March   ...   **Actions at the Somme Crossings** [1st Cav. Div. with XIX (on 24/3) ; and 2nd Cav. and 3rd Cav. Divs. with XVIII Corps—Fifth Army].

25 March   ...   ...   **First Battle of Bapaume** [1st Cav. Div. with VII Corps—Third Army].

4 and 5 April   ...   ...   **Battle of the Avre** [3rd Cav. Div. with XIX Corps—Fourth Army].

BATTLE OF THE LYS.

13–15 April   ...   ...   **Battle of Hazebrouck** [2nd Cav. Div., in Reserve to XV Corps—Second Army].

THE ADVANCE TO VICTORY.

8–11 August   ...   ...   **Battle of Amiens** [1st Cav., 2nd Cav., and 3rd Cav. Divs. ; with 3rd (Whippets) Bn. and 6th [Whippets] Bn. and 17th (A.-C.) Bn., 3rd Tank Bde., under Cavalry Corps—Fourth Army].

1918 *(Contd.)*

THE ADVANCE TO VICTORY *(Contd.).*

SECOND BATTLES OF THE SOMME.

21–23 August ... ... **Battle of Albert** [1st Cav. and 2nd Cav. Divs.—Third Army].

31 August–3 September **Second Battle of Bapaume** [2nd Cav. Div.—Third Army].

BATTLES OF THE HINDENBURG LINE.

27 September–1 October **Battle of the Canal du Nord** [3rd and 4th Cav. Bdes. (2nd Cav. Div.)—Third Army].

29 September–2 October **Battle of the St. Quentin Canal** [5th Cav. Bde. (2nd Cav. Div.)— Fourth Army].

3–5 October ... ... **Battle of the Beaurevoir Line** [5th Cav. Bde. (2nd Cav. Div.)— Fourth Army].

8 and 9 October ... **Battle of Cambrai** [1st Cav. Div. (with XIII and II Am. Corps) ; and 5th Cav. Bde. (2nd Cav. Div.) and 3rd Cav. Div.— —Fourth Army ; and 2nd Cav. Div. (less 5th Bde.)— Third Army].

9–12 October ... ... **Pursuit to the Selle** [1st Cav. Div., 5th Cav. Bde. (2nd Cav. Div.), and part 3rd Cav. Div.—Fourth Army ; 4th Cav. Bde. (2nd Cav. Div.) and part 3rd Cav. Div.— Third Army ; and 3rd Cav. Bde. (2nd Cav. Div.)— First Army ; 17th (A.-C. Bn.) with Cavalry Corps].

THE FINAL ADVANCE.

17 Oct.–11 Nov. ... **A. IN PICARDY** [1st Cav. Div. (17/10–6/11), and 5th Cav. Bde. (2nd Cav. Div.)—Fourth Army ; and 4th Cav. Bde. (2nd Cav. Div.)—Third Army].

4 November ... ... **Battle of the Sambre** [5th Cav. Bde. (2nd Cav. Div.)—Fourth Army ; and 4th Cav. Bde. (2nd Cav. Div.)—Third Army].

5 Nov.–11 a.m. 11 Nov. **Final Operations** [5th Cav. Bde. (2nd Cav. Div.)—Fourth Army].

1918 *(Contd.)*

THE FINAL ADVANCE.

2 Oct.–11 Nov.	**B. IN ARTOIS** [3rd Cav. Bde. (2nd Cav. Div.)—First Army ; and, from 7–11/11, 1st Cav. Div. with I and III Corps—Fifth Army].
11 November	**Capture of Mons** [5th R. Lcrs. and 1 Sec. D.R.H.A. (3rd Cav. Bde., 2nd Cav. Div.), with 3rd Cdn. Div., Cdn. Corps—First Army].
9–11 November	**C. IN FLANDERS** [3rd Cav. Div. (from 9–11/11)—Second Army].

When the Armistice brought hostilities to a close on the Western Front at 11 a.m. on the 11th November, the Divisions of the Cavalry Corps had reached the following positions : 2nd Cavalry Division—Clairfayts (8 miles east of Avesnes) with the 5th Cavalry Brigade, Erquelinnes (8 miles east of Maubeuge) with the 4th Cavalry Brigade, and Havre (on the canal) and St. Denis (4 miles beyond Mons)with the 3rd Cavalry Brigade ; the 1st Cavalry Division (with I Corps, Fifth Army) was well beyond Ath ; and the 3rd Cavalry Division (with the Second Army) had reached the line of the River Dendre at Lessines and below that town.

The Cavalry Corps (1st, 2nd, and 3rd Cavalry Divisions, together with the 17th Armoured-Car Battalion of the Tank Corps) was now detailed to cover the Second and Fourth Armies as they advanced to the German Frontier.

The advance began on the 17th November : the 1st and 3rd Cavalry Divisions covered the Second Army, and the 2nd Cavalry Division and the 17th (A.-C.) Battalion screened the Fourth Army. The German Frontier was reached on the 29th, and a further reorganization of the force which was to enter Germany became necessary.

The 1st Cavalry Division and the 17th (A.-C.) Battalion were now placed under the Second Army to cover its advance to the Rhine, and on the 1st December this Cavalry Division crossed the frontier and entered Germany. On the 6th, the 2nd Cavalry Brigade marched into Cologne and the 17th (A.-C.) Battalion piqueted the Rhine bridges. On the next day, the 1st and 9th Cavalry Brigades reached the Rhine, both above and below Cologne ; and on the 12th December the 1st Cavalry Division crossed the Rhine by the Hohenzollern Bridge (2nd and 9th Cavalry Brigades) as well as by the bridge at Bonn (1st Cavalry Brigade).

I CORPS

G.O.C.

5 August, 1914	... ...	Lieut.-General Sir D. Haig.
26 December, 1914	... ...	Lieut.-General Sir C. C. Monro.
13 July, 1915	... ...	Lieut.-General H. de la P. Gough.
1 April, 1916	... ...	Lieut.-General C. T. McM. Kavanagh.
4 September, 1916	... ...	Major-General H. Hudson (acting).
30 September, 1916	... ...	Lieut.-General Sir C. A. Anderson.
11 February, 1917	... ...	Major-General J. E. Capper (acting).
19 February, 1917	... ...	Lieut.-General A. E. A. Holland.
19 September, 1918	... ...	Major-General Sir H. S. Jeudwine (acting).
4 October, 1918	... ...	Lieut.-General Sir A. E. A. Holland.

B.-G.G.S.

5 Aug., 1914...Br.-Gen. J. E. Gough, V.C.
26 Dec., 1914...Br.-Gen. R. D. Whigham.
16 July, 1915...Br.-Gen. A. S. Cobbe, V.C.
27 Jan., 1916...Br.-Gen. G. V. Hordern.

D.-A. and Q.-M.-G.

5 Aug., 1914...Br.-Gen. P. E. F. Hobbs.
26 Dec., 1914...Br.-Gen. H. N. Sargent.
28 May, 1916...Br.-Gen. F. F. Ready.
6 Aug., 1916...Br.-Gen. N. G.
Anderson.

G.S.O. 1.

5 Aug., 1914...Col. H. S. Jeudwine.
1 Nov., 1914⎫
−12 Jan., 1915⎭Lt.-Col. N. Malcolm.

B.-G.R.A.

5 Aug., 1914...Br.-Gen. H. S. Horne.
1 Jan., 1915...Br.-Gen. R. A. K.
Montgomery.
19 July, 1915...Br.-Gen. J. F. N. Birch.
29 Jan., 1916...Br.-Gen. C. M. Ross-
Johnson.
18 June, 1916...Br.-Gen. F. C. Poole.
19 Dec., 1916...Br.-Gen. M. Peake
(killed, 27/8/17).
27 Aug., 1917...Br.-Gen. E. F.
Delaforce (tempy.).
4 Sept., 1917...Br.-Gen. H. C. Sheppard.

C.H.A.

*
....

11 Mar., 1916...Br.-Gen. W. J. Napier.
21 April, 1916...Br.-Gen. W. F.
Cockburn.
21 Feb., 1917...Br.-Gen. A. Ellershaw.
14 Feb., 1918..Br.-Gen. F. G.
Maunsell.

---

* First Army Heavy Arilllery Group (formerly No. 5 H.A.R. Group—G.H.Q. Artillery) joined I Corps on 11/3/16, and its designation was then changed to I Corps Heavy Artillery (see Appendix 3).

I CORPS

C.E.

5 Aug., 1914...Br.-Gen. S. R. RICE.
11 April, 1915...Br.-Gen. C. GODBY.
14 Sept., 1915...Br.-Gen. R. P. LEE.
18 May, 1916...Br.-Gen. E. H. DE V.
　　　　　　　　　　　　　ATKINSON.
31 Oct., 1917...Br.-Gen. H. W. GORDON.

A.-D. Signals.

5 Aug., 1914...Major M. G. E. BOWMAN-
　　　　　　MANIFOLD (i/c Army Signals).
20 Mar., 1915...Major D. C. JONES
　　　　　　　　　　(i/c Army Signals).
1 June, 1915...Major D. C. JONES
　　　　　　　　　　(i/c Corps Signals).
6 Feb., 1916...Major W. L. DE M.
　　　　　　　　　　　　　CAREY.
20 Nov., 1916...Lt.-Col. W. L. DE M.
　　　　　　　　　　　　　CAREY.
26 Nov., 1916...Lt.-Col. E. F. W.
　　　　　　　　　　　　　BARKER.
30 Dec., 1917...Lt.-Col, M. T. PORTER.
[12 Dec., 1918...Lt.-Col. H. G. GILCHRIST.]

D.-D.M.S.

5 Aug., 1914...Major E. RYAN (M.O.).
15 Sept., 1914...Lt.-Col. N. C. FERGUSON
　　　　　　　　　　　　(D.-D.M.S.).
7 Jan., 1915...Major P. G. EASTON (M.O.).
8 April, 1915...Col. S. WESTCOTT.
22 July, 1917...Col. C. A. YOUNG.

A.-D.V.S.

....

16 June, 1917...Lt.-Col. W. A. MC
　　　　　　　　　　　DOUGALL.

I CORPS

FORMATION.

I Corps was formed in England and began mobilization on the 5th August, 1914.

I Corps was composed of the 1st and 2nd Divisions (the Aldershot Divisions).

I Corps crossed to France between the 11th and 16th August ; and the Corps concentrated to the east of Bohain, with Corps Headquarters at Wassigny. On the 21st August I Corps began to move northward into Belgium.

BATTLES AND ENGAGEMENTS.

1914

23 and 24 August ...	**Battle of Mons** [1st and 2nd Divisions ; and 5th Cav. Bde. and J. R.H.A.].

RETREAT FROM MONS.

25 August	**Landrecies** [4th (Guards) Bde., 2nd Division].
26 August	**Le Grand Fayt** [2/Conn. Rgrs., 5th Inf. Bde., 2nd Div.].
27 August	**Étreux** [15/Hsrs., and 1 Sec. 118 R.F.A., and 2/R.M.F., (1st Guards Bde.) 1st Division].
28 August	**Cerizy** [5th Cav. Bde. and J. R.H.A.].
1 September	**Villers Cottérêts** [2nd Division and 3rd Cav. Bde.].

7–10 September	**Battle of the Marne*** [1st and 2nd Divisions].
12–15 September ...	**Battle of the Aisne**** [1st and 2nd Divisions].
20 September	**Actions on the Aisne Heights** [1st and 2nd Divisions ; and 18th Inf. Bde. (6th Div.), and 2nd Cav. Bde.].
26 September	**Chivy** [1st Division].

---

* The Battle of the Marne (7–10/9) includes the Passage of the Petit Morin (8/9) and the Passage of the Marne (9/9).

** The Battle of the Aisne (12–15/9) includes the Passage of the Aisne (13/9) and the Capture of the Aisne Heights (14/9).

1914 *(Contd.)*

BATTLES OF YPRES.

21–24 October ... ... **Battle of Langemarck** [1st and 2nd Divisions].

29–31 October ... ... **Battle of Gheluvelt** [1st, 2nd, and 7th Divisions, and 2nd Cav. and 3rd Cav. Divisions].

11 November ... ... **Battle of Nonne Bosschen** [1st, 2nd, and 3rd* Divisions, 14/Lond. (Lond. Scottish), and 3rd Cav. Div.].

1915

25 January ... ... **First Action of Givenchy** [1st Div.—First Army].

29 January ... ... **Cuinchy** [1st Div.—First Army].

1 and 6 February ... **Cuinchy** [2nd Div.—First Army].

9 May ... ... { **Battle of Aubers Ridge**
{ **Attack at Rue du Bois** [1st and 47th Divs.—First Army].

15–25 May ... ... **Battle of Festubert** [2nd, 7th, 47th, and 1st Cdn. Divs., and 51st Div. (until 22/5)—First Army].

25 Sept.–8 Oct. ... ... **Battle of Loos** [2nd, 7th, 9th, and 28th Divs.—First Army].

13–19 October ... ... **Hohenzollern Redoubt** [2nd Division—First Army].

1916

2–18 March ... ... **Hohenzollern Craters** [12th Div.—First Army].

27–29 April ... ... **German Gas Attacks, Hulluch** [15th and 16th Divs.—First Army].

11 May ... ... **Loss of the Kink** [15th Div.—First Army].

---

* In the Battle of Nonne Bosschen the 3rd Division consisted of two of its own brigades (7th and 9th) and one from the 5th Division (15th).

1917

BATTLES OF ARRAS.

9–14 April ... ... **Battle of Vimy Ridge** [24th Div.—First Army].

---

1 July ... ... **Attack on Liévin** [46th Div.—First Army].

15–25 August ... ... **Battle of Hill 70, Lens** [6th and 46th Divs —First Army].

1918

BATTLES OF THE LYS.

12–15 April ... ... **Battle of Hazebrouck** [3rd Inf. Bde. (1st Div.], and 3rd, 4th, and 55th Divs.—First Army].

12–15 April ... ... **Defence of Hinges Ridge** [3rd and 4th Divs.—First Army].

12–17 April ... ... **First Defence of Givenchy** [55th Div.*—First Army].

18 April ... ... **Battle of Béthune** [1st, 3rd, and 4th Divs.—First Army].

18 and 19 April ... **Second Defence of Givenchy** [1st Div.—First Army].

THE ADVANCE TO VICTORY.

18 Aug.–18 Sept. ... **THE ADVANCE IN ARTOIS AND FLANDERS** [1st, 11th, 15th, 16th, and 55th Divs.—First Army].

24 August ... ... **Capture of Givenchy Craters** [55th Div.—First Army].

17 September ... ... **Capture of Canteleux Trench** [165th Bde., 55th Div.—First Army**].

2 Oct.–11 Nov. ... ... **THE FINAL ADVANCE IN ARTOIS** [15th, 16th, 55th*** and 58th*** Divs. ; and, from 7–11/11, part of 1st Cav. Div.—Fifth Army].

---

* 55th Div. was transferred (in the line) from XI Corps (First Army) at 8 a.m. on 12/4/18.
** I Corps was transferred (in the line) from First Army to Fifth Army at Noon on 19/9/18. I Corps had served continuously in First Army from 26/12/14.
*** 55th Division was transferred to III Corps, Fifth Army, on 8/10/18 ; and 58th Division joined I Corps at Noon on 14/10/18, from VIII Corps First Army.

1918 *(Contd.)*

The Germans started to withdraw on the I Corps front on the 2nd October, and the 55th Division at once occupied La Bassée. Thereafter, for over 5 weeks, the I Corps (now in the Fifth Army) pressed steadily eastward in contact with the retiring enemy.

On the 11th November, when hostilities ceased, the I Corps, on the right of the Fifth Army, had advanced to a line four miles to the eastward of the Schelde–Dendre Canal and was covered by the advanced posts of the 1st Cavalry Division, established to the east of Ath.

In the 86 days, since the 18th August, the I Corps had advanced nearly 50 miles.

II CORPS

G.O.C.

5 August, 1914	... ...	Lieut.-General Sir J. M. GRIERSON (died, 17/8/14).
19 August, 1914	... ...	Major-General Sir C. FERGUSSON, Bt. (acting).
21 August, 1914	... ...	General Sir H. L. SMITH-DORRIEN.
1 January, 1915	... ...	Lieut.-General Sir C. FERGUSSON, Bt.
28 May, 1916	... ...	Lieut.-General C. W. JACOB.

B.-G.G.S.

5 Aug., 1914...Br.-Gen. G. T. FORESTIER-
WALKER.
1 Jan., 1915...Br.-Gen. W. T. FURSE.
2 Oct., 1915...Br.-Gen. P. P. DE B.
RADCLIFFE.
4 June, 1916...Br.-Gen. P. HOWELL
(killed, 7/10/16).
12 Oct., 1916...Br.-Gen. S. H. WILSON.
27 Oct., 1918...Br.-Gen. C. BONHAM-
CARTER.

D.-A. and Q.-M.-G.

5 Aug., 1914...Maj.-Gen. L. G.
DRUMMOND.
20 Aug., 1914...Br.-Gen. W. B. HICKIE.
30 Sept., 1914...Br.-Gen. W. H. RYCROFT.
4 Jan., 1915...Br.-Gen. H. P.
SHEKLETON.
24 Dec., 1916...Br.-Gen. R. S. MAY.
3 Nov., 1917...Br.-Gen. R. M. FOOT.

G.S.O. 1.

5 Aug., 1914 }
-27 Dec., 1914 } Col. R. S. OXLEY.

_____

13 April, 1918 }
- July, 1918 } Col. H. R. HOPWOOD.

B.-G. R.A.

5 Aug., 1914...Br.-Gen. A. H. SHORT.*
17 Nov., 1915...Br.-Gen. G. McK. FRANKS.
26 Dec., 1915...Br.-Gen. C. E. LAWRIE.
19 Feb., 1917...Br.-Gen. A. D. KIRBY.

C.H.A.

.........**

10 April, 1916...Br.-Gen. B. M. BATEMAN.
1 Aug., 1916...Br.-Gen. D. F. H. LOGAN.

---

* Injured in France on 16/8/1914 ; but returned to duty.
** Formed in France on 10/4/16.

II CORPS

C.E.

5 Aug., 1914...Br.-Gen. A. E. SANDBACH.
7 May, 1915...Br.-Gen. G. M. HEATH.
14 Sept., 1915...Br.-Gen. C. GODBY.
8 Jan., 1918...Br.-Gen. G. H. BOILEAU
(tempy.).
6 Feb., 1918...Br.-Gen. C. GODBY.

A.-D. Signals.

5 Aug., 1914...Maj. A. B. R. HILDE-
BRAND (i/c Army Signals).
8 April, 1915...Maj. H. G. GANDY
(i/c Army Signals).
1 June, 1915...Capt. J. DAY
(i/c Corps Signals).
6 Feb., 1916...Maj. J. DAY.
20 Nov., 1916...Lt.-Col. J. DAY.
4 Feb., 1917...Lt.-Col. A. St. J. YATES.
29 Dec., 1917...Lt.-Col. C. V. MONIER-
WILLIAMS.
27 Aug., 1918...Lt.-Col. E. DE W. H.
BRADLEY.

D.-D.M.S.

5 Aug., 1914...Capt. E. L. MOSS (M.O.).
Nov., 1914...Col. R. PORTER
(D.-D.M.S.).
7 Jan., 1915...Capt. E. L. MOSS (M.O.).
4 April, 1915...Col. R. J. GEDDES.
18 Jan., 1917...Col. S. G. MOORES.
1 April, 1918...Col. G. St. C. THOM.

A.-D.V.S.

....

16 June, 1917...Lt.-Col. J. J. GRIFFITH.

II CORPS

FORMATION.

II Corps was formed in England and began mobilization on the 5th August, 1914. One of the two divisions composing the II Corps came from the Southern Command (3rd Division), and the other division (5th) from Ireland. The units mobilized at their peace stations. The Corps Commander (Lt.-Gen. Sir J. M. Grierson) came from the Eastern Command; but, on the way to the concentration area in N. France, he died in the train on the 17th August, and the G.O.C. Southern Command (Gen. Sir H. L. Smith-Dorrien) was then selected to replace him.

The 3rd Division crossed to France between the 11th and the 16th August and the 5th Division (from Ireland) followed between the 13th and 17th August. II Corps effected its concentration to the eastward and southward of the Forest of Mormal, between Avesnes and the River Sambre, with the Corps Headquarters at Landrecies.

On the 21st August II Corps began to move northward into Belgium.

BATTLES AND ENGAGEMENTS.

1914

23 and 24 August ... **Battle of Mons** [3rd and 5th Divisions].

RETREAT FROM MONS.

24 August ... ... **Élouges** [1/Norf. and 1/Ches. (15th Inf. Bde.), and 119 R.F.A. : 5th Division].

25 August ... ... **Solesmes** [7th Inf. Bde. (3rd Div.), and 19th* Inf. Bde.].

26 August ... ... **Battle of Le Cateau** [3rd and 5th Divisions; with 4th Div., 19th Inf. Bde., and Cavalry Div.].

1 September ... ... **Crépy en Valois** [13th Inf. Bde. and XXVII R.F.A. : 5th Division].

7–10 September ... ... **Battle of the Marne**** [3rd and 5th Divisions].

12–15 September ... **Battle of the Aisne***** [3rd and 5th Divisions].

20 September ... ... **Action on the Aisne Heights** [3rd Division].

---

* Formed at Valenciennes on 22 and 23/8/14, and consisted of : 2/R.W.F., 1/Sco. Rif., 1/Middx., and 2/A. and S. H. ; with 19th Bde. Ammn. Column, Field Ambulance, and Train.
** Includes Passage of the Petit Morin (8/9), and passage of the Marne (9/9).
*** Includes Passage of the Aisne (13/9), and Capture of the Aisne Heights (14/9).

K

II CORPS

1914 *(Contd.)*

10–30 October ... ... **Battle of La Bassée*** [3rd and 5th Divisions].

14 December ... ... **Attack on Wytschaete** [3rd Division].

1915

17–22 April ... ... **Capture of Hill 60** [5th Division—Second Army].

BATTLES OF YPRES.

22 and 23 April ... **Battle of Gravenstafel Ridge** [5th Division—Second Army].

24 April–1 May ... ... **Battle of St. Julien** [5th Division—Second Army**].

1916

BATTLES OF THE SOMME.

24 July†–3 September **Battle of Pozières Ridge** [12th, 25th, 48th, and 49th Divs.—Reserve Army].

6 August–3 September **Fighting for Mouquet Farm** [12th, 25th, and 48th Divs.—Reserve Army].

14 September ... ... **Capture of the Wonder Work** [32nd Bde. (11th Div.)—Reserve Army].

15–22 September ... **Battle of Flers-Courcelette** [11th and 49th Divs.—Reserve Army].

26–28 September ... **Battle of Thiepval Ridge** [11th and 18th Divs.; with 6 tanks C. Coy.—Reserve Army].

26 September ... ... **Capture of Mouquet Farm** [11th Div.; with 2 tanks C. Coy.—Reserve Army].

---

* Indian Corps—3rd (Lahore) and 7th (Meerut) Divs.—took over from II Corps and was in the line from Night 29–30/10/14 until the end of the Battle on 2/11/14   3rd (Lahore) Div., which had disembarked at Marseilles on 26/9/14, went into the line under II Corps on 23/10/14. Its 7th (Ferozepore) Brigade served with the Cavalry Corps in the Battle of Messines from 22–27/10/14 ; and its 9th (Sirhind) Bde., which had been left in Egypt, only rejoined the Div. on 9/12/14. 7th (Meerut) Div. went into the line on the Night 30–31/10/14, under Indian Corps.

** 13th Inf. Bde. in " Plumer's Force " 28/4–7/5/15, see Second Army (p. 82 and footnote).

† Took over (in the line) at Noon on 24/7/16, from X Corps.

1916 *(Contd.)*

BATTLES OF THE SOMME *(Contd.)*.

1 Oct.–11 Nov. ... ... **Battle of the Ancre Heights** [18th, 19th, 25th, 39th,* and 4th Cdn. Divs. ; and 4 tanks A. Coy. (on 21/10) with 18th Div.—Reserve Army, until 30/10 ;** then Fifth Army].

9 October ... ... **Capture of Stuff Redoubt** [25th Div.—Reserve Army].

14 October ... ... **Capture of Schwaben Redoubt** [39th Div.–Reserve Army].

21 October ... ... **Capture of Regina Trench and Redoubt** [18th and 25th Divs. ; with 4 tanks A. Coy. with 18th Div.—Reserve Army].

21 October ... ... **Capture of Stuff Trench** [39th Div.—Reserve Army].

13–18 November ... **Battle of the Ancre** [18th, 19th, 39th, and 4th Cdn. Divs. ; with 3 tanks A. Coy. with 39th Div. (on 13/11) ; and 3 tanks A. Coy. with 19th Div. (on 18/11)—Fifth Army**].

1917

11 Jan.–13 March ... **Operations on the Ancre** [2nd, 18th, and 63rd Divs.—Fifth Army].

17 and 18 February ... **Miraumont** [2nd, 18th, and 63rd Divs.—Fifth Army].

25 February–2 March **Capture of the Thilloys** [2nd Div.—Fifth Army].

10 March ... ... **Capture of Grévillers Trench** (near Irles) [2nd Div.—Fifth Army].

10 March ... ... **Capture of Irles** [18th Div.—Fifth Army].

14–20 March ... ... **German Retreat to the Hindenburg Line** [2nd and 18th Divs.—Fifth Army].

BATTLES OF YPRES.

31 July–2 August ... **Battle of Pilckem Ridge** [8th, 18th, 24th, 25th, and 30th Divs. ; with A. and B. Bns., 2nd Tank Bde.—Fifth Army].

10 August ... ... **Capture of Inverness Copse** [18th Div.—Fifth Army].

10 August ... ... **Capture of Westhoek** [25th Div.—Fifth Army].

---

* Transferred (in the line) on 5/10/16 from V Corps.
** On 30/10/16 the Reserve Army became the Fifth Army.

II CORPS

1917 *(Contd.)*

BATTLES OF YPRES *(Contd.)*.

16–18 August ... ... **Battle of Langemarck** [8th, 14th, 18th, 24th, and 56th Divs.; with part of 20 Coy. G. Bn., 1st Tank Bde.—Fifth Army.].

22 August ... ... **Fighting in front of St. Julien** [14th Div. (less 41st Bde.) and 47th Div.; with 4 tanks, 2nd Tank Bde.—Fifth Army].

22 and 23 August ... **Fighting on the Menin Road** [41st Bde. (14th Div.) and 23rd and 24th Divs.; with A Bn., 2nd Tank Bde.—Fifth Army].

2–10 November ... ... **Second Battle of Passchendaele** [1st, 58th, and 63rd Divs.—Second Army*].

1918

THE ADVANCE TO VICTORY.

18 August–6 September **THE ADVANCE IN FLANDERS**** [14th, 34th, 35th, and 49th Divs., and 30th Am. Div.—Second Army].

THE FINAL ADVANCE IN FLANDERS.

28 Sept–2 Oct. ... ... **Battle of Ypres** [9th, 29th, and 36th Divs.—Second Army].

14–19 October ... ... **Battle of Courtrai** [9th, 29th, and 36th Divs.—Second Army].

25 October ... ... **Ooteghem** [9th and 36th Divs.—Second Army].

31 October ... ... **Tieghem** [31st and 34th Divs.—Second Army].

The II Corps, on the left of the B.E.F. was withdrawn from the front line on the 5th November, owing to the necessary contraction of the Second Army front after the Action of Tieghem. When hostilities ceased on the 11th November the divisions of the II Corps were engaged in refitting and reorganizing in the Lys valley, between Comines and Courtrai. Since the 18th August the II Corps fought in two battles and had advanced 28 miles in 80 days.

---

* II Corps (then in Second Army) took over 58th and 63rd Divs. and its battle-front from XVIII Corps, Fifth Army, at 10 a.m. on 2/11/1917.
** II Corps held the left flank of the Second Army whilst this Advance took place.

1918 *(Contd.)*

The II Corps, to be composed of 9th, 29th, 34th, and 41st Divisions, was selected to form part of the Second Army in the advance to the German Frontier. This advance began on the 18th November ; and by the end of the month II Corps had closed up on the frontier and was ready to enter Germany. Owing, however, to the narrow front on the Rhine which had been allotted to the B.E.F. it became necessary to reorganize the force which would march into Germany and occupy the Rhine bridgeheads.

The II Corps, now composed of the 9th, 29th, and New Zealand Divisions, was detailed to accompany the Second Army in the Advance to the Rhine. At the beginning of December this final advance was opened ; and on the 7th December, in response to an urgent summons, the leading infantry brigade (28th) of the 9th Division reached Cologne by train. On the 13th the Division crossed the Rhine at Mulheim, and became responsible for the left divisional sector of the Cologne bridgehead.

III CORPS

G.O.C.

5 August, 1914	... ...	Lieut.-General W. P. PULTENEY.
16 February, 1918	... ...	Major-General R. P. LEE (acting).
26 February, 1918	... ...	Lieut.-General Sir R. H. K. BUTLER.
11 August, 1918	... ...	Lieut.-General Sir A. J. GODLEY (tempy.).
11 September, 1918 ...	...	Lieut.-General Sir R. H. K. BUTLER.

B.-G.G.S.

5 Aug., 1914...Br.-Gen. J. P. DuCANE.
25 Jan., 1915...Br.-Gen. G. F. MILNE.
25 Feb., 1915...Br.-Gen. A. L. LYNDEN-BELL.
13 July, 1915...Br.-Gen. C. F. ROMER.
11 April, 1917...Br.-Gen. C. BONHAM-CARTER.
15 Oct., 1917...Br.-Gen. C. G. FULLER.

D.-A. and Q.-M.-G.

5 Aug., 1914...Br.-Gen. C. R. R. McGRIGOR.
6 Oct., 1914...Br.-Gen. W. CAMPBELL.
13 July, 1915...Br.-Gen. A. A. CHICHESTER.
10 Nov., 1915...Br.-Gen. N. W. H. DuBOULAY.
15 Dec., 1915...Br.-Gen. P. O. HAMBRO.
11 Jan., 1918...Br.-Gen. J. F. I. H. DOYLE.

G.S.O. 1.

5 Aug., 1914...Col. F. S. MAUDE.
2 Nov., 1914⎱
–7 Jan., 1915⎰ Col. H. S. SLOMAN.

B.-G.R.A.

5 Aug., 1914...Br.-Gen. E. J. PHIPPS-HORNBY, V.C.
5 June, 1915...Br.-Gen. A. STOKES.
1 April, 1916...Br.-Gen. G. H. W. NICHOLSON (tempy.).
4 April, 1916...Br.-Gen. H. C. C. UNIACKE.
26 July, 1916...Br.-Gen. T. A. TANCRED.
29 May, 1918...Br.-Gen. C. M. ROSS-JOHNSON.

C.H.A.

.........*

[26 June, 1915] Br.-Gen. A. C. CURRIE.
5 April, 1916...Lt.-Col. P. D. HAMILTON (acting).
7 April, 1916...Br.-Gen. A. E. J. PERKINS.

---

* Second Army H.A. Group (formerly No. 3 H.A.R. Group—G.H.Q. Artillery) joined III Corps on 5/4/16, and its designation was then changed to III Corps Heavy Artillery (see Appendix 3).

III CORPS

C.E.

5 Aug., 1914...Br.-Gen. F. M. GLUBB.
9 May, 1915...Br.-Gen. J. E. CAPPER.
14 July, 1915...Br.-Gen. A. L. SCHREIBER.
29 Nov., 1917...Br.-Gen. A. ROLLAND.

A.-D. Signals.

5 Aug., 1914...Maj. W. P. E. NEWBIGGING (i/c Army Signals).
29 Mar., 1915...Maj. A. B. CUNNINGHAM (i/c Army Signals).
1 June, 1915...Maj. A. B. CUNNINGHAM (i/c Corps Signals).
6 Feb., 1916...Maj. A. B. CUNNINGHAM.
20 Nov., 1916...Lt.-Col. A. B. CUNNINGHAM.
20 Aug., 1917...Lt.-Col. A. C. ALLAN.
8 Oct., 1918...Lt.-Col. N. F. HITCHINS.

D.-D.M.S.

5 Aug., 1914...Maj. P. DAVIDSON (M.O.).
6 Jan., 1915...Col. M. W. O'KEEFFE (D.-D.M.S.).
7 Jan., 1915...Capt. M. B. H. RITCHIE (M.O.).
6 April, 1915...Col. B. M. SKINNER.
2 Nov., 1916...Col. S. MACDONALD (sick, 12/4/18).
12 April, 1918...Col. J. POE (tempy.).
14 April, 1918...Col. C. W. PROFEIT.

A.-D.V.S.

....

16 June, 1917...Lt.-Col. J. A. B. McGOWAN.

III CORPS

FORMATION.

III Corps Headquarters began to form in England on the 5th August, 1914. Originally it was intended that the Corps should be composed of the 4th Division and the 6th Division

Events, however, moved too rapidly in Belgium : on the 22nd August the 4th Division was sent independently to France and on the 26th August fought at Le Cateau, under II Corps. During the subsequent Retreat the Division remained under that Corps until 30th August.

On the 27th August III Corps Headquarters crossed to France ; and on the 31st the III Corps was formed in the field (at Verberie), composed of the 4th Division and the 19th Infantry Brigade.*

Between the 15th–21st August the 6th Division crossed from Ireland to England and the division concentrated in the neighbourhood of Cambridge and Newmarket. On the 7th September, the Retreat to the Marne having terminated and the Advance to the Aisne having started, the 6th Division began to move to France, disembarking at St. Nazaire ; and by the 13th September, as the Battle of the Aisne opened, the 6th Division completed concentration around Coulommiers (on the Grand Morin). On the next day the 6th Division advanced northward towards the Aisne, and on arrival at the front was employed to reinforce the I and II Corps which were heavily engaged in that Battle. It was not until the beginning of October that the 6th Division was free to join the III Corps, in preparation for the move of the B.E.F. to the north.

BATTLES AND ENGAGEMENTS.

1914

RETREAT FROM MONS [4th Div. and 19th Inf. Bde.].

1 September ... ... **Néry** [Part of 10th Inf. Bde. (4th Div.), and 19th Inf. Bde.-- from 8 a.m.].**

---

* 19th Inf. Bde. was formed at Valenciennes on 22 and 23/8/14, from L. of C. Battalions (see p. 139 fn.) From 12/10/14–31/5/15 the 19th Inf. Bde. was attached to the 6th Div. ; from 31/5–19/8/15 to the 27th Div. ; from 19/8–25/11/15 to the 2nd Div. ; and from 25/11/15 to the 33rd Div.
** Also 1st Cav. Bde. (1st Cav. Div.) and L Bty., R.H.A. from 5.40 a.m. ; and, in addition, I Bty. R.H.A. from 8 a.m.

1914 (*Contd.*)

7–10 September ... ...   **Battle of the Marne*** [4th Div. and 19th Inf. Bde.].

12–15 September   ...   **Battle of the Aisne**** [4th Div. and 19th Inf. Bde.].

13 Oct.–2 Nov. ...   ...   **Battle of Armentières** [4th Div. (less 11th and 12th Inf. Bdes.), 6th Div., and 19th Inf. Bde.; with, on 13–17/10, 2nd Cav. Div.; and, on 1 and 2/11, 3/Worc. (7th Bde., 3rd Div.) and 1/Dorset (15th Bde., 5th Div.)].

13 October ... ...   **Capture of Meteren** [10th Bde., 4th Div.].

19 Oct.–22 Nov.   ...   **Battles of Ypres** [11th and 12th Inf. Bdes., 4th Div.*****].

1915

25 September   ...   **Bois Grenier** [8th Div.—First Army].

1916

BATTLES OF THE SOMME.

1–13 July ... ...   **Battle of Albert** [1st, 8th, 12th, 19th, 23rd, and 34th Divs.—Fourth Army].

2–4 July   ...   ...   **Capture of La Boisselle** [19th Div.—Fourth Army].

10 July   ...   ...   **Capture of Contalmaison** [23rd Div.—Fourth Army].

14–17 July ...   ...   **Battle of Bazentin Ridge** [1st, 5th, and 34th† Divs.—Fourth Army].

20–25 July ...   ...   **Attacks on High Wood** [19th Div.—Fourth Army].

---

* Includes Passage of the Grand Morin (7/9) and Passage of the Marne (9/9).
** Includes Passage of the Aisne (13/9) and Capture of the Aisne Heights (14/9).
*** Holding the line from the R. Lys (near Frelinghien)—in front of Ploegsteert Wood—St. Yves.
† From 6/7–22/8/16 111th and 112th Inf. Bdes. of 37th Div. were attached to 34th Div., in exchange for 102nd and 103rd Inf. Bdes., which had suffered heavy losses in the Battle of Albert on 1–3/7/16.

1916 (*Contd.*)

BATTLES OF THE SOMME (*Contd.*).

23 July–3 September	**Battle of Pozières Ridge** [1st, 15th, 19th, 23rd, and 34th Divs.—Fourth Army].
15–22 September ...	**Battle of Flers-Courcelette** [1st, 15th, 23rd, 47th, and 50th Divs., and 103rd Inf. Bde. (34th Div.) attd. to 15th Div. ; with 8 tanks D Coy. : 15th (4), 47th (2), and 50th (2)—Fourth Army].
15 September	**Capture of Martinpuich** [15th Div. ; with 4 tanks D Coy.—Fourth Army].
15 September	**Capture of High Wood** [47th Div.—Fourth Army].
25–28 September ...	**Battle of Morval** [1st, 23rd, and 50th Divs. ; with 2 tanks D Coy. with 23rd Div.—Fourth Army].
1–18 October	**Battle of the Transloy Ridges** [9th, 15th, 23rd, 47th, and 50th Divs.—Fourth Army].
1–3 October	**Capture of Eaucourt l'Abbaye** [47th Div.—Fourth Army].
7 October	**Capture of Le Sars** [23rd Div.—Fourth Army].
7 October–5 November	**Attacks on the Butte de Warlencourt,** [9th, 23rd, 47th, 48th, and 50th Divs.—Fourth Army].
3–11 November	**Battle of the Ancre Heights** [48th Div.—Fourth Army].
13–18 November ...	**Battle of the Ancre** [48th Div.—Fourth Army].

1917

14 March–5 April ...	**German Retreat to the Hindenburg Line** [1st, 48th, and 59th Divs.—Fourth Army].
18 March	**Occupation of Péronne** [48th Div.—Fourth Army].

1917 *(Contd.)*

BATTLE OF CAMBRAI.

20 and 21 November	**The Tank Attack** [6th, 12th, 20th, and 29th Divs. ; with 2nd and 3rd Tank Bdes. (204 tanks)—Third Army].
21 November	**Recapture of Noyelles** [6th Div. ; with 2 tanks B Bn., 2nd Tank Bde.—Third Army].
23–28 November ...	**Capture of Bourlon Wood** [6th, 12th, and 20th Divs. ; with part of 2nd Tank Bde.—Third Army].
30 Nov.–3 Dec.	**The German Counter-Attacks** [Gds., 6th, 12th, 20th, 29th, 36th, and 61st, Divs., and 1st, 2nd, 4th (Ind.), and 5th (Ind.) Cav. Divs. ; with 1st and 2nd Tank Bdes.-Third Army].
30 November	**Attack on Gouzeaucourt** [Gds. Div. ; with 22 tanks 2nd Tank Bde.—Third Army].
1 December	**Attack on Villers Guislain and Gauche Wood** [Gds. and 12th Divs., and 4th (Ind.) and 5th (Ind.) Cav. Divs. ; with 19 tanks, 2nd Tank Bde.—Third Army].

1918

21–25 March	**FIRST BATTLES OF THE SOMME.**
21–23 March	**Battle of St. Quentin** [14th, 18th, and 58th Divs., and 2nd and 3rd Cav. Divs.—Fifth Army].

---

24 and 25 April ...	**Villers Bretonneux** [8th, 18th, and 58th, Divs. ; with 13 Heavy and 7 Whippet Tanks, 3rd Tank Bde.—Fourth Army].
8 Aug.–1 Oct. ; ... ... } and 8 Oct.–11 Nov. ... }	**THE ADVANCE TO VICTORY.**
8–11 August	**Battle of Amiens** [12th, 18th, and 58th Divs., and, on 8/8, 131st Am. Inf. Regt. (transferred on 9/8 to Aus. Corps)—Fourth Army].

1918 *(Contd.)*

THE ADVANCE TO VICTORY *(Contd.).*

SECOND BATTLES OF THE SOMME.

21–23 August	**Battle of Albert** [12th, 18th, 47th, and 48th Divs. ; with 66 tanks, 1st, 4th, and 5th Bns., 4th Tank Bde.—Fourth Army].
31 Aug.–3 Sept. ...	**Second Battle of Bapaume** [18th, 47th, 58th, and 74th Divs.— Fourth Army].

BATTLES OF THE HINDENBURG LINE.

18 September	**Battle of Epéhy** [12th, 18th, 58th, and 74th Divs. ; with 8 tanks, 2nd Bn., 5th Tank Bde.—Fourth Army].
21 September	**The Knoll, Ronssoy** [12th and 18th Divs. ; with 9 tanks 2nd Bn., 5th Tank Bde.—Fourth Army].
29 Sept.–1 Oct.* ...	**Battle of the St. Quentin Canal** [12th and 18th Divs., and, on Night 30/9–1/10, 149th Bde. (50th Div.)—Fourth Army].
8 Oct.**–11 Nov. ...	**THE FINAL ADVANCE IN ARTOIS** [55th and 74th Divs. ; and from 7–11/11, part of 1st Cav..Div.—Fifth Army].

In the Final Advance the III Corps forced the line of the Haute Deule Canal on the 14th–16th October and early on the 11th November captured Ath. During its service in the Fourth Army from the 8th August to the 1st October the III Corps took part in 5 battles ; and, by almost continuous fighting during the 54 days, the Corps advanced nearly 30 miles through the German positions between Albert on the Ancre and Vendhuille on the Schelde. Then, after joining the Fifth Army, the III Corps, in 35 more days, took part in a further advance of 45 miles ; and, when the Armistice brought hostilities to a close, the III Corps was established on a line 4 miles to the eastward of Ath and astride the highway to Enghien.

On the 15th November the III Corps (8th, 15th, 55th, and 74th Divisions) was ordered to form part of the Second Army in the advance to the German Frontier. On the 21st November this order was cancelled and the divisions were transferred to the Fifth Army— the 55th Division moving up to Brussels.

---

* At Noon on 1/10/18 III Corps handed over (in the line) to XIII Corps.
** At 10 a.m. 8/10/18 III Corps came into the line in the Fifth Army, and took over 55th Div. from I Corps and 74th Div. from XI Corps. (74th Div. served in III Corps from 30/8–30/9/18 ; and from 8/10/18 until Armistice.)

IV CORPS

G.O.C.

5 October, 1914	... ...	Lieut.-General Sir H. S. RAWLINSON, Bt.*
22 December, 1915	... ...	Lieut.-General Sir H. H. WILSON.**
1 December, 1916	... ...	Lieut.-General Sir C. L. WOOLLCOMBE.
11 March, 1918	... ...	Lieut.-General Sir G. M. HARPER.

B.-G.G.S.

8 Oct., 1914...Br.-Gen. R. A. K. MONTGOMERY.
30 Dec., 1914...Br.-Gen. A. G. DALLAS.
19 Aug., 1915...Br.-Gen. A. A. MONTGOMERY.
5 Feb., 1916...Br.-Gen. H. D. DE PREE.
19 Mar., 1918...Br.-Gen. R. G. PARKER.

D.-A. and Q.-M.-G.

6 Oct., 1914...Br.-Gen. W. L. WHITE.
24 Dec., 1916...Br.-Gen. W. H. V. DARELL.

G.S.O. 1.

10 Oct., 1914
−29 Dec., 1914 } Col. A. G. DALLAS.

8 May, 1918
— July, 1918 } Lt.-Col. W. H. DIGGLE.

B.-G.R.A.

5 Oct., 1914...Br.-Gen. A. H. HUSSEY.
10 Oct., 1915...Br.-Gen. C. E. D. BUDWORTH.
26 Mar., 1916...Br.-Gen. J. G. GEDDES.

C.H.A.

.........***

5 April, 1916 Br.-Gen. F. C. POOLE.
18 June, 1916...Br.-Gen. T. E. MARSHALL.

---

* Became G.O.C. First Army on 22/12/15.
** From 17/3/17–25/6/17 General Wilson was Head of the British Mission with G.Q.G. ; on 1/9/17 he became G.O.C. Eastern Command (Home Forces), and C.I.G.S. on 19/2/18.
*** Formed in France on 5/4/16.

IV CORPS

C.E.

5 Oct., 1914...Br.-Gen. R. U. H. BUCKLAND.
13 Feb., 1916...Br.-Gen. E. R. KENYON.
16 July, 1916...Lt.-Col. H. B. DESVŒUX (acting).
24 July, 1916...Br.-Gen. S. F. WILLIAMS.
8 April, 1918...Br.-Gen. C. M. CARPENTER.

A.-D. Signals.

10 Oct., 1914...Maj. J. C. M. KERR (i/c Army Signals).
1 June, 1915...Maj. J. C. M. KERR (i/c Corps Signals).
6 Feb., 1916...Maj. J. C. M. KERR.
20 Nov., 1916...Lt.-Col. J. C. M. KERR.
29 Jan., 1918...Lt.-Col. J. STEVENSON.

D.-D.M.S.

6 Oct., 1914...Col. R. J. GEDDES.
7 Jan., 1915...Capt. R. GALE (M.O.).
7 April, 1915...Col. J. MEEK.
15 Feb., 1918...Col. C. E. POLLOCK.
19 July, 1918...Col. T. W. GIBBARD.

A.-D.V.S.

....

16 June, 1917...Lt.-Col. C. B. M. HARRIS.

IV CORPS

FORMATION.

On the 5th October, 1914, Lieut.-General Sir H. Rawlinson (who had been in temporary command of the 4th Division since the 23rd September) was sent by the F.-M. C.-in-C. to ascertain the situation in the area between Antwerp and Ypres, and he was appointed to command the forces about to land—the 7th Division and the 3rd Cavalry Division.

Early on the 8th October General Rawlinson was informed that the retirement from Antwerp would begin on the next day.

Meanwhile, on the 6th October, the 7th Division had landed at Zeebrugge, and on the 7th the Division moved forward to Bruges, so as to cover the disembarkation of the 3rd Cavalry Division at Ostend on the next day. On the 9th the 7th Division occupied a position at Ghent and the 3rd Cavalry Division collected at Bruges.

On the 10th October General Rawlinson's command was given the title of IV Corps, and the C.-in-C. ordered the IV Corps to cover and protect the withdrawal of the Belgian Army from the line Ghent—Selzaete to the area Ostend—Thourout—Dixmude. This task accomplished, the IV Corps would then form the left column of the B.E.F., of which the remainder was detraining at St. Omer.

At 3 a.m. on the 10th October the " Q " Staff of IV Corps (4 officers), Administrative Services (6 officers), with the B.-G.R.A., C.E., and Signals Officer embarked (with transport) at Southampton, reached Ostend at 4 a.m. on the 11th, and completed disembarkation by 4 p.m. On the 12th the " G " Staff and the D.-A. & Q.-M.-G. went to Thourout and the remainder of the Corps Staff moved to Nieuport.

To carry out the C.-in-C.'s orders the 3rd Cavalry Division moved to Thourout on the 10th, but the 7th Division remained at Ghent until the night of 11th/12th October.

On the 12th the 7th Division moved via Aeltre to Thielt, and the 3rd Cavalry Division marched to Roulers. On the 13th Cavalry patrols were at Kemmel and Corps H.Q. and the 7th Division retired to Roulers. On the 14th October the 3rd Cavalry Division established contact with the Cavalry Corps, and IV Corps H.Q. and the 7th Division reached Ypres. On the 15th Corps H.Q. (now complete) moved to Poperinghe ; and IV Corps, having reached its required position on the left of the B.E.F., was ordered to advance between Courtrai and Roulers.

L

BATTLES AND ENGAGEMENTS.

1914

9 and 10 October ... **Antwerp Operations** [7th Div. and 3rd Cav. Div.].

19–27 October ... ... **BATTLES OF YPRES.**

21–24 October ... ... **Battle of Langemarck** [7th Div. and 3rd Cav. Div.].

On the 26th October the 3rd Cavalry Division was transferred to serve with the I Corps in the Battles of Ypres. On the 27th the 7th Division was placed temporarily under the I Corps, and on the same day the C.-in-C. ordered General Rawlinson to cross to England and take charge of the final battle-training of the 8th Division (which was to become part of the IV Corps). At 3 a.m. on the 28th General Rawlinson with Br.-Gen. R. A. K. Montgomery (B.-G.G.S.) and Colonel A. G. Dallas (G.S.O. 1) left for England (via Calais) ; and on the 31st Br.-Gen. A. H. Hussey (B-G., R.A.) was ordered to report to the Corps Commander on Salisbury Plain.

Early in November the 8th Division was ready to move to France, and on the 6th and 7th November the Division disembarked at Le Havre. On the 12th the 8th Division completed its concentration around IV Corps Headquarters, then at Merville, and now the Corps was composed of the 7th and 8th Divisions. On the night of the 14th/15th November the two divisions (7th and 8th) moved forward to take over that part of the British Front which was opposite Aubers, that is between the left of the Indian Corps and the right of the III Corps.

18 December ... ... **Neuve Chapelle-Moated Grange Attack** [8th Division].

18 December ... ... **Rouges Bancs—Well Farm Attack** [7th Division).

1915

10–13 March	**Battle of Neuve Chapelle** [7th and 8th Divs.—with 5th Cav. Bde. (2nd Cav. Div.) in Army Reserve—First Army].
9 May	{ **Battle of Aubers Ridge.** **Attack at Fromelles** [7th, 8th, and 49th Divs—First Army].
15 and 16 June ...	**Second Action of Givenchy** [7th, 51st and 1st Cdn. Divs.—First Army].
25 Sept.–8 Oct.	**Battle of Loos** [1st, 15th, and 47th Divs., and 3rd Cav. Div.—First Army].
13–19 October	**Hohenzollern Redoubt** [1st and 47th Divs.—First Army].

1916

21 May	**German Attack on Vimy Ridge** [47th Div.—First Army].*

1917

11–19 January	**Operations on the Ancre** [2nd, 11th, and 61st Divs.—Fifth Army].
14 March–5 April ...	**German Retreat to the Hindenburg Line** [32nd, 35th, and 61st Divs.—Fourth Army].
26 May–16 June ...	**Actions on the Hindenburg Line** [20th Div.—Fifth Army, until 10 a.m. 31/5 ; then Third Army].

BATTLE OF CAMBRAI.

20 and 21 November	**The Tank Attack** [36th, 51st, 56th, 62nd Divs., and 1st Cav. Div. ; with 120 tanks, 1st Tank Bde.—Third Army].
21 November	**Capture of Cantaing** [51st Div., with 12 tanks B Bn., 2nd Tank Bde.—Third Army].
21 November	**Capture of Tadpole Copse** (¾-mile W. of Mœuvres) [56th Div.—Third Army].

---

* Also see XVII Corps and Third Army.

1917 *(Contd.)*

BATTLE OF CAMBRAI *(Contd.)*.

23–28 November ... **Capture of Bourlon Wood** [Gds., 2nd, 36th, 40th, 47th, 51st, 56th,* 59th, and 62nd Divs., and 1st and 2nd Cav. Divs. ; with 1st and 3rd Tank Bdes., and part 2nd Tank Bde.—Third Army].

30 Nov. and 1 Dec.** **German Counter-Attacks** [2nd, 47th, and 59th ; with 3rd Tank Bde.—Third Army].

1918

FIRST BATTLES OF THE SOMME.

21–23 March ... ... **Battle of St. Quentin** [6th, 19th, 25th, 41st, and 51st Divs. ; with 1 Coy. 8th Bn., 2nd Tank Bde.—Third Army].

22 March ... ... **Counter-Attack at Beugny** [19th Div. ; with 25 tanks 2nd Bn., 2nd Tank Bde.—Third Army].

24 and 25 March ... **First Battle of Bapaume** [19th, 25th, 41st, 51st, and 62nd Divs. ; with 10th Bn., 2nd Tank Bde.—Third Army].

28 March ... ... **First Battle of Arras** [41st, 42nd, 62nd, and N.Z. Divs., and 4th Aus. Bde. (4th Aus. Div.) ; with defnt. 2nd Tank Bde.—Third Army].

5 April ... ... **Battle of the Ancre** [37th, 42nd, and N.Z. Divs., and 4th Aus. Bde. (4th Aus. Div.] ; with 1 tank 10th Bn., 4th Tank Bde.—Third Army].

Night 22/23 June ... **Bucquoy*** [5 pltns. 5/K.O.Y.L.I., 62nd Div. ; and party R.E. with 5 female tanks C Coy. 10th Bn., 4th Tank Bde.—Third Army].

---

* At Midnight 24/11/17 56th Div. was transferred (in the line) to VI Corps.
** On 1/12/17 IV Corps handed over (in the line) to V Corps.
*** First night raid in which tanks were engaged.

1918 *(Contd.)*

THE ADVANCE TO VICTORY.

SECOND BATTLES OF THE SOMME.

21–23 August ... ... **Battle of Albert** [5th, 37th, 42nd, 63rd, and N.Z. Divs.; with 3rd (Whippets), and 7th and 10th Tank Bns., and 17th (A.-C.) Bn., 1st Tank Bde.—Third Army].

31 Aug.–3 Sept. ... **Second Battle of Bapaume** [5th, 42nd, and N.Z. Divs.; with 3rd (Whippets), and 7th and 10th Bns., and 17th (A.-C.) Bn., 1st Tank Bde.—Third Army].

BATTLES OF THE HINDENBURG LINE.

12 September ... ... **Battle of Havrincourt** [37th and N.Z. Divs.—Third Army].

18 September ... ... **Battle of Epéhy** [5th Div.—Third Army].

27 Sept.—1 Oct. ... **Battle of the Canal du Nord** [5th, 37th, 42nd, and N.Z. Divs.; with (part) 11th Tank Bn., 1st Tank Bde.—Third Army].

8 and 9 October ... **Battle of Cambrai** [37th and N.Z. Divs.; with (part) 12th Bn., 1st Tank Bde.—Third Army].

9–12 October ... ... **Pursuit to the Selle** [5th, 37th, 42nd, and N.Z. Divs.—Third Army].

THE FINAL ADVANCE IN PICARDY.

17–25 October ... ... **Battle of the Selle** [5th, 37th, 42nd, and N.Z. Divs.; with, on 23/10, (part) 11th and 12th Bns., 1st Tank Bde.—Third Army].

23 October ... ... **Capture of Grand Champ Ridge** [5th Div.; with 2 tanks 12th Bn., 1st Tank Bde.—Third Army].

4 November ... ... **Battle of the Sambre** [37th and N.Z. Divs.; with (part) 2nd Tank Bde.—Third Army].

4 November ... ... **Capture of Le Quesnoy** [N.Z. Div.—Third Army].

On the 10th November the 42nd Division (which had been in IV Corps Reserve from 24/10–3/11) showed that its strength and energy were repaired by capturing Hautmont

1918 *(Contd.)*

and Fort Hautmont (south of Maubeuge). At 11 a.m. on the next day, when the Armistice brought hostilities to a close, the front line of the IV Corps was established some 8 miles eastward of Maubeuge.

For 83 days the IV Corps had been almost continuously engaged. In that period it had fought in 8 battles and advanced more than 60 miles.

Soon after Armistice the IV Corps (5th, 37th, 42nd, and New Zealand Divisions) was informed that it had been selected to form part of the Fourth Army in the advance to the German frontier. Shortly afterwards this order was cancelled, and three of the selected divisions—5th, 37th, and 42nd—then moved into billets in the Charleroi—Namur—Wavre area, to await demobilization. The New Zealand Division, however, did eventually enter Germany in the II Corps.

V CORPS

G.O.C.

8 January, 1915	... ...	Lieut.-General Sir H. C. O. Plumer.
8 May, 1915	... ...	Lieut.-General Sir E. H. H. Allenby.
23 October, 1915	... ...	Lieut.-General H. D. Fanshawe.
5 July, 1916	... ...	Lieut.-General E. A. Fanshawe.
11 August, 1916	... ...	Maj.-General O. S. W. Nugent (acting).
17 August, 1916	... ...	Lieut.-General E. A. Fanshawe.
28 April, 1918	... ...	Lieut.-General C. D. Shute.

B.-G.G.S.

8 Jan., 1915...Br.-Gen. H. S. Jeudwine.
6 Oct., 1915...Br.-Gen. A. R. Hoskins.
13 Feb., 1916...Br.-Gen. A. Blair.
24 June, 1916...Br.-Gen. G. F. Boyd.
14 July, 1918...Br.-Gen. R. H. Mangles.

D.-A. and Q.-M.-G.

8 Jan., 1915...Br.-Gen. A. E. J. Cavendish.
21 April, 1915...Br.-Gen. L. W. Atcherley.
22 June, 1916...Br.-Gen. H. M. de F. Montgomery.

G.S.O. 1.

27 Mar., 1918...Lt.-Col. J. M. Blair.
6 May, 1918...Lt.-Col. W. R. Pinwill.
14 May, 1918⎱ Lt.-Col. J. M. R.
— Aug., 1918⎰ Harrison.

B.-G. R.A.

8 Jan., 1915...Br.-Gen. S. D. Browne.
16 Nov., 1915...Br.-Gen. H. C. C. Uniacke.
24 Mar., 1916...Br.-Gen. A. Stokes.
15 Jan., 1917...Br.-Gen. R. P. Benson.

C.H.A.

.........*
[16 Nov., 1915] Br.-Gen. R. P. Benson.
15 Jan., 1917...Br.-Gen. T. R. C. Hudson (sick, 20/6/17).
20 June, 1917...Lt.-Col. W. A. Edmeads (acting).
16 July, 1917...Br.-Gen. A. M. Tyler.

---

* No. 2 H.A.R. Group (G.H.Q. Artillery) joined V Corps on 9/4/16, and changed its designation to V Corps Heavy Artillery (see Appendix 3).

V CORPS

C.E.

8 Jan., 1915...Br.-Gen. R. D. PETRIE.
27 Mar., 1917...Lt.-Col. G. H. BOILEAU
(acting).
4 April, 1917...Br.-Gen. A. J. CRAVEN.
6 April, 1918...Br.-Gen. A. G.
STEVENSON.

A.-D. Signals.

23 Jan., 1915...Maj. W. C. MACFIE
(i/c Army Signals).
1 June, 1915...Maj. W. C. MACFIE
(i/c Corps Signals).
6 Feb., 1916...Maj. J. WATSON.
20 Nov., 1916...Lt.-Col. J. W.
DANIELSEN.

D.-D.M.S.

8 Jan., 1915...Maj. G. B. RUSSELL (M.O.).
Mar., 1915...Lieut. E. H. WORTH (M.O.).
5 April, 1915...Col. C. E. NICHOL.
3 July, 1916...Col. D. M. O'CALLAGHAN.
[16 Nov., 1918...Col. R. W. CLEMENTS].

A.-D.V.S.

....

16 June, 1917...Lt.-Col. M. St. G. GLASSE
(sick, 20/8/18).
20 Aug., 1918...Maj. W. R. NEALE
(acting).
25 Sept., 1918...Lt.-Col. G. CONDER.

V CORPS

FORMATION.

Part of V Corps Headquarters began to assemble in England on the 27th December, 1914, and early in January, 1915, the remainder formed in France. On the 10th January, 1915, the part which had collected in England crossed to France, and the formation of V Corps Headquarters was completed.

On the 18th February, 1915, V Corps took over the 27th and 28th Divisions, and with them that part of the British front (opposite St. Eloi) which these divisions were then holding.

BATTLES AND ENGAGEMENTS.

1915

14 and 15 March ... **St. Eloi** [27th Div.—Second Army].

BATTLES OF YPRES.

22 and 23 April ... **Battle of Gravenstafel Ridge** [27th, 28th, and 1st Cdn. Divs., and " Geddes's Detnt.,"* and 13th Bde. (5th Div.)—Second Army].

22 April ... ... **The Gas Attack** [1st Cdn. Div., and B Coy. 2/Buffs (85th Bde., 28th Div.)—Second Army].

24 April–4 May ... ... **Battle of St. Julien** [4th, 27th, 28th, 50th, Lahore, and 1st Cdn. Divs., and Geddes's Detnt.,* and 13th Bde. (5th Div.), and 2nd Cav. Div.—Second Army, until 7.50 a.m. 28/4 ; then Plumer's Force,** until 6 a.m. 7/5/15].

8–13 May ... ... **Battle of Frezenberg Ridge** [4th, 27th, 28th, and 50th Divs., and 1st Cav. and 3rd Cav. Divs.—Second Army].

24 and 25 May ... ... **Battle of Bellewaarde Ridge** [4th, 27th, 28th, and 50th Divs., and 1st Cav. and 2nd Cav. Divs.—Second Army].

---

* " Colonel A. D. Geddes's Detachment " was formed (without any Staff) on 23/4/15 of 4 battalions from 28th Div.—2/Buffs (less B Coy.), 3/Middx., 5/K.O., and 1/Y. and L.—and was reinforced by another battalion from 28th Div. (2/E. York.) and two from 27th Div. (9/R. Scots and 2/D.C.L.I.). After 27/4/15 the units of Geddes's Detachment returned to their respective divisions. Col. A. D. Geddes (2/Buffs) was killed by a shell on the morning of 28/4/15.
** See Second Army (p. 82 and footnote) for detail of " Plumer's Force."

1915 *(Contd.)*

16 June ... ... **First Attack on Bellewaarde** [3rd Div.—Second Army].

19 July ... ... **Hooge** [3rd Div.—Second Army].

30 and 31 July ... ... **German Liquid Fire Attack, Hooge** [139th Bde. (46th Div.)—Second Army].*

25 September ... ... **Second Attack on Bellewaarde** [3rd Div.—Second Army].*

1916

14 February ... ... **Loss of The Bluff** [17th Div.—Second Army].

2 March ... ... **Recapture of The Bluff** [17th Div. and 76th Bde. (3rd Div.)—Second Army].

27 March–4 April** ... **Capture of St. Eloi Craters** [3rd Div.—Second Army].

30 April ... ... **Wulverghem (German Gas Attack)** [3rd and 24th Divs.—Second Army].

BATTLES OF THE SOMME.***

3 September ... ... **Fighting on the Ancre** [39th Div.—Reserve Army].

26–28 September ... **Battle of Thiepval Ridge** [39th Div.—Reserve Army].

1—5 October ... ... **Battle of the Ancre Heights** [39th Div.†—Reserve Army††].

13–18 November ... **Battle of the Ancre** [2nd, 3rd, 32nd, 37th, 51st, and 63rd Divs. ; with 2 tanks D Coy. (51st) on **13/11** ; 3 tanks D Coy. (63rd) on **14/11** ; 2 tanks D Coy. (2nd) on **16/11** ; 5 tanks D Coy. (4 with 32nd ; and 1 with 51st) on **18/11**—Fifth Army††].

13 November ... ... **Capture of Beaumont Hamel** [51st Div. ; with 2 tanks D Coy.—Fifth Army].

14 November ... ... **Capture of Beaucourt** [190th Bde. (63rd Div.) ; with 2 tanks D Coy.—Fifth Army].

---

* Also see VI Corps.
** On 4/4/16 2nd Cdn. Div. relieved 3rd Div., and fighting (on this front) continued under Cdn. Corps until 16/4/16.
*** At Noon on 16/8/16 V Corps took over (in the line) from XIV Corps.
† Transferred to II Corps on 5/10/16.
†† Reserve Army became Fifth Army on 30/10/16.

1917

11 January–13 March	**Operations on the Ancre** [7th, 31st, 32nd, 46th, and 62nd Divs.—Fifth Army].
12 March	**Attack on Rettemoy Graben** [46th Div.*—Fifth Army].
14 March–5 April ...	**German Retreat to the Hindenburg Line** [7th, 46th, and 62nd Divs.—Fifth Army].

---

11 April	**First Attack on Bullecourt** [62nd Div.—Fifth Army].
15 April	**German Attack on Lagnicourt** [62nd Div.—Fifth Army].
3–17 May	**Battle of Bullecourt** [7th, 58th,,** and 62nd Divs. ; with 12 tanks, 1st Tank Bde.—Fifth Army].
20 May–16 June ...	**Actions on the Hindenburg Line** [58th and 62nd Divs.—Fifth Army, until 10 a.m. 31/5/17, then Third Army].

BATTLES OF YPRES.***

20–25 September ...	**Battle of the Menin Road Ridge** [3rd, 9th, 55th, and 59th Divs. ; with 18 tanks, C and F Bns., 3rd Tank Bde.—Fifth Army].
26–28 September† ...	**Battle of Polygon Wood** [3rd and 59th Divs.—Fifth Army].

BATTLE OF CAMBRAI.††

1–3 December	**The German Counter-Attacks** [2nd, 47th, and 59th Divs. ; and, on Night 2nd–3rd/12/17, 51st Div. (from VI Corps)—Third Army].

---

30 and 31 December	**Welch Ridge**††† [63rd Div.—Third Army].

---

* Transferred on 7/3/17 from XVIII Corps.
** From 16/5/17.
*** At Noon on 7/9/17 V Corps took over (in the line) from XIX Corps.
† At 10 a.m. on 28/9/17 V Corps (Fifth Army) handed over (in the line) to II Anzac Corps (Second Army).
†† On 1/12/17 V Corps took over (in the line) from IV Corps.
††† Also see VII Corps, Fifth Army.

1918

FIRST BATTLES OF THE SOMME.

21–23 March	**Battle of St. Quentin** [2nd, 17th, 47th, and 63rd Divs.—Third Army].
24 and 25 March ...	**First Battle of Bapaume** [2nd, 12th* 17th, 47th, and 63rd Divs. with 8th Bn. ; 2nd Tank Bde.—Third Army].
28 March	**First Battle of Arras** [2nd and 12th Divs. ; with Tank Detnt., 2nd and 3rd Tank Bdes.—Third Army].
5 April	**Battle of the Ancre** [12th, 47th, and 63rd Divs., and 38th Div. (in Reserve)—Third Army].

THE ADVANCE TO VICTORY.

SECOND BATTLES OF THE SOMME.

21–23 August	**Battle of Albert** [17th, 21st, and 38th Divs.—Third Army].
31 Aug.–3 Sept. ...	**Second Battle of Bapaume** [17th, 21st, and 38th Divs.—Third Army].

BATTLES OF THE HINDENBURG LINE.

12 September	**Battle of Havrincourt** [38th Div.—Third Army].
18 September	**Battle of Epéhy** [17th, 21st, 33rd, and 38th Divs.—Third Army].
29 Sept.–2 Oct.	**Battle of the St. Quentin Canal** [21st and 33rd Divs. ; with part 11th Bn., 1st Tank Bde.—Third Army].
3–5 October	**Battle of the Beaurevoir Line** [33rd and 38th Divs.—Third Army].
8 and 9 October ...	**Battle of Cambrai** [17th, 21st, 33rd, and 38th Divs. ; with 2 Comp. Cos., 11th Bn., 1st Tank Bde.—Third Army].
8 October	**Capture of Villers Outréaux** [38th Div., with tanks of 11th Bn., 1st Tank Bde.—Third Army].

9–12 October	**Pursuit to the Selle** [17th and 33rd Divs.—Third Army].

---

* Between 8.20 p.m.–11.35 p.m. on 25/3/18 the 12th Div. was transferred to V Corps from VII Corps.

1918 *(Contd.)*

THE FINAL ADVANCE IN PICARDY.

17–25 October ... ... **Battle of the Selle** [17th, 21st, 33rd, and 38th Divs. ; with 11th Bn. (on **20/10**) and part 11th and 12th Bns. (on **23/10**), 1st Tank Bde.—Third Army].

20 October ... ... **Crossing of the Selle** [17th and 38th Divs. ; with 4 tanks 11th Bn., 1st Tank Bde.—Third Army].

23 October ... ... **Attack on Forest and Ovillers** [21st and 33rd Divs. ; with 6 tanks 11th Bn., 1st Tank Bde.—Third Army].

4 November ... ... **Battle of the Sambre** [17th and 38th Divs. ; with (part) 10th Bn. and 301st Am. Bn., 2nd Tank Bde.—Third Army].

After the conclusion of the Battle of the Sambre the V Corps continued to advance steadily eastward, and by 11 a.m. on the 11th November, when the Armistice brought hostilities to a close, the Corps had established a line to the south-east of Maubeuge and close to the Belgian frontier.

In its advance between the 21st August and the 11th November, a period of 83 days, the V Corps had fought in 9 battles and driven back the enemy nearly 70 miles across fortified France.

VI CORPS

G.O.C.

27 May, 1915 ... ... Lieut.-General Sir J. L. Keir.
8 August, 1916 ... ... Lieut.-General J. A. L. Haldane.

B.-G.G.S.

27 May, 1915...Br.-Gen. Lord Loch.
21 July, 1917...Br.-Gen. R. H. Kearsley.

D.-A. and Q.-M.-G.

27 May, 1915...Br.-Gen. E. R. O.
Ludlow.
13 Mar., 1917...Br.-Gen. J. B. G.
Tulloch.

G.S.O. 1.

25 Mar., 1918
–10 June, 1918 } Lt.-Col. P. B. O'Connor.

B.-G.R.A.

27 May, 1915...Br.-Gen. W. L. H. Paget.
9 Aug., 1916...Br.-Gen. J. G. Rotton.

C.H.A.

.........*
5 April, 1916...Br.-Gen. H. de T.
Phillips.
25 June, 1918...Br.-Gen. A. Ellershaw.

---

* Corps Heavy Artillery was formed (under Colonel H. de T. Phillips) on 8/3/16.

VI CORPS

C.E.

8 June, 1915...Br.-Gen. C. Hill.
4 Jan., 1918...Br.-Gen. R. N. Harvey.

A.-D. Signals.

1 June, 1915...Maj. A. H. W. Grubb
      (i/c Corps Signals).
12 Nov., 1915...Capt. A. N. Paxton
      (i/c Corps Signals).
6 Feb., 1916...Maj. A. N. Paxton.
7 Oct., 1916...Maj. H. Lee Wright.
20 Nov., 1916...Lt.-Col. H. Lee Wright.
Aug., 1918...Lt.-Col. P. R. Bald.

D.-D.M.S.

29 May, 1915...Col. H. N. Thompson.
21 July, 1917...Col. J. P. Jones (tempy.).
2 Aug., 1917...Col. S. Westcott.
17 Dec., 1917...Col. E. W. Bliss (tempy.).
1 Jan., 1918...Col. S. Westcott
     (to England, 2/1/18).
3 Jan., 1918...Col. H. A. Hinge.
28 Jan., 1918...Col. L. Humphry (tempy.).
7 Feb., 1918...Col. E. W. Bliss (tempy.).
27 Feb., 1918...Col. H. A. Hinge.
9 Aug., 1918...Col. C. E. Pollock.

A.-D.V.S.

....

16 June, 1917...Lt.-Col. O. S. Fisher.

VI CORPS

FORMATION.

VI Corps Headquarters began to form in France at the end of May, 1915; and on the 1st June the VI Corps took over the left of the British front (to the north-east of Ypres) with the 4th and 6th Divisions.

BATTLES AND ENGAGEMENTS.

1915

30 and 31 July	**German Liquid Fire Attack, Hooge** [14th Div.—Second Army].*
9 August	**Hooge** [6th Div.—Second Army].
25 September	**Second Attack on Bellewaarde** [14th Div.—Second Army].*
19 December	**First Phosgene Gas Attack** [49th Div.—Second Army].

1916

1 Jan.–31 Dec.	[In Second Army until 10 a.m. 5/2/16; then in Third Army].**

1917

BATTLES OF ARRAS.

9–14 April	**First Battle of the Scarpe** [3rd, 12th, 15th, 17th, 29th, and 37th Divs.; with part of 1st Tank Bde.—Third Army].
11 April	**Capture of Monchy le Preux** [37th Div. and 3rd Cav. Div.; with 7 tanks 8 and 9 Cos. C Bn., 1st Tank Bde.—Third Army].
23 and 24 April ...	**Second Battle of the Scarpe** [3rd, 15th, 17th, and 29th Divs.; with part of 1st Tank Bde.—Third Army].
23 April	**Capture of Guémappe** [15th Div.—Third Army].
28 and 29 April ...	**Battle of Arleux** [3rd and 12th Divs.—Third Army].
3 and 4 May	**Third Battle of the Scarpe** [3rd, 12th, 29th, and 56th Divs.—Third Army].

---

* Also see V Corps.

** Corps H.Q. opened at Toutencourt (8 miles W.N.W. of Albert) and took over 49th Div. (9/2/16), 56th Div. (10/2/16), and 14th Div. (20/2/16). On 29/2/16 VI Corps was reconstituted with 5th, 14th, and 56th Divs. On 2/3/16 VI Corps H.Q. moved to Avesnes le Comte in Third Army.

1917 *(Contd.)*

12 May ... ... **Attack on Devil's Trench** [12th Div.—Third Army].

13 and 14 May ... ... **Capture of Rœux** [3rd Div.—Third Army].

BATTLE OF CAMBRAI.

20 November ... ... **Attack at Bullecourt*** [3rd and 16th Divs.—Third Army].

25–28 November ... **Capture of Bourlon Wood** [56th Div.**–Third Army].

30 Nov.–3 Dec. ... ... **The German Counter-Attacks** [3rd, 51st,*** and 56th Divs.—Third Army].

1918

FIRST BATTLES OF THE SOMME.

21–23 March ... ... **Battle of St. Quentin** [Gds., 3rd, 31st, 34th, 40th, and 59th† Divs. ; with 6th Bn., 3rd Tank Bde.—Third Army].

24 and 25 March ... **First Battle of Bapaume** [Gds., 3rd, 31st, 40th, 42nd, and 59th† Divs.—Third Army].

28 March ... ... **First Battle of Arras** [Gds., 3rd, and 31st Divs., and 97th Bde. (32nd Div.), and 2nd Cdn. Div.—Third Army].

5 April ... ... **Battle of the Ancre** [32nd Div.—Third Army].

THE ADVANCE TO VICTORY.

SECOND BATTLES OF THE SOMME.

21–23 August ... ... **Battle of Albert** [Gds., 2nd, 3rd, 52nd, 56th, and 59th Divs. ; with 6th (Whippets), 12th, and 15th Bns., 2nd Tank Bde., and 9th and 11th Bns., 3rd Tank Bde.—Third Army].

---

* Subsidiary attack on northern flank of Battle of Cambrai.
** Transferred at Mn. 24/11/17 from IV Corps.
*** 51st Div. relieved 56th Div. on night of 2nd/3rd/12/17, and was then taken over by V Corps.
† 177th Bde. and 59th Div. Artillery remained in action from 22–25/3/18 under 40th Div. ; and on 27/3/18 59th D.A. was transferred to 42nd Div. (IV Corps), and fought with it until 5/4/18.

1918 *(Contd.)*

THE ADVANCE TO VICTORY *(Contd.)*.

SECOND BATTLES OF THE SOMME *(Contd.)*.

24 August ... ... **Capture of Mory Copse** [99th Bde. (2nd Div.)—Third Army].

25 August ... ... **Capture of Behagnies and Sapignies** [5th Bde. (2nd Div.)—Third Army].

31 Aug.–3 Sept. ... **Second Battle of Bapaume** [Gds., 2nd, 3rd, and 62nd Divs. ;* with 6th (Whippets), 12th, and 15th Bns., 2nd Tank Bde.—Third Army].

SECOND BATTLES OF ARRAS.

26–30 August ... ... **Battle of the Scarpe** [Gds. and 62nd Divs.—Third Army].

3 September ... ... **Assault of the Drocourt-Quéant Line** [2nd Div.—Third Army].

BATTLES OF THE HINDENBURG LINE.

12 September ... ... **Battle of Havrincourt** [Gds., 2nd, and 62nd Divs.—Third Army].

27 Sept.–1 Oct. ... ... **Battle of the Canal du Nord** [Gds., 2nd, 3rd, and 62nd Divs.—Third Army].

1 October ... ... **Capture of Mont sur l'Œuvre** [2nd Div.—Third Army].

8 and 9 October ... **Battle of Cambrai** [Gds., 2nd, and 3rd Divs. ; with part of 12th Bn., 1st Tank Bde.—Third Army].

8 October ... ... **Capture of Forenville** [2nd Div.—Third Army].

9–12 October ... ... **Pursuit to the Selle** [Gds. Div.—Third Army].

THE FINAL ADVANCE IN PICARDY.

17–25 October ... ... **Battle of the Selle** [Gds., 2nd, 3rd, and 62nd Divs.—Third Army].

20 October ... ... **Capture of Solesmes** [62nd Div.—Third Army].

---

* Henceforward in the Advance to Victory the composition of VI Corps remained unchanged : Guards, 2nd, 3rd, and 62nd Divisions.

1918 *(Contd.)*

THE FINAL ADVANCE IN PICARDY *(Contd.)*.

4 November ... ... **Battle of the Sambre** [Gds. and 62nd Divs.—Third Army].

5–7 November ... ... **Passage of the Grande Honnelle** [Gds. and 62nd Divs. ; with 6th (Whippets) Bn., 2nd Tank Bde.—Third Army].

9 November ... ... **Occupation of Maubeuge** [Guards Div.—Third Army].

At 11 a.m. on the 11th November, when the Armistice brought hostilities to a close, the VI Corps, in the left Centre of the Third Army Front, was on the south bank of the R. Sambre and some 5 miles to the eastward of Maubeuge.

When the victorious advance of the Third Army began on the 21st August the VI Corps was in position astride the Cojeul facing Boiry ; and during the 83 days of this advance the VI Corps fought in 8 battles and advanced some 60 miles.

When the selection was made of those Corps which should carry out the march to the German frontier, the VI Corps was one of those selected.

At first the VI Corps formed part of the Fourth Army, and on the 18th November the advance began from the Armistice Line. Ten days later the 62nd Division was transferred to the Second Army and joined the IX Corps.

On reaching the German Frontier the VI Corps (Guards, 2nd, and 3rd Divisions) was transferred from the Fourth Army to the Second Army, and in this Army the VI Corps entered Germany between the 9th–11th December. The 2nd Guards Brigade was sent by train to Cologne and reached that city on the 14th December ; on the 18th the Guards Division Headquarters opened in Cologne, and on the 19th December the remainder of the Guards Division arrived at the Rhine bridgehead. The 2nd and 3rd Divisions reached their allotted area, between Cologne and Düren, on the 27th and 20th December respectively. VI Corps Headquarters was at Düren.

VII CORPS

G.O.C.

15 July, 1915	Lieut.-General Sir T. D'O. Snow.
3 January, 1918	Lieut.-General Sir W. N. Congreve, V.C.
13 April, 1918	Major-General Sir R. D. Whigham.
–19 June, 1918	

*

B.-G.G.S.

14 July, 1915...	Br.-Gen. F. Lyon.
9 Feb. 1917...	Br.-Gen. J. T. Burnett-Stuart.
26 Dec., 1917...	Br.-Gen. Hon. A. G. A. Hore-Ruthven, V.C.
1 Aug., 1918...	Br.-Gen. C. Bonham-Carter.
8 Aug., 1918...	Br.-Gen. C. F. Aspinall.
11 Sept., 1918...	Br.-Gen. C. Bonham-Carter.
28 Oct., 1918...	Br.-Gen. W. J. Maxwell-Scott.

D.-A. and Q.-M.-G.

14 July, 1915...	Br.-Gen. A. F. Sillem.
11 Mar., 1916...	Br.-Gen. R. E. Vaughan.
30 April, 1916...	Br.-Gen. R. J. Tudway.
30 Aug., 1916...	Br.-Gen. A. A. McHardy.
31 Aug., 1918...	Lt.-Col. A. R. G. Gordon (acting).
Oct., 1918...	Lt.-Col. P. F. Fitz-Gerald (acting).
Nov., 1918...	Lt.-Col. Hon. M. A. Wingfield (acting).

G.S.O. 1.

2 May, 1918	Lt.-Col. E. H. Kelly.
– June, 1918	

B.-G.R.A.

19 July, 1915...	Br.-Gen. A. E. A. Holland.
4 Sept., 1915...	Br.-Gen. R. F. Fox.
16 June, 1916...	Br.-Gen. C. M. Ross-Johnson.
6 Sept., 1917...	Br.-Gen. K. K. Knapp.

C.H.A.

....

**

[7 Mar., 1916]...	Br.-Gen. C. R. Buckle.
10 July, 1916...	Br.-Gen. J. G. Wynne.
21 Aug., 1916...	Col. C. Brownlow (acting).
23 Aug., 1916...	Br.-Gen. K. K. Knapp.
5 Sept., 1917...	Br.-Gen. F. H. Metcalfe.
8 Nov., 1918...	Br.-Gen. W. B. Anley.

---

* VII Corps was in back areas from 7/4/18 to 11/11/18 ; and no appointment as G.O.C. was made between 19/6–11/11/18.
** No. 6 H.A.R. Group (G.H.Q. Artillery) joined VII Corps on 1/4/16, and changed its designation to VII Corps Heavy Arillery (see Appendix 3).

VII CORPS

C.E.

20 July, 1915...Br.-Gen. W. Huskisson.
7 Oct., 1915...Br.-Gen. J. A. Tanner
(killed, 23/7/17).
23 July, 1917...Lt.-Col. C. E. G. Vesey
(acting).
7 Aug., 1917...Br.-Gen. R. D. Petrie.
9 July, 1918...Br.-Gen. R. A. Gillam.
4 Nov., 1918...Br.-Gen. C. J.
Armstrong.

A.-D. Signals.

14 July, 1915...Major T. G. Moore
(i/c Corps Signals).
6 Feb., 1916...Major T. G. Moore.
17 June, 1916...Major D. C. Jones.
20 Nov., 1916...Lt.-Col. D. C. Jones.
8 June, 1918...Lt.-Col. C. H. Walsh.
16 Aug., 1918...Capt. H. F. Dallison
(acting).
Oct., 1918...Capt. A. McK. Johnston
(acting).

D.-D.M.S.

14 July, 1915...Col. W. T. Swan.
5 Jan., 1918...Col. E. W. Slayter.
9 Oct., 1918...Maj. E. C. Beddows
(acting).

A.-D.V.S.

....
16 June, 1917...Lt.-Col. G. Conder.
24 Sept., 1918...Capt. W. Marshall
(acting).

VII CORPS

FORMATION.

VII Corps Headquarters began to form in France on the 14th July, 1915. After formation, VII Corps took over the 4th and 48th Divisions, and with them joined the newly-formed Third Army. VII Corps held the left of the Third Army front, and was in touch near Hébuterne with the right of the French Tenth Army.

BATTLES AND ENGAGEMENTS.

1915

14 July–31 December   [Third Army].

1916

BATTLES OF THE SOMME.

1 July   ... ...   **Attack on the Gommecourt Salient** [46th and 56th Divs.—Third Army].

1917

14 March–5 April   ...   **German Retreat to the Hindenburg Line** [14th, 21st, 30th, 56th, and 58th* Divs.—Third Army].

BATTLES OF ARRAS.

9–14 April ... ...   **First Battle of the Scarpe** [14th, 21st, 30th, 33rd,** 50th,*** and 56th Divs. ; with part of 1st Tank Bde.—Third Army].

11 April   ... ...   **Capture of Wancourt** [14th Div. ; with 4 tanks D Bn., 1st Tank Bde.—Third Army].

13–15 April   ... ...   **Capture of Wancourt Ridge** [50th Div.***—Third Army].

23 and 24 April   ...   **Second Battle of the Scarpe** [30th, 33rd, and 50th Divs. ; with part of 1st Tank Bde.—Third Army].

3 and 4 May   ... ...   **Third Battle of the Scarpe** [14th, 18th, and 21st Divs. ; with 4 tanks, 1st Tank Bde.—Third Army].

---

* 58th Div. was transferred to VII Corps from XVIII Corps, Third Army, on 19/3/17.
** 19th Inf. Bde. (33rd Div.) fought under 21st Div.
*** On 11/4/17 50th Div. was transferred from XVIII Corps to VII Corps.

1917 *(Contd.)*

20 May–16 June   ...   **Actions on the Hindenburg Line** [21st and 33rd Divs.—Third Army].

BATTLE OF CAMBRAI.

20 and 21 November   **The Tank Attack** [55th Div.—Third Army].

30 Nov.–3 Dec. ...   ...   **The German Counter-Attacks** [21st, 24th, and 55th Divs.—Third Army].

---

30 December   ...   ...   **Welch Ridge** [Part of 26th Bde. (9th Div.)—Fifth Army*].

1918

FIRST BATTLES OF THE SOMME.

21–23 March   ...   ...   **Battle of St. Quentin** [9th, 16th, 21st, and 39th Divs. ; with part of 4th Tank Bde.—Fifth Army].

24 and 25 March   ...   **Actions at the Somme Crossings** [39th Div. (less 116th Bde.) ; with part of 4th Tank Bde.—Fifth Army**].

24 and 25 March   ...   **First Battle of Bapaume** [9th, 12th,*** 21st, and 35th Divs., and 116th Bde. (39th Div.), and 1st Cav. Div. ; with part of 4th Tank Bde.—Fifth Army**].

5 April   ...   .   **Battle of the Ancre** [10th and 11th Aus. Bdes., 3rd Aus. Div., and 12th and 13th Aus. Bdes., 4th Aus. Div., and 35th Div. (in Reserve) ; with 18 teams of Lewis Guns, 4th Bn., 4th Tank Bde.—Third Army].

On the 7th April VII Corps Headquarters was withdrawn from the line and, until early in May, was located in the Bernaville area. VII Corps H.Q. then moved north and took over the battle-training of divisions which were resting and recuperating in the St. Omer area. VII Corps H.Q. remained near St. Omer until late in September when it moved southward, and it was in the neighbourhood of Fruges when the Armistice brought hostilities to a close on the 11th November.

---

* Also see 63rd Div., V Corps, Third Army.

** At 4 a.m. on 25/3/18 VII Corps was transferred (in the line) from Fifth Army to Third Army; but 39th Div. (less 116th Bde.) was transferred to XIX Corps, Fifth Army.

*** 12th Div. came under VII Corps in a.m. of 25/3/18 ; and between 8.20 p.m.–11.35 p.m. on 25/3/18 12th Div. was transferred to V Corps.

VIII CORPS*

G.O.C.

24 May, 1915	Lieut.-General A. G. HUNTER-WESTON (invalided, 17/7/15).
17 July, 1915	Lieut.-General Hon. Sir F. W. STOPFORD (tempy.).
24 July, 1915	Major-General W. DOUGLAS (acting).
8 August, 1915 ... –27 January, 1916 ...	} Lieut.-General Sir F. J. DAVIES.**

....

18 March, 1916 ... ... –22 June, 1918	} Lieut.-General Sir A. G. HUNTER-WESTON.**

....

2 July, 1918	Lieut.-General Sir A. G. HUNTER-WESTON.**

B.-G.G.S.

24 May, 1915...Br.-Gen. H. E. STREET.

....

7 Mar., 1916...Br.-Gen. Hon. W. P. HORE-RUTHVEN.
1 Jan., 1917...Br.-Gen. E. L. ELLINGTON.
18 Nov., 1917...Br.-Gen. C. F. ASPINALL.

....

2 July, 1918...Br.-Gen. C. F. ASPINALL.
10 Aug., 1918...Br.-Gen. C. BONHAM-CARTER.
11 Sept., 1918...Br.-Gen. C. F. ASPINALL.

D.-A. and Q.-M.-G.

24 May, 1915...Br.-Gen. A. J. TUDWAY.

....

12 Mar., 1916...Br.-Gen. J. C. G. LONGMORE.
4 Sept., 1916...Lt.-Col. B. J. LANG (acting).
3 Nov., 1916...Br.-Gen. B. ATKINSON.
17 April, 1918...Br.-Gen. E. V. D. RIDDELL.

....

2 July, 1918...Br.-Gen. L. H. ABBOTT.***
1 Sept., 1918...Br.-Gen. A. A. McHARDY.

G.S.O. 1.

2 July, 1918...Lt.-Col. G. BLEWITT.***
7 July, 1918...Major P. D. STIRLING.

---

* When this Corps was formed at Helles on 24/5/15, it was styled " British Army Corps "; it became VIII Corps on 5/6/15.)

** On 17/1/16 VIII Corps H.Q. arrived at Alexandria and it was temporarily broken up at Cairo on 27/1/16. On 7/3/16 VIII Corps H.Q. began to re-form in France, at Marieux. On 24/6/18 VIII Corps H.Q. was broken up in France. On 2/7/18 XVIII Corps H.Q. (then in First Army, at Camblain l'Abbé) was merged in and became VIII Corps H.Q.

*** Transferred from XVIII Corps H.Q.

VIII CORPS

B.-G.R.A.

24 May, 1915...Br.-Gen. H. A. D. SIMPSON-BAIKIE.
2 Aug., 1915...Br.-Gen. C. H. DE ROUGEMONT.

7 Mar., 1916...Br.-Gen. T. A. TANCRED.
13 July, 1916...Br.-Gen. W. STRONG.
13 May, 1917...Br.-Gen. H. D. O. WARD.

2 July, 1918...Br.-Gen. D. J. M. FASSON.**
19 July, 1918...Br.-Gen. H. D. O. WARD.

C.H.A.

....
*

10 April, 1916...Br.-Gen. D. F. H. LOGAN.
28 July, 1916...Br.-Gen. C. DE S. BURNEY (tempy.).
30 July, 1916...Br.-Gen. B. M. BATEMAN.
1 Feb., 1918...Lt.-Col. H. DE L. WALTERS (acting).
11 Feb., 1918...Br.-Gen. A. ELLERSHAW.

2 July, 1918...Br.-Gen. L. J. CHAPMAN.**

C.E.

24 May, 1915...Br.-Gen. E. A. TUDOR.
17 Aug., 1915...Br.-Gen. J. A. GIBBON.

7 Mar., 1916...Br.-Gen. G. S. CARTWRIGHT.
23 Sept., 1917...Br.-Gen. H. W. RUSHTON.
31 Dec., 1917...Br.-Gen. R. A. GILLAM.

2 July, 1918...Br.-Gen. H. G. JOLY DE LOTBINIÈRE **
19 Oct., 1918...Br.-Gen. H. BIDDULPH (tempy.).
23 Oct., 1918...Br.-Gen. A. B. CAREY.

A.-D. Signals.

....

13 Mar., 1916...Maj. R. V. DOHERTY HOLWELL.
20 Nov., 1916...Lt.-Col. R. V. DOHERTY HOLWELL.
1 Feb., 1917...Lt.-Col. J. W. COHEN.
4 May, 1918...Lt.-Col. J. A. F. MAIR.

2 July, 1918...Lt.-Col. W. L. DE M. CAREY.**
16 Sept., 1918...Lt.-Col. M. G. PLATTS.

D.-D.M.S.

4 June, 1915...Col. M. T. YARR.

7 Mar., 1916...Col. J. M. IRWIN.
7 April, 1916...Col. J. B. WILSON.
22 June, 1916...Col. J. J. GERRARD.
5 Jan., 1918...Col. J. THOMSON.
16 Mar., 1918...Col. D. D. SHANAHAN.

2 July, 1918...Col. H. V. PRYNNE.**

A.-D.V.S.

....

16 June, 1917...Lt.-Col. A. ENGLAND.

2 July, 1918...Lt.-Col. W. H. NICOL.**

---

* Formed on 10/4/16 in France.
** Transferred from XVIII Corps H.Q.

VIII CORPS

FORMATION.

On the 24th May, 1915, the War Office decided that the three British divisions at Helles—29th, 42nd, and Royal Naval Divisions—should be grouped together in one Corps, and selected Lieut.-General A. G. Hunter-Weston to command it. For a time, however, only a skeleton staff could be provided, and, as a temporary measure, the three divisions remained for administration directly under G.H.Q., M.E.F. From its formation on the 24th May until the 5th June the new corps was styled " British Army Corps "; but on the latter date a number was allotted to it, and it became the VIII Corps.

The VIII Corps served on the Gallipoli Peninsula, then in Egypt, and finally on the Western Front in France and Belgium.

BATTLES AND ENGAGEMENTS.

1915

24 May–6 June	**BATTLES OF HELLES.**
4 June	**Third Battle of Krithia** [29th, 42nd, and R.N. Divs., and 29th Ind. Inf. Bde., and 8 Armoured Cars, R.N.A.S.; with 78 guns].
28 June–2 July	**Gully Ravine** [29th Div., and 156th Bde. (52nd Div.), and 29th Ind. Inf. Bde.].
12 and 13 July	**Achi Baba Nullah** [52nd Div.].
6–13 August	**Krithia Vineyard** [29th and 42nd Divs.].
29 December	**Krithia Nullahs** [52nd Div.].

1916

7 January	**The Last Turkish Attacks** [13th Div.].
The Last Night, 8–9 Jan. }	**EVACUATION OF HELLES*** ...[Part of 13th, 29th, 52nd, and R.N. Divs.—16,918 men and 37 guns and hows.].

* The Divisions went first of all to Mudros, and were then transhipped to Egypt.
13th Div. went from Egypt to Mesopotamia in Feb., 1916.
29th Div. went to France in April, 1916.
52nd Div. remained in the E.E.F. until April, 1918, and then was sent to France.
R.N. Div. was employed at first on garrison duty in the Ægean; it was transferred on 29/4/16 from the Admiralty to the War Office; went to France in May, 1916; and on 19/7/16 became 63rd (Royal Naval) Division.

1916 *(Contd.)*

After the Evacuation of Helles VIII Corps Headquarters moved to Egypt in January and disembarked on the 17th at Alexandria. On the 27th January VIII Corps H.Q. was temporarily broken up at Cairo ; and on the 7th March it began to re-form in France at Marieux (5 m. S.E. of Doullens).

For the remainder of the Great War VIII Corps served on the Western Front in France and Belgium and was engaged in the following operations :

BATTLES OF THE SOMME.

1 and 2 July ... ... **Battle of Albert** [4th, 29th, 31st, and 48th Divs.—Fourth Army, until 4/7/16, then Reserve Army].

At 4 p.m. on 30/7/16 XIV Corps took over VIII Corps front, in the Reserve Army ; and at 6 p.m. on 29/7/16 VIII Corps took over, from XIV Corps, the left of the Second Army front, to the north-east of Ypres.*

1917

1 January–31 Dec.   [In Second Army until mid-June, then in back-area in Belgium until mid-November, and then in Second Army (designated Fourth Army on 20/12/17)].

1918

1 January–15 June ... [In Fourth Army until 17/3/18, then in Second Army until 14/4/18 ; and then, until 15/6/18, holding rear defences in back-area in Belgium].

On 22/6/18 the Corps Commander was transferred to take command of XVIII Corps (20th, 24th, and 52nd Divisions), which was part of the First Army and was holding the front line to the south of Lens. On 24/6/18 VIII Corps H.Q. was broken up at Long in the Fourth Army area.**

On 2/7/18 the XVIII Corps H.Q. was renumbered VIII ; it still remained composed of the 20th, 24th, and 52nd Divisions, and still held the same sector of the First Army front. Corps H.Q. was located at Camblain l'Abbé.

This renumbered VIII Corps thereafter took part in the Advance to Victory (in

---

* VIII Corps H.Q. was at La Lovie Château (3 m. N.W. of Poperinghe).
** VIII Corps H.Q. had moved to Long at Noon on 16/6/18.

1918 (*Contd.*)

the First Army) and in the same Army's Final Advance in Artois. During this time the VIII Corps was engaged in the following operations :

THE ADVANCE TO VICTORY.

SECOND BATTLES OF ARRAS.

26–30 August	**Battle of the Scarpe** [8th Div.—First Army].
2 Oct.–11 Nov.	**THE FINAL ADVANCE IN ARTOIS** [8th, 12th, 20th (until 6/10),* and 52nd Divs.; and 58th Div. (until *Noon, 14/10,* when it was transferred to I Corps); and 3rd Cav. Bde. (2nd Cav. Div.)—First Army].
7 and 8 October ...	**Forcing the Rouvroy—Fresnes Line** [8th Div.—First Army].
17 October	**Capture of Douai** [8th Div.—First Army].

At 11 a.m. on the 11th November, when the Armistice brought hostilities to a close, the VIII Corps, on the left of the First Army front, had secured the Nimy—Turbise road to the north of Mons. In the final 78 days of the Great War the VIII Corps had advanced 50 miles eastward across France and Belgium.

---

* On 31/10/18 20th Div. moved to the Cambrai area and was transferred to XVII Corps, Third Army.

IX CORPS*

G.O.C.

17 June, 1915	Lieut.-General Hon. Sir F. W. Stopford.
16 August, 1915	Major-General H. de B. de Lisle (tempy.).
24 August, 1915	Lieut.-General Hon. Sir J. H. G. Byng.
8 February, 1916	Lieut.-General Sir F. J. Davies.

....

20 June, 1916	Lieut.-General A. Hamilton Gordon.
16 July, 1918	Major-General Sir R. D. Whigham (tempy.).
22 July, 1918	Major-General H. W. Higginson (tempy.).
30 July, 1918	Lieut.-General Sir A. Hamilton Gordon.
10 September, 1918	Major-General E. P. Strickland (tempy.).
13 September, 1918	Lieut.-General Sir W. P. Braithwaite.

B.-G.G.S.

24 June, 1915...Br.-Gen. H. L. Reed, V.C.
8 Feb., 1916...Br.-Gen. H. E. Street.

D.-A. and Q.-M.-G.

17 June, 1915...Br.-Gen. J. H. Poett.
28 Sept., 1915...Br.-Gen. A. B. Hamilton.
29 Sept., 1915...Lt.-Col. A. G. P. McNalty (acting).
13 Oct., 1915...Br.-Gen. J. H. Poett.
21 Nov., 1915...Lt.-Col. A. G. P. McNalty (acting).
2 Dec., 1915...Br.-Gen. A. G. P. McNalty.
8 Feb., 1916...Br.-Gen. C. D. H. Moore.

....

21 June, 1916...Br.-Gen. A. F. Home.
4 Sept., 1916...Br.-Gen. J. S. J. Percy.**
25 Dec., 1917...Br.-Gen. W. J. Maxwell-Scott.
24 Sept., 1918...Br.-Gen. A. R. Cameron.

20 June, 1916...Br.-Gen. B. F. Burnett Hitchcock.
3 Dec., 1916...Br.-Gen. B. H. H. Cooke.
26 Feb., 1918...Br.-Gen. J. C. Harding Newman.

G.S.O. 1.

....

---

* After the Evacuation of Suvla in December, 1915, the IX Corps H.Q. went to Egypt on 4/1/1916 and until 22/4/16 the IX Corps was at Suez (Canal Defence Zone). IX Corps H.Q. was then transferred to France, and re-formed at Bailleul on 20/6/16.
** In October, 1917, this surname was taken instead of Baumgartner.

B.-G.R.A.

16 June, 1915...Br.-Gen. S. C. U. SMITH.
11 Oct., 1915...Br.-Gen. W. GILLMAN.
24 Nov., 1915...Br.-Gen. F. B. JOHNSTONE.
18 Jan., 1916...Br.-Gen. J. L. PARKER.
10 Feb., 1916...Br.-Gen. C. H. DE
ROUGEMONT.

....

22 June, 1916...Br.-Gen. G. HUMPHREYS.

C.H.A.

*

20 June, 1916...Br.-Gen. J. G. E. WYNNE.
14 Aug., 1916...Br.-Gen. R. P. BENSON
(tempy.).
17 Aug., 1916...Br.-Gen. H. E. B. LANE.
26 Feb., 1917...Br.-Gen. G. B.
MACKENZIE.

C.E.

16 June, 1915...Br.-Gen. A. C. PAINTER.
12 Aug., 1915...Br.-Gen. E. H. BLAND.

....

20 June, 1916...Br.-Gen. G. P. SCHOLFIELD.
6 April, 1918...Br.-Gen. G. S.
CARTWRIGHT.
28 Oct., 1918...Br.-Gen. R. A. GILLAM.

A.-D. Signals.

June, 1915...Major M. McC. BIDDER.

....

20 June, 1916...Major O. C. MORDAUNT.
Oct., 1916...Major R. H. WILLAN.
20 Nov., 1916...Lt.-Col. R. H. WILLAN.
18 Jan., 1918...Lt.-Col. H. W. EDWARDS.

D.-D.M.S.

20 June, 1915...Capt. T. S. BLACKWELL
(M.O.).
6 July, 1915...Col. C. C. REILLY.
25 Dec., 1915...Col. J. GIRVIN.

A.-D.V.S.

....

22 June, 1916...Col. J. B. WILSON.
17 May, 1918...Col. R. J. BLACKHAM.
1 Nov., 1918...Col. H. W. GRATTAN.

16 June, 1917...Lt.-Col. E. B. BARTLETT.

---

* Formed on 20/6/16 in France.

IX CORPS

FORMATION.

At the beginning of June, 1915, it was decided to send out a substantial reinforcement of four divisions to the M.E.F. on the Gallipoli Peninsula, so as to ensure that a decisive blow was struck in that theatre. These four divisions were to be sent as a Corps—the IX Corps—the divisions were the 10th, 11th, 53rd, and 54th.

To this end, IX Corps Headquarters began to form in the Tower of London on the 16th June, 1915; and, at 3 p.m. on the 20th, Corps H.Q. embarked at Avonmouth. The transport left Avonmouth at 9 p.m. on the 22nd June and reached Mudros at 10 a.m. on the 9th July.

BATTLES AND ENGAGEMENTS.

1915

BATTLES OF SUVLA.

6–15 August	**THE LANDING AT SUVLA** [10th and 11th Divs.; and 53rd Div. (from 9/8) and 54th Div. (from 10/8)].
7 August	**Capture of Karakol Dagh** [34th Bde. (11th Div.)].
Night, 7/8 August ...	**Capture of Chocolate Hill** [" Hill's Force ":—31st Bde. and 7/R.D.F. of 30th Bde. (10th Div.)].
21 August	**Battle of Scimitar Hill** [11th and 29th Divs.; and 2nd Mtd. Div.*].
21 August	**Attack on " W " Hills** [11th Div. and 2nd Mtd. Div.].

The Last Night, 19/20 December**	**EVACUATION OF SUVLA***** [2nd Mtd. Div., 11th, and 13th Divs., 88th Bde. (29th Div.), and 4/Gurkhas (29th Ind. Inf. Bde.)—10,612 men with 21 guns and hows.].

---

* Landed on Night of 17–18/8/15.
** On this same night (of 19–20/12/15) 10,040 men with 8 guns and hows. were evacuated from Anzac.
*** On leaving Suvla the divisions, at first, went either to Imbros or Mudros. Thereafter the divisions served as follows : *10th Div.* served in Macedonia 5/10/15–1/9/17, and thenceforth in the E.E.F. until Armistice. *11th Div.* was in Egypt from Feb.–July, 1915, and then went to France. *13th Div.* went to Helles, 27–31/12/15 and joined VIII Corps ; and *29th Div.* returned to VIII Corps at Helles, between 1/10–22/12/15. *53rd and 54th Divs.* went to Egypt in December, 1915 and served until Armistice in the E.E.F. *2nd Mtd. Div.* returned to Egypt by 27/12/15 and was broken up by 21/1/16.

1916

After the Evacuation of Suvla, IX Corps Headquarters went to Egypt on the 4th January, and was in charge of a sector of the Suez Canal Defences until the 22nd April. IX Corps H.Q. was then ordered to France and re-formed at Bailleul in the latter half of June.

For the remainder of the Great War IX Corps served on the Western Front in France and Belgium and was engaged in the following operations :

1916

3 July*–31 December   [In Second, Fourth, Reserve, and Second Armies].**

1917

7–14 June ... ...   **Battle of Messines** [11th, 16th, 19th, and 36th Divs. ; with 16 tanks, and 12 tanks from Army Reserve, 2nd Tank Bde.—Second Army].

7 June   ... ...   **Capture of Wytschaete** [16th and 36th Divs. ; with part of 2nd Tank Bde.—Second Army].

BATTLES OF YPRES.

31 July–2 August   ...   **Battle of Pilckem Ridge** [37th Div.—Second Army].

20–25 September   ...   **Battle of Menin Road Ridge** [19th and 37th Divs.—Second Army].

26 September–3 October **Battle of Polygon Wood** [19th and 37th Divs.—Second Army].

4 October ... ...   **Battle of Broodseinde** [19th and 37th Divs.—Second Army].

9 October ... ...   **Battle of Poelcappelle** [19th and 37th Divs.—Second Army].

12 October   ... ...   **First Battle of Passchendaele** [19th and 37th Divs.—Second Army].

26 Oct.–10 Nov.   ...   **Second Battle of Passchendaele** [19th Div.—Second Army].

---

* On 3/7/16 IX Corps took over part of Second Army front to the N.E. of Bailleul.
** At 5 p.m. on 16/7/16 IX Corps H.Q. was transferred from Mt. Noir (Second Army) to Talmas (Fourth Army) ; and at 3 p.m. on 23/7/16 IX Corps H.Q. relieved II Corps at Villers Bocage (7 miles N. of Amiens). On 1/8/16 IX Corps H.Q. was transferred to Reserve Army, and at 2.30 p.m. Corps H.Q. opened at Domart (24 miles W.N.W. of Albert). On 14/8/16 IX Corps H.Q. was transferred back to Second Army and opened at Bailleul. At mn. 13–14/8/16 IX Corps took over the centre sector of the Second Army front, from V Corps, and held this part of the line for the remainder of the year and during 1917.

1918

BATTLES OF THE LYS.*

10 and 11 April... ... **Battle of Messines** [9th and 19th Divs., 25th Div. (less 74th Bde.], and 62nd Bde. (21st Div.), 88th Bde. (29th Div.), 108th Bde. (36th Div.) and 148th Bde. (49th Div.) ; and on 11/4 100th Bde. (33rd Div.)—Second Army].

11 April ... ... **Loss of Hill 63** [7th Bde. (25th Div.)—Second Army].

12–15 April ... ... **Battle of Hazebrouck** [33rd Div.—Second Army].

13–15 April ... ... **Battle of Bailleul** [19th, 25th, 34th,** 49th, and 59th Divs., and 71st Bde. (6th Div.), S. African Bde. (9th Div.), 88th Bde. (29th Div.), 100th Bde. (33rd Div.), and 108th Bde. (36th Div.)—Second Army].

13 and 14 April ... **Defence of Neuve Église** [100th Bde. (33rd Div.) and 148th Bde. (49th Div.)].

17–19 April ... ... **First Battle of Kemmel Ridge** [19th, 25th, 33rd, 34th, and 59th Divs., and 49th Div. (less 146th Bde.), and 71st Bde. (6th Div.), 89th Bde. (30th Div.), 108th Bde. (36th Div.), and " James's Force,"† and " Wyatt's Force ";†† with 34th (Fr.), and 133rd (Fr.) Divs ; and 2nd (Fr.), 3rd (Fr.), and 6th (Fr.) Cav. Divs.—Second Army].*

GERMAN OFFENSIVE IN CHAMPAGNE.

27 May–6 June ... ... **Battle of the Aisne** [8th, 19th, 21st, 25th, and 50th Divs., and " Gater's Force "†††—under Sixth (Fr.) Army until 29/5 ; then under Fifth (Fr.) Army].

---

*By the morning of 21/4/18 the French XXXVI Corps (34th, 133rd, and 2nd Cav. Divs.) and the French II Cavalry Corps (3rd Cav., 6th Cav., and 28th and 154th Divs.) had taken over the IX Corps front in the Second Army. The front line was at that time to the east of Kemmel Hill.

** At 6 p.m. on 12/4/18 34th Div. was transferred to IX Corps from XV Corps.

† *James's Force*—2,000 of 59th Div. placed under Br.-Gen. C. H. L. James (177th Bde.)—served from 16–19/4/18 under 49th Div.

†† *Wyatt's Force*—1,400 rifles and 12 m. guns under Br.-Gen. L. J. Wyatt (116th Bde., 39th Div.)—from 13/4/18. Formed from IX Corps Details.

††† *Gater's Force*—Br.-Gen. G. A. Gater (62nd Bde., 21st Div.) commanded a Force made up of composite battalions of the three brigades of the 21st Div. Gater's Force was formed on 31/5/18 and broken up on 19/6/18.

189

1918 *(Contd.)*

THE ADVANCE TO VICTORY.

BATTLES OF THE HINDENBURG LINE.

18 September	**Battle of Epéhy** [1st and 6th Divs.—Fourth Army*].
24 September	**Attack on Quadrilateral and Fresnoy** [1st and 6th Divs. ; with 20 tanks 13th Bn., 5th Tank Bde.—Fourth Army].
29 Sept.–2 Oct.	**Battle of the St. Quentin Canal** [1st, 6th, 32nd, and 46th Divs. ; with 5th, 6th (Whippets), and 9th Bns., 3rd Tank Bde.—Fourth Army].
29 September	**Passage at Bellenglise** [46th Div. ; with 2 Cos. 9th Bn., 3rd Tank Bde.—Fourth Army].
3–5 October	**Battle of the Beaurevoir Line** [1st, 6th, 32nd, and 46th Divs. ; with 5th Bn. and detnt. 6th (Whippets) Bn., 3rd Tank Bde.—Fourth Army].
8 and 9 October ...	**Battle of Cambrai** [6th and 46th Divs. ; with 5th Bn., 3rd Tank Bde.—Fourth Army].

9–12 October	**The Pursuit to the Selle** [6th and 46th Divs. ; with 5th Bn. and detnt. 6th (Whippets) Bn., 3rd Tank Bde.—Fourth Army].

THE FINAL ADVANCE IN PICARDY.

17–25 October	**Battle of the Selle** [1st, 6th, and 46th Divs. ; with 6th Bn. (12 Whippets), and 16th Bn. (12 tanks), 4th Tank Bde.,** on 17–19/10/18 ; and on 19–23/10/18, part of 2nd Tank Bde.** (6th (Wh.), 10th, and 301st (Am.) Bns.)—Fourth Army].
2 November	**Attack S. W. of Landrecies (Happegarbes Spur)** [96th Inf. Bde. (32nd Div.) ; with 3 tanks, 10th Bn., 2nd Tank Bde.—Fourth Army].

---

* On 4/9/18 IX Corps H.Q. arrived in Fourth Army, and on 11/9/18 took over 1st and 6th Divisions in the line. For the remainder of the Campaign IX Corps was composed of 1st, 6th, 32nd, and 46th Divisions.
** 4th Tank Bde. handed over (in the line) to 2nd Tank Bde. on 19/10/18.

190

1918 (*Contd.*)

THE FINAL ADVANCE IN PICARDY (*Contd.*).

4 November	**Battle of the Sambre** [1st, 32nd, and 46th Divs. ; with 5 tanks 10th Bn., 2nd Tank Bde.—Fourth Army].
4 November	**Passage of the Sambre—Oise Canal** [1st and 32nd Divs. ; with tanks of 10th Bn., 2nd Tank Bde.—Fourth Army].
5 November— 11 a.m., 11 Nov.	**Final Operations** [1st, 32nd, and 46th Divs., and 5th Cav. Bde. (2nd Cav. Div.) ; with, on 5–7/11/18, part of 9th and 14th Bns., 2nd Tank Bde.—Fourth Army].

In accordance with Fourth Army instructions, on the 9th November the IX Corps (on the right of the Army front) halted with its head on La Capelle—Avesnes—Maubeuge highway, and covered itself by an outpost line to the east of this main road. To continue the pursuit of the retiring German forces a comparatively small mobile force (" Bethell's Force "*) was formed and placed under the commander of the 66th Division, XIII Corps. On the morning of the 10th November, " Bethell's Force " took up the pursuit on the whole of the Fourth Army front and maintained the pressure until 11 a.m. on the 11th November, when the Armistice brought hostilities to a close.

Since the 11th September, when the IX Corps had come into line on the right of the Fourth Army front, the Corps had fought its way forward across France for 59 days, and in that time had advanced more than 50 miles and taken part in six battles.

The IX Corps (composed of the 1st, 6th, 32nd, and 66th Divisions) was selected to advance under the Fourth Army up to the German frontier. This advance began on the 18th November ; but, owing to the narrowing front, a reorganization of the Army of Occupation took place ten days later, and the IX Corps was then transferred to the Second Army, which had been selected to carry out the further advance across Germany to the Rhine. The IX Corps was reorganized for this task : the 32nd and 66th Divisions remained on the Meuse to act as a reserve to the Army of Occupation, and the 62nd Division** was transferred from the VI Corps to the IX Corps. The reorganized IX Corps (1st, 6th, and 62nd Divisions) entered Germany between the 13th—16th December and reached its allotted area, around Bonn, between the 23rd—25th December, 1918.

---

* *Bethell's Force* was formed on 9/11/18 and broken up after Armistice (for its composition see p. 213).
** The only Territorial Force Division to enter Germany.

X CORPS

G.O.C.

15 July, 1915	Lieut.-General Sir T. L. N. MORLAND.
15 April, 1918	Lieut.-General Sir W. N. CONGREVE, V.C. (tempy.).
24 May, 1918	Lieut.-General Sir W. E. PEYTON.
3 July, 1918	Lieut.-General R. B. STEPHENS.

B.-G.G.S.

14 July, 1915...Br.-Gen. G. DE S. BARROW.
23 Aug., 1915...Br.-Gen. P. HOWELL.
21 Oct., 1915...Br.-Gen. A. R. CAMERON.
2 July, 1918...Br.-Gen. W. J. MAXWELL-
           SCOTT (tempy.).
13 July, 1918...Br.-Gen. C. EVANS.

D.-A. and Q.-M.-G.

14 July, 1915...Lt.-Col. G. D. JEBB
           (acting).
25 July, 1915...Br.-Gen. H. H. BURNEY.
31 Dec., 1915...Br.-Gen. G. D. JEBB.
1 Dec., 1916...Br.-Gen. W. K. LEGGE.

G.S.O. 1.

....

B.-G.R.A.

19 July, 1915...Br.-Gen. F. E. JOHNSON.
9 Oct., 1915...Br.-Gen. J. G. GEDDES.
26 Mar., 1916...Br.-Gen. C. E. D.
           BUDWORTH.
29 May, 1916...Br.-Gen. C. C. VAN
           STRAUBENZEE.
3 Jan., 1917...Br.-Gen. H. L. REED, V.C.
11 Oct., 1917...Br.-Gen. G. GILLSON.
12 Sept., 1918...Br.-Gen. W. P. MONKHOUSE.

C.H.A.

....

*

[9 Dec., 1915] Br.-Gen. H. O. VINCENT.
17 July, 1918...Br.-Gen. A. H. OLLIVANT

---

* Third Army H. A. Group (formerly No. 4 H.A.R. Group—G.H.Q. Artillery) joined X Corps on 2/3/1916, and its designation was then changed to X Corps Heavy Artillery (see Appendix 3).

X CORPS

C.E.

14 July, 1915...Br.-Gen. J. A. S. TULLOCH
(sick, 31/10/16).
31 Oct., 1916...Col. E. N. STOCKLEY
(acting).
30 Nov., 1916...Br.-Gen. J. A. S. TULLOCH.
16 Nov., 1917...Br.-Gen. G. H. BOILEAU.

A.-D. Signals.

23 July, 1915...Capt. R. M. POWELL
(i/c Corps Signals).
6 Feb., 1916...Maj. R. M. POWELL.
20 Nov., 1916...Lt.-Col. R. M. POWELL.
Dec., 1916...Lt.-Col. F. A. ILES
(sick, 16/12/16).
27 Dec., 1916...Maj. A. Yates (acting).
7 Feb., 1917...Lt.-Col. F. A. ILES.
12 May, 1918...Lt.-Col. R. F. B.
NAYLOR.

D.-D.M.S.

14 July, 1915...Col. R. L. R. MACLEOD.

A.-D.V.S.

....
13 June, 1917...Lt.-Col. G. P. KNOTT.

X CORPS

FORMATION.

X Corps Headquarters began to form at St. Omer on the 14th July, 1915. The X Corps, with the 5th, 18th, and 51st Divisions, then joined the newly-formed Third Army (VII and X Corps) which was relieving part of the French Second Army (French XI and XIV Corps) on the front from Curlu on the Somme to Hébuterne.

In this relief X Corps took over the right of the Third Army front ; and, when the relief was completed, X Corps was in touch on the Somme with the left of the French Sixth Army.*

BATTLES AND ENGAGEMENTS.

20 July–31 December	**1915**	[Third Army]

1916

1–24 July	**BATTLES OF THE SOMME.**
1–13 July	**Battle of Albert** [12th, 25th, 32nd, 36th, and 49th Divs.—Fourth Army**].
14–17 July	**Battle of Bazentin Ridge** [25th, 32nd, 48th, and 49th Divs.——Reserve Army**].
17 July	**Capture of Ovillers** [48th Div.—Reserve Army].
23 and 24 July	**Battle of Pozières Ridge** [48th and 49th Divs.—Reserve Army].***

1917

7–14 June	**Battle of Messines** [23rd, 24th, 41st, and 47th Divs. ; with 12 tanks, 2nd Tank Bde.,—Second Army].

---

* French Sixth Army relieved right of French Second Army (south of R. Somme) from 1/7/15.
** On 1/3/16 X Corps (32nd, 36th, 48th, and 49th Divs.) was taken over by the newly-formed Fourth Army. On 4/7/16 X Corps (25th, 32nd, 36th, and 49th Divs.) was taken over (in the line) by the Reserve Army.
*** At Noon on 24/7/16 X Corps handed over (in the line) to II Corps.

1917 *(Contd.)*

BATTLES OF YPRES.

31 July–2 August ...	**Battle of Pilckem Ridge** [41st and 47th Divs.—Second Army].
16–18 August	**Battle of Langemarck** [39th Div.—Second Army].
20–25 September ...	**Battle of the Menin Road Ridge** [23rd, 33rd, 39th, and 41st Divs.—Second Army].
26 Sept.–3 Oct. ...	**Battle of Polygon Wood** [5th 7th, 21st, 23rd, 33rd, and 39th Divs.—Second Army].
4 October	**Battle of Broodseinde** [5th, 7th, and 21st Divs.—Second Army].
9 October	**Battle of Poelcappelle** [5th and 7th Divs.—Second Army].
12 October	**First Battle of Passchendaele** [23rd Div.—Second Army].
26 Oct.–10 Nov. ...	**Second Battle of Passchendaele** [5th, 7th, 21st, and 39th Divs.—Second Army].

*

1918

THE ADVANCE TO VICTORY.

18 Aug.–6 Sept. ...	**THE ADVANCE IN FLANDERS** [30th and 36th Divs.—Second Army].
1 September	**Capture of Neuve Église** [89th Bde. (30th Div.)—Second Army].
2 September ... ,...	**Capture of Wulverghem** [21st Bde. (30th Div.)—Second Army].
	THE FINAL ADVANCE IN FLANDERS [29th, 30th, and 34th Divs.—Second Army].
28 Sept.–2 Oct.	**Battle of Ypres** [30th and 34th Divs.—Second Army].
14–19 October	**Battle of Courtrai** [30th and 34th Divs.—Second Army].
25 October	**Ooteghem** [34th Div.—Second Army].

The X Corps (on the right of the Second Army) pushed on steadily eastwards, and on the night of the 7th/8th November its then front-line divisions (29th and 30th) were

---

* On the conclusion of the Battles of Ypres, 1917, X Corps was withdrawn from the line, and until July, 1918, the Corps remained in the back area. Then, on 8/7/18, X Corps (30th, 35th, and 36th Divs.) took over part of the Second Army front, relieving the Fr. XVI Corps (*D.A.N.*).

1918 *(Contd.)*

in position along the left bank of the Schelde. On the next night the divisions crossed the river and secured the right bank. On the 9th Renaix was taken. Still further progress was made, and before hostilities ceased, at 11 a.m. on the 11th November, the 29th Division and part of the 3rd Cavalry Division* had seized Lessines and secured the passage across the Dendre. The 30th Division and part of the 3rd Cavalry Division prolonged the X Corps front line to the north-west of Lessines.

Since the 18th August the X Corps had fought in two battles and had advanced across Flanders nearly 50 miles in eighty-six days.

---

* 3rd Cavalry Division joined the Second Army on the 9th November and co-operated with the X and XIX Corps in the last stage of the Final Advance.

XI CORPS*

G.O.C.

29 August, 1915	... ...	Major-General EARL OF CAVAN (tempy.).
4 September, 1915	... ...	Lieut.-General R. C. B. HAKING.
13 August, 1916	... ...	Lieut.-General Sir C. A. ANDERSON (tempy.).
30 September, 1916	... ...	Lieut.-General Sir R. C. B. HAKING.

B.-G.G.S.

30 Aug., 1915...Br.-Gen. H. M. DE F. MONTGOMERY.
25 Oct., 1915...Br.-Gen. W. H. ANDERSON.
27 Sept., 1916...Lt.-Col. A. SYMONS (acting).
10 Nov., 1916...Br.-Gen. H. W. STUDD.
27 Nov., 1917...Br.-Gen. J. E. S. BRIND.

D.-A. and Q.-M.-G.

29 Aug., 1915...Br.-Gen. R. FORD.
4 Nov., 1915...Br.-Gen. H. C. HOLMAN.
11 Nov., 1916...Br.-Gen. A. F. U. GREEN.

G.S.O. 1.

....

B.-G.R.A.

12 Sept., 1915...Br.-Gen. G. G. S. CAREY.
31 May, 1917...Br.-Gen. E. W. ALEXANDER, V.C.
23 Oct., 1917...Br.-Gen. W. A. M. THOMPSON (tempy.).
16 Nov. 1917...Br.-Gen. E. W. ALEXANDER, V.C.
1 April, 1918...Br.-Gen. S. F. METCALFE.

C.H.A.

....

**

[15 Nov., 1915] Br.-Gen. F. H. CRAMPTON.
10 Nov., 1917...Br.-Gen. R. H. F. McCULLOCH.
9 Sept., 1918...Br.-Gen. F. A. TWISS.

---

* XI Corps H.Q. was ordered to Italy on 16/11/17, and served there from 1/12/17. Ordered back to France on 22/2/18, XI Corps H.Q. left Italy on 10/3/18, reached Aire (in First Army) on 13/3/18, and XI Corps H.Q. opened at Hinges on 16/3/18.
** No. 1 H.A.R. Group (G.H.Q. Artillery) joined XI Corps on 11/3/16, and its designation was then changed to XI Corps Heavy Artillery (see Appendix 3).

XI CORPS

C.E.

11 Sept., 1915...Br.-Gen. L. JONES.
22 Nov., 1917...Br.-Gen. H. J. M.
MARSHALL.

A.-D. Signals.

6 Sept., 1915...Capt. J. D. MURDOCH
(i/c Corps Signals).
6 Feb., 1916...Maj. J. D. MURDOCH.
22 May, 1916...Maj. G. E. B. DOBBS.
20 Nov., 1916...Lt.-Col. G. E. B. DOBBS.
15 Jan., 1917...Lt.-Col. A. H. FRENCH.
13 June, 1917...Capt. J. W. ORANGE-
BROMHEAD (acting).
15 Feb., 1918...Maj. J. W. ORANGE-
BROMHEAD (acting).
14 May, 1918...Lt.-Col. J. A. F. MAIR.

D.-D.M.S.

8 Sept., 1915...Col. R. H. FIRTH.
12 May, 1917...Col. R. W. WRIGHT.

A.-D.V.S.

... .
16 June, 1917...Lt.-Col. R. C. COCHRANE.
30 June, 1918...Lt.-Col. A. ENGLAND.

XI CORPS

FORMATION.

XI Corps Headquarters began to form in France on the 29th August, 1915. The new Corps took over two New Army Divisions : the 24th, which completed its concentration near St. Pol on the 4th September, and the 21st, which only reached France on the 13th September. Strengthened by the addition of the Guards Division (which had collected and formed in France between the 15th and the 30th August), the XI Corps was launched in a night-attack at the end of the first day of the Battle of Loos.

BATTLES AND ENGAGEMENTS.

1915

25 Sept.–8 Oct.	**Battle of Loos** [Guards, 12th, 21st, and 24th Divs.—First Army].
13–19 October	**Hohenzollern Redoubt, and the Hulluch Quarries** [Guards, 12th, and 46th Divs.—First Army].

1916

1 January–31 December	[In First Army].
19 July	**Attack at Fromelles** [61st and 5th Aus. Divs.—First Army].

1917

1 January–28 November	[In First Army].

On the 16th November XI Corps Headquarters received orders to move to Italy ; on the 28th Corps Headquarters left Lillers and reached Mantua on the 1st December.

1918

On the 27th January the XI Corps (5th and 48th Divisions) took over the Arcade Sector on the Piave. But on the 24th February orders were received that the XI Corps, with the 7th* and 41st* Divisions, was to return to France ; and on the 10th March XI Corps H.Q. left Merlengo. XI Corps H.Q. reached Aire (in the First Army

---

* On 22/2/18 the 7th Div. received orders to return to France, and this accounts for the 48th Div. relieving the 7th Div. in the Montello Sector. On the 24th March, however, the order to the 7th Div. was countermanded, and the 5th Div. was then substituted for the 7th Div.

41st Div. began entraining for France on the 1st March, and on arrival joined IV Corps (Third Army). The 5th Div. began entraining on the 1st April, and on arrival rejoined XI Corps, in the First Army.

1918 *(Contd.)*

area) on the 13th March ; and, on the 16th, Corps H.Q. opened at Hinges (3 miles N.N.W. of Béthune). On the 19th March XI Corps took over the front-line sector, then held by the 55th Division, from La Bassée Canal to north-east of Festubert, in the centre of the First Army.

Thereafter XI Corps was engaged in the following operations on the Western Front :

BATTLES OF THE LYS.

9–11 April ... ... **Battle of Estaires** [3rd, 51st, 55th, and 61st Divs., and 2nd Bde. (1st Div.), and 2nd Port. Div. and 3rd Bde. (1st Port. Div.), and King Edward's Horse (XI Corps Cav.)—First Army].

9–12 April ... ... **First Defence of Givenchy** [55th Div.—transferred in the line at 8 a.m. on 12/4 to I Corps—First Army].

12–15 April ... ... **Battle of Hazebrouck** [5th, 50th*, 51st, and 61st Divs., and King Edward's Horse—First Army].

12–15 April ... ... **Defence of Hinges Ridge** [51st Div.—First Army].

12–15 April ... ... **Defence of Nieppe Forest** [5th Div.—First Army].

18 April ... ... **Battle of Béthune** [61st Div.—First Army].

———

28 June ... ... **La Becque** [5th and 31st** Divs.—First Army].

10 a.m. 1 July ... ... Fifth Army took over XI Corps in the line.

THE ADVANCE TO VICTORY.

18 Aug.–6 Sept. ... **THE ADVANCE IN FLANDERS** [59th, 61st, and 74th*** Divs.—Fifth Army].

---

* At 8 a.m. on 12/4/18 the 50th Div. was transferred from XV Corps to XI Corps.
** 31st Div. (of XV Corps, Second Army) was placed under XI Corps, First Army, for this operation.
*** 74th Div. (from E.E.F.) went into the line near Merville (on the right of the XI Corps) on 14/7/18. On 30/8/18 the 74th Division joined III Corps, Fourth Army ; on 30/9/18 it rejoined XI Corps ; and on 8/10/18 74th Div. was transferred back to III Corps.

1918 (*Contd.*)

2 Oct.–11 Nov. ... **THE FINAL ADVANCE IN ARTOIS** [47th, 57th, 59th, and 74th* Divs.—Fifth Army].

17th October ... ... **Occupation of Lille** [57th Div.—Fifth Army].

28 October ... ... **Official Entry into Lille** [47th Div.—Fifth Army].

When hostilities ceased at 11 a.m. on the 11th November, the leading troops of the XI Corps (on the left of the Fifth Army) were on a line running south from Lessines. In the eighty-six days which had elapsed since the 18th August, when the attack through Flanders and Artois opened, the XI Corps had advanced more than 55 miles.

---

* At 10 a.m. on 8/10/18 the 74th Division was transferred to III Corps, Fifth Army.

XII CORPS

G.O.C.

5 September, 1915 ... ... Lieut.-General Sir H. F. M. Wilson.
4 January, 1917 ... ... Major-General E. C. W. Mackenzie-Kennedy (tempy.).
11 January, 1917 ... ... Lieut.-General Sir H. F. M. Wilson.

B.-G.G.S.

8 Sept., 1915...Br.-Gen. L. J. Bols.
21 Oct., 1915
–15 Nov., 1915 } Br.-Gen. P. Howell.*
23 Jan., 1916...Br.-Gen. F. G. Fuller (sick, 7/6/18).
7 June, 1918...Lt.-Col. T. G. G. Anderson (acting).
30 June, 1918...Br.-Gen. F. G. Fuller.
12 July, 1918...Lt.-Col. P. L. Hanbury (acting).
23 Aug., 1918...Br.-Gen. F. G. Fuller (sick, 16/9/18).
16 Sept., 1918...Lt.-Col. P. L. Hanbury (acting).
26 Sept., 1918...Br.-Gen. F. G. Fuller.

D.-A. and Q.-M.-G.

6 Sept., 1915
–15 Nov., 1915 } Br.-Gen. Travers E. Clarke.
20 Dec., 1915...Br.-Gen. G. S. Richardson.
9 Mar., 1916...Br.-Gen. H. L. N. Beynon.
26 Dec., 1917...Br.-Gen. E. J. F. Vaughan.

B.-G. R.A.

19 Sept., 1915
–15 Nov., 1915 } Br.-Gen. W. H. Onslow.
17 Jan., 1916...Br.-Gen. D. Arbuthnot.
29 July, 1916...Br.-Gen. H. E. T. Kelly (tempy.).
20 Sept., 1916...Br.-Gen. H. D. White-Thomson.
22 June, 1917...Br.-Gen. T. Bruce (tempy.).
12 Aug., 1917...Br.-Gen. H. D. White-Thomson.
27 Sept., 1917...Br.-Gen. H. H. Bond (tempy.).
5 Nov., 1917...Br.-Gen. H. D. White-Thomson.

CORPS M.G.O.

....

22 Dec., 1916...Lt.-Col. K. A. Plimpton.

---

* Br.-Gen. C. J. Perceval was appointed to succeed Br.-Gen. P. Howell as B.-G. G.S. ; but on 19/1/16 was evacuated to Hospital from the Transport, and never reported for duty.

Note.—There was no Corps Heavy Artillery Commander. The Heavy Artillery Groups were under Br.-Gen. P. L. Holbrooke, at G.H.Q. British Salonika Army.

C.E.

10 Sept., 1915
–4 Nov., 1915 } Br.-Gen. G. GODBY.
15 Jan., 1916...Br.-Gen. F. K. FAIR.
 9 July, 1916...Lt.-Col. C. G. W. HUNTER
(acting).
12 July, 1916...Br.-Gen. G. WALKER.
12 July, 1916...Lt.-Col. C. G. W. HUNTER
(acting).
26 July, 1916...Br.-Gen. G. WALKER
(sick, 8/8/16).
 8 Aug., 1916...Lt.-Col. C. G. W. HUNTER
(acting).
15 Nov., 1916...Br.-Gen. G. WALKER
(sick, 30/11/17).
30 Nov., 1917...Lt.-Col. C. G. W. HUNTER
(acting).
25 Dec., 1917...Br.-Gen. C. G. W. HUNTER.

A.-D. Signals.

24 Sept., 1915...Capt. G. G. RAWSON
(i/c Corps Signals).
20 Nov., 1915...Maj. G. G. RAWSON
(i/c Army Signals).
19 April, 1917...Lt.-Col. G. G. RAWSON.
13 Nov., 1917...Lt.-Col. H. C. SAUNDERS.

D.-D.M.S.

14 Sept., 1915...Col. N. C. FERGUSON.
30 July, 1916...Col. G. T. RAWNSLEY.
11 June, 1918...Col. W. H. S. NICKERSON,
V.C.

A.-D.V.S.

....

XII CORPS

FORMATION.

XII Corps Headquarters began to form at Doullens (France) on the 5th September, 1915, and joined the Third Army on the Somme front.

For the remainder of the Great War XII Corps served on the Western Front and then in Macedonia and was employed as follows :

1915

On the 25th September (the opening day of the Battle of Loos) the XII Corps (22nd and 27th Divisions) supported with its artillery the attack delivered on the Arras front by the French Tenth Army.

On the 20th October, 1915, the XII Corps (22nd and 28th Divisions) was ordered to move to Marseilles, preparatory to embarkation, and on the 4th November XII Corps H.Q. entrained for that port. On the 7th, Corps H.Q. embarked on the *Minneapolis*, sailed at noon, and reached Salonika at 8 a.m. on the 12th November. Three days later XII Corps Headquarters Staff was directed to take over the duties of British H.Q. Staff in Macedonia, with the exception of the Corps Commander who was to await further instructions.

On the 28th December, XII Corps was re-formed at Lembet Camp (3 miles N.N.E. of Salonika), and at this time was composed of the 22nd, 26th, and 28th Divisions.

BATTLES AND ENGAGEMENTS.

1916

10–18 August ... ... **Horseshoe Hill** (2¼ miles S.W. of Dojran) [22nd and 26th Divs.].

13 and 14 September **Machukovo** [22nd Div.].

1917

24 and 25 April ; ... }**BATTLE OF DOJRAN** [22nd, 26th, and 60th Divs.].
and 8 and 9 May ...

1918

THE OFFENSIVE.

1 and 2 September ...   **Capture of the Roche Noire Salient** (4 miles W. of the R. Vardar) [27th Div.].

18 and 19 September   **BATTLE OF DOJRAN** [22nd and 26th Divs., and 83rd Bde. (less 2 Bns.—28th Div.), and Greek Seres Div. and 2° bis Régt. de Zouaves].*

22–30 September   ...   **Pursuit to the Strumica Valley** [22nd and 28th Divs.].

On the 26th September the two divisions of the XII Corps occupied the crest of the Belašica Planina : the right division (22nd) was at the Signal Allemand, and the head of the left division (28th) was on the ridge to the east of Dorlobos.**

The two divisions were still in the same positions at Noon on the 30th September, when the Armistice with Bulgaria brought hostilities to a close in this theatre of operations.

---

   * The following British Heavy, Siege, and Mountain Artillery was attached to XII Corps for this Battle of Dojran :
      3, 6″ guns ; 10, 60-pdr. batteries ; 1, 2.75″ (10-pdr.) mountain battery (Bute Mtn. Bty.) ; 1, 8″ howitzer battery ; and 8, 6″ howitzer batteries.
Headquarters, Heavy Artillery G.H.Q., was attached to XII Corps for this Battle of Dojran.

   ** The Strumica Valley is about 5 miles northward of the crest of the Belašica Planina at Dorlobos.

NOTE.—The moves of the British Divisions in Macedonia from September, 1918, until the Armistice with Germany on the 11th November, are briefly detailed in G.H.Q. British Salonika Army (pp. 61, 62).

XIII CORPS

G.O.C.

15 November, 1915	Lieut.-General W. N. Congreve, V.C.
	(sick, 10/8/16).
10 August, 1916	Lieut.-General Earl of Cavan (tempy.).
16 August, 1916	Lieut.-General W. N. Congreve, V.C.
	(wounded, 12/6/17).
17 June, 1917	Lieut.-General Sir W. F. N. McCracken.
13 March, 1918	Lieut.-General Sir H. de B. de Lisle.
12 April, 1918	Lieut.-General Sir T. L. N. Morland.

B.-G.G.S.

15 Nov., 1915...Br.-Gen. W. H. Greenly.
16 Nov., 1916...Br.-Gen. I. Stewart.

D.-A. and Q.-M.-G.

12 Nov., 1915...Br.-Gen. P. G. Twining.
28 Oct., 1916...Br.-Gen. S. W. Robinson

G.S.O. 1.

....

B.-G.R.A.

13 Nov., 1915...Br.-Gen. R. St. C. Lecky.

19 Feb., 1917...Br.-Gen. L. W. P. East.
3 April, 1917...Br.-Gen. G. H. Sanders
(tempy.).
13 May, 1917...Br.-Gen. R. A. C.
Wellesley.

C.H.A.

....
*

15 Mar., 1916...Br.-Gen. L. W. P. East.
19 Feb., 1917...Br.-Gen. A. F. S. Scott.
8 June, 1917...Br.-Gen. L. W. P. East
(killed, 6/9/18).
18 Sept., 1918...Br.-Gen. J. D. Sherer.

* Formed in France on 15/3/16.

XIII CORPS

C.E.

15 Nov., 1915...Br.-Gen. S. H. POWELL.
 7 July, 1916...Br.-Gen. E. P. BROOKER.
26 Nov., 1917...Br.-Gen. H. R. S. CHRISTIE.
17 Feb., 1918...Br.-Gen. C. A. ELLIOTT.

A.-D. Signals.

15 Nov., 1915...Capt. P. R. BALD
                  (i/c Corps Signals).
 6 Feb., 1916...Maj. P. R. BALD.
20 Nov., 1916...Lt.-Col. P. R. BALD.
18 Jan., 1918...Lt.-Col. T. W. VIGERS.

D.-D.M.S.

15 Nov., 1915...Col. G. CREE.
11 Jan., 1918...Col. T. P. JONES.

A.-D.V.S.

....
16 June, 1917...Lt.-Col. H. GAMBLE.

XIII CORPS

FORMATION.

XIII Corps Headquarters was formed in France between the 12th and 15th November, 1915. The newly-formed Corps took over the 30th and 36th Divisions and joined the Third Army on the Somme front.*

BATTLES AND ENGAGEMENTS.

15 Nov.–31 Dec.   **1915**   [Third Army].

1916

BATTLES OF THE SOMME.**

1–13 July	**Battle of Albert** [3rd. 9th, 18th, 30th, and 35th Divs.—Fourth Army*].
1 July	**Capture of Montauban** [30th Div.—Fourth Army].
3 July	**Capture of Bernafay Wood** [9th Div.—Fourth Army].
7–13 July	**Fighting in Trônes Wood** [30th Div.—Fourth Army].
14–17 July	**Battle of Bazentin Ridge** [3rd, 9th, and 18th Divs.—Fourth Army].
14 July	**Capture of Trônes Wood** [54th Bde. (18th Div.)—Fourth Army].
14–18 July	**Attack of Longueval** [3rd and 9th Divs.—Fourth Army].
15 July–16 August**	**Battle of Delville Wood** [2nd, 3rd, 9th, 18th, and 24th*** Divs.—Fourth Army].
27 and 28 July	**Capture and Consolidation of Delville Wood** [2nd Div.—Fourth Army].
8 and 9 August ...	**Attack of Waterlot Farm—Guillemont** [2nd Div.—Fourth Army].
13–18 November** ...	**Battle of the Ancre** [31st Div. with 120th Bde. (40th Div.)—Fifth Army].

---

* On 1/3/16 XIII Corps (7th, 18th, and 30th Divs.) was taken over by the newly-formed Fourth Army.
** At Midnight 16–17/8/16 XIII Corps was relieved (in the line) by XIV Corps. Until 4/10/16 XIII Corps remained at Domart (24 miles W.N.W. of Albert), and then XIII Corps took over left of Reserve (later Fifth) Army, from opposite Serre to Hébuterne.
*** 24th Div. was transferred to XIV Corps at Mn. 16–17/8/16.

211

1917

BATTLES OF ARRAS.

9–14 April ... ... **Battle of Vimy Ridge*** [Until night 11–12/4/17 in Reserve with 2nd, 31st, and 63rd Divs.; then 2nd Div.—First Army].

23 and 24 April... ... **Second Battle of the Scarpe** [63rd Div.—First Army].

23 April ... ... **Capture of Gavrelle** [63rd Div.—First Army].

28 and 29 April ... **Battle of Arleux** [2nd and 63rd Divs.—First Army].

3 and 4 May ... ... **Third Battle of the Scarpe** [2nd and 31st Divs.—First Army].

---

28 June ... ... **Capture of Oppy Wood** [5th and 31st Divs.—First Army].

1918

FIRST BATTLES OF THE SOMME.

28 March ... ... **First Battle of Arras** [56th and 3rd Cdn. Divs.—First Army].

THE ADVANCE TO VICTORY.

18 Aug.–6 Sept. ... **THE ADVANCE IN FLANDERS** [4th, 19th, and 46th Divs.—Fifth Army**].

BATTLES OF THE HINDENBURG LINE.

1*** and 2 October ... **Battle of St. Quentin Canal** [18th and 50th Divs.—Fourth Army].

3–5 October ... ... **Battle of the Beaurevoir Line** [25th and 50th Divs.—Fourth Army].

5 October ... ... **Capture of Beaurevoir** [25th Div.; with 6 tanks, 4th Bn., 4th Tank Bde.—Fourth Army].

8 and 9 October ... **Battle of Cambrai** [25th, 50th, and 66th Divs.; with part of 1st, 3rd (Whippets), 4th, 6th (Whippets) 10th, and 16th Bns., and 301st Am. Bn., 4th Tank Bde.—Fourth Army].

9–12 October ... ... **Pursuit to the Selle** [25th, 50th, and 66th Divs.—Fourth Army].

---

* XIII Corps came into the line between XVII Corps and Canadian Corps.
** At 10 a.m. on 1/7/18 Fifth Army took over XIII Corps from First Army.
*** At Noon on 1/10/18 XIII Corps took over (in the line) from III Corps, Fourth Army III Corps then moved to Fifth Army and took over a front-line sector on 8/10/18.

1918 *(Contd.)*

THE FINAL ADVANCE.

IN PICARDY.

17–25 October ... ... **Battle of the Selle** [18th, 25th, 50th, and 66th Divs.; with 1st Bn. (12 tanks), 4th Tank Bde., on *17–19/10;* and, from *19–23/10*, part of 6th (Whippets), and 10th Bns., and 301st Am. Bn., 2nd Tank Bde.—Fourth Army].

23 October ... ... **Capture of Bousies** [18th Div.; with 6 tanks 10th Bn., 2nd Tank Bde.—Fourth Army].

4 November ... ... **Battle of the Sambre** [18th, 25th, and 50th Divs.; with 21 tanks 9th and 14th Bns., 2nd Tank Bde.—Fourth Army].

4 November ... ... **Passage of the Sambre—Oise Canal** [25th Div.; with tanks of 9th, 10th, and 14th Bns., 2nd Tank Bde., and 6 cars 17th (A.-C.) Bn.—Fourth Army].

5 Nov.–11 a.m. 11 Nov. **Final Operations** [18th, 25th, 50th, and 66th Divs., and 5th Cav. Bde. (2nd Cav. Div.); with part of 9th and 14th Bns., 2nd Tank Bde. on *5–7/11*, and 17th (A.-C.) Bn.; and 5 cars 17th (A.-C.) Bn. with XIII until *9/11;* then, until Armistice, the cars were with " Maj.-Gen. H. K. Bethell's Force*"—Fourth Army].

In accordance with Fourth Army instructions, on the 9th November the XIII Corps (on the left of the Army front) halted with its head on La Capelle—Avesnes—Maubeuge highway, covered by an outpost line to the east of the main road. To keep touch with and press back the rapidly retreating Germans, a comparatively small mobile force was formed and placed under the command of Major-General H. K. Bethell (G.O.C. 66th Division).*

On the morning of the 10th " Bethell's Force " advanced and established contact with the Germans near Hestrud and Sivry; and when the Armistice brought hostilities

---

* *Bethell's Force* (formed on 9/11/18) was composed as follows :—G.O.C., Maj.-Gen. H. K. Bethell (Comdg. 66th Div.), with 2 Sqdns. R.A.F., 5th Cav. Bde., A and B, and 2 secs. D(H.) CCCXXXI, 1 Sec. A.-A., 430th, 431st, 432nd Fd. Cos., 66th Div. Signal Coy., 5 cars 17th (A.-C.) Bn., IX Corps and XIII Corps Cyclist Bns., 1 Coy. 9/Glouc. (P.), 1 Coy. 100th Bn. M.G.C., S. African Inf. Bde. Group, 1st S. African Fd. Amb., and Detnts. from 2/2 and 2/3 Lanc. Fd. Amb.

On 10/11/18 Bethell's Force was reinforced by 199th Inf. Bde. (66th Div). After the Armistice Bethell's Force was broken up, and the troops returned to their own formations.

1918 *(Contd.)*

to a close, at 11 a.m. on the 11th November, " Bethell's Force " had established a line along the front of the Fourth Army, running from Pont de la République—eastern edge of Grandrieu—east of Sivry—Montbliart.   On its right, or southern, flank " Bethell's Force " was in touch with French troops—French 51st Division, XV Corps, French First Army—near Eppé Sauvage (12 miles east of Avesnes).

Since joining the Fourth Army on the 1st October, in the midst of the Battle of the St. Quentin Canal, the XIII Corps had been engaged in 5 Battles and had advanced some 45 miles in 42 days of active operations.

XIV CORPS*

G.O.C.

11 January, 1916	Lieut.-General EARL OF CAVAN.
11 August, 1916	Lieut.-General E. A. FANSHAWE (tempy.).
17 August, 1916	Lieut.-General Sir T. L. N. MORLAND (tempy.).
10 September, 1916 ... ...⎫	
–10 March, 1918 ... ...⎭	Lieut.-General EARL OF CAVAN.

....

15 October, 1918 ... ... Lieut.-General Sir J. M. BABINGTON.

B.-G.G.S.

3 Jan., 1916⎫ Br.-Gen. Hon. J. F.
–13 Mar., 1918⎭   GATHORNE-HARDY.

....

9 Oct., 1918...Br.-Gen. W. W. PITT-
          TAYLOR.

D.-A. and Q.-M.-G.

3 Jan., 1916...Br.-Gen. B. H. H. COOKE.
3 Dec., 1916...Br.-Gen. B. F. BURNETT-
            HITCHCOCK.
7 May, 1917⎫ Br.-Gen. H. L.
–10 Mar., 1918⎭   ALEXANDER.

....

9 Oct., 1918...Br.-Gen. C. OGSTON.

G.S.O. 1.

5 Feb., 1918⎫
–10 Mar., 1918⎭ Lt.-Col. W. W. PITT-TAYLOR.

B.-G.R.A.

5 Jan., 1916...Br.-Gen. H. K. JACKSON.
29 Feb., 1916⎫
–10 Mar., 1918⎭ Br.-Gen. A. E. WARDROP.

....

16 Oct., 1918...Br.-Gen. T. R. C. HUDSON
           (tempy.).
23 Oct., 1918...Br.-Gen. E. S. HOARE
           NAIRNE.

C.H.A.**

10 April, 1916...Br.-Gen. P. DE S.
           BURNEY.
15 Nov., 1916⎫
–2 Nov., 1917⎭ Br.-Gen. F. G. MAUNSELL.

Artillery Adviser to G.O.C. Corps.

6 Nov., 1917⎫
–10 Mar., 1918⎭ Br.-Gen. P. D. HAMILTON.

---

  * XIV Corps H.Q. was ordered to Italy on 29/10/17 and served in Italy from 5/11/17–18/4/18, when XIV Corps merged in and became G.H.Q. British Force in Italy. Between 9–16/10/18 XIV Corps was re-formed in Italy (see G.H.Q. Italy, pp. 63 and 67).
  ** Corps Hy. Arty. H.Q. was established on 7/2/16, under Lt.-Col. B. M. Bateman ; and on 10/4/16 XIV Corps H.A. was formed. XIV Corps H.A. H.Q. did not accompany XIV Corps H.Q. to Italy on 2/11/17, and on 12/2/18 was broken up in France.

C.E.

3 Jan., 1916...Br.-Gen. H. R. GALE.
4 Mar., 1916 ⎱
-18 Mar., 1918 ⎰ Br.-Gen. C. S. WILSON.

....

9 Oct., 1918...Br.-Gen. E. BARNARDISTON.

D.-D.M.S.

3 Jan., 1916...Col. J. M. F. SHINE.
10 Aug., 1916 ⎱
-10 Mar., 1918 ⎰ Col. T. DU B. WHAITE.

....

9 Oct., 1918...Col. T. DU B. WHAITE.

A.-D. Signals.

3 Jan., 1916...Maj. J. W. DANIELSEN (i/c Corps Signals).
6 Feb., 1916...Maj. J. W. DANIELSEN.
2 Oct., 1916...Maj. O. C. MORDAUNT.
20 Nov., 1916 ⎱
-10 Mar., 1918 ⎰ Lt.-Col. O. C. MORDAUNT.

....

25 Oct., 1918...Lt.-Col. J. A. ARROWSMITH-BROWN.

A.-D.V.S.

16 June, 1917 ⎱
-10 Mar., 1918 ⎰ Lt.-Col. H. S. MOSLEY.

....

9 Oct., 1918...Capt. W. L. LITTLE (tempy.).
29 Oct., 1918...Lt.-Col. S. F. G. PALLIN.

XIV CORPS

FORMATION.

XIV Corps Headquarters formed in France between the 3rd and the 11th January, 1916. The Corps, at first composed of the Guards, 36th, and 55th Divisions, joined the Third Army, which at this time held the line from Curlu on the Somme to Ransart (8 miles south of Arras).

BATTLES AND ENGAGEMENTS.

1916

2–13 June ... ... **Battle of Mount Sorrel*** [20th Div.—Second Army].

BATTLES OF THE SOMME.**

17 Aug.–3 Sept. ... **Battle of Delville Wood** [20th and 24th*** Divs.—Fourth Army].

3–6 September ... ... **Battle of Guillemont** [5th, 16th, and 20th Divs.—Fourth Army].

9 September ... ... **Battle of Ginchy** [15th and 56th Divs.—Fourth Army].

15–22 September ... **Battle of Flers-Courcelette** [Guards, 5th, 6th, 20th, and 56th Divs.; with 17 tanks C Coy.—Gds. (10), 6th (3), and 56th (4)—and in Reserve, 1st Cav. and 5th (Ind.) Cav. Divs.—Fourth Army].

25–28 September ... **Battle of Morval** [Guards, 5th, 6th, 20th, and 56th Divs.; with 2 tanks C Coy. with 56th on 26/9—Fourth Army].

25 September ... ... **Capture of Lesbœufs** [Guards and 6th Divs.—Fourth Army].

26 September ... ... **Capture of Combles** [56th Div.; with 2 tanks C Coy.—Fourth Army].

1–18 October ... ... **Battle of the Transloy Ridges** [4th, 6th, 20th, and 56th Divs.; with 3 tanks C Coy. on 17 and 18/10—4th Div. (1) and 6th Div. (2)—Fourth Army].

---

* 1½ miles S. of Hooge.
** At 4 p.m. 30/7/16 XIV Corps took over VIII Corps front (opp. Beaumont Hamel) in Reserve Army; and at Noon 16/8/16 handed over this front to V Corps. XIV. Corps H.Q. then took over (in the line) from XIII Corps, from midnight 16–17/8/16.
*** 24th Div. was transferred from XIII Corps at Midnight 16–17/8/16; and on 31/8/16 was transferred from XIV Corps to XV Corps.

1917

14–25 March ... ... **German Retreat to the Hindenburg Line** [Guards and 20th* Divs.—Fourth Army].

BATTLES OF YPRES.

31 July–2 August ... **Battle of Pilckem Ridge** [Guards and 38th Divs.—Fifth Army].

16–18 August ... ... **Battle of Langemarck** [20th and 29th Divs.—Fifth Army].

27 August ... ... **Fighting north of St. Julien** [38th Div.—Fifth Army].

20–25 September ... **Battle of the Menin Road Ridge** [Guards, 20th, and 29th Divs.— Fifth Army].

26 Sept.–3 Oct. ... ... **Battle of Polygon Wood** [4th, 20th, and 29th Divs.—Fifth Army].

4 October ... ... **Battle of Broodseinde** [4th and 29th Divs.—Fifth Army].

9 October ... ... **Battle of Poelcappelle** [Guards, 4th, and 29th Divs.—Fifth Army].

12 October ... ... **First Battle of Passchendaele** [Guards, 4th, and 17th Divs.— Fifth Army].

22 October ... ... **Fighting in the Houthulst Forest** [34th and 35th Divs.—Fifth Army].

26–29** October ... **Second Battle of Passchendaele** [35th, 50th, and 57th Divs.— Fifth Army].

On the 29th October XIV Corps Headquarters received orders to move to Italy, and it handed over its Corps front (to the N.E. of Ypres) at 2 p.m. to XIX Corps.

XIV Corps H.Q. left Eperlecques on the 2nd November, reached Pavia on the 5th November ; and, with the 7th, 23rd, and 41st Divisions, XIV Corps took over the Montello Sector of the Piave front on the 4th December.

------

* At 2 p.m. on 25/3/17 the 20th Div. was transferred from XIV Corps to XV Corps, Fourth Army
** At 2 p.m. on 29/10/17 XIV Corps handed over (in the line) to XIX Corps, Fifth Army.

1918

On the 24th February, when the XI Corps was ordered to return to France with the 7th and 41st Divisions, the 48th Division relieved the 7th Division in the Montello Sector on the 28th February.*

On the 9th March XIV Corps took over the Arcade Sector on the Piave from the XI Corps ;** and on the 29th March the XIV Corps took over the Asiago Sector on the mountain front.

Then, on the 18th April, XIV Corps merged in and became G.H.Q. British Force in Italy, under Lieut.-General the Earl of Cavan.

....

Between the 9th and 16th October XIV Corps was re-formed in Italy, and the Corps took part in the final Italian Offensive. In this Offensive the XIV Corps was engaged in the following operations :***

BATTLE OF VITTORIO VENETO [7th and 23rd Divs., XIV (Br.) Corps—Tenth (Italian) Army†].

23–26 October ...   ...   **Capture of the Grave di Papadopoli** [7th Div.].

Night, *26/27–and   28⎫
    October   ⎬ **Passage of the Piave** [7th and 23rd Divs.].

29 October ...   .   **Passage of the Monticano** [23rd Div.].

3 November   ...   ...   **Crossing of the Tagliamento** [7th Div.].

At 3 p.m. on the 4th November the Armistice with Austria brought hostilities to a close on the Italian Front. At this time the 7th Division had reached a line about one-third

---

* See XI Corps and footnote on page 201. On 24/3/18 the 5th Div. was substituted for the 7th Div.

** XIV Corps was relieved in the right sub-sector of the Montello front and in the Arcade sector by the Italian VIII Corps ; and in the left sub-sector of the Montello front by the Italian XXVII Corps.

*** The 7th, 23rd, and 48th Divisions, which fought in the Battle of the Piave, in June, 1918, were under the Italian Sixth Army (see page 67) ; and for the engagement of the 48th Div in the Battle of Vittorio Veneto, under Italian Sixth Army (see footnote, p. 67).

† From 14/10/18 the Italian Tenth Army was commanded by General the Earl of Cavan. The Tenth Army included both XIV (Br.) and XI (Italian) Corps.

1918 *(Contd.)*

of the way between the Tagliamento and Udine ; and on the left of the Corps front the 23rd Division, to the east of Sacile, was midway between the rivers Livenza and Meduna.

XV CORPS
(EGYPT)

G.O.C.

12 January, 1916 ... ... ⎱
–12 April, 1916 ... ... ⎰ Lieut.-General H. S. HORNE.

B.-G.G.S.

12 Jan., 1916...Lt.-Col. P. W. GAME.
25 Jan., 1916...Br.-Gen. P. W. GAME.
8 Feb., 1916⎱ Br.-Gen. C. N.
–12 April,1916⎰ MACMULLEN.

D.-A. and Q.-M.-G.

18 Jan., 1916...Br.-Gen. G. F. MACMUNN.
24 Mar., 1916⎱ Br.-Gen. R. FORD.
–12 April,1916⎰

B.-G.R.A.

18 Jan., 1916⎱ Br.-Gen. J. G. E. WYNNE.
–12 April, 1916⎰

C.E.

12 Jan., 1916...Lt.-Col. P. G. GRANT.
25 Jan., 1916⎱
–12 April, 1916⎰ Br.-Gen. P. G. GRANT.

A.-D. Signals.

13 Jan., 1916...Maj. H. L. MACKWORTH.
8 Mar., 1916⎱ Lt.-Col. H. L. MACKWORTH.
–12 April, 1916⎰

D.-D.M.S.

18 Jan., 1916⎱ Col. C. C. REILLY.
–24 Feb., 1916⎰

NARRATIVE.

Headquarters of XV Corps began to form in Egypt, at Port Said, on the 12th January, 1916.

After formation, XV Corps took over No. 3 (Northern) Section, Canal Zone Defences,* and held this section with the 11th, 13th, and 31st Divisions until the end of February. By that time the garrison of this section was reduced to two divisions—11th and 52nd— and the front was now covered by patrols which were pushed out half-way to Qatia.

On the 8th April, 1916, a telegram from G.H.Q. informed the XV Corps Commander that he and the General Staff of the Corps were to move at once to France, and the command of No. 3 Section of the Canal Zone Defences would be taken over by the G.O.C. 52nd Division. In accordance with this order, Lieut.-General H. S. Horne handed over

---

* Ferdan—Port Said.

1916 *(Contd.)*

command of No 3 Section to Major-General Hon. H. A. Lawrence at 8.15 a.m. on the 12th April. General Horne then left Port Said to proceed to France ; and, as well as the Corps Commander, the D.-A. & Q.-M.-G., Chief Engineer, and Staff Officer R.A.,* also left for France. In due course these four officers joined the new XV Corps which began to form at Vignacourt on the 22nd April, 1916.

XV Corps (Egypt) " ceased to exist " on the 12th April, 1916.**

---

* Major J. D. Byrne. In France he took up, on 24/4/16, the appointment of B.-M. Heavy Artillery.
** The last word of the G.S. Diary is " Finis " (12/4/16) ; and on the same date the Q Diary states : " The XV Corps is disbanded."

XV CORPS
(FRANCE)

G.O.C.

22 April, 1916 ... ... Lieut.-General H. S. HORNE.*
29 September, 1916 ... ... Lieut.-General Sir J. P. DuCANE.
9 a.m. 12 April, 1918 ... Lieut.-General Sir H. DE B. DE LISLE.

B.-G.G.S.

22 April, 1916...Br.-Gen. L. R. VAUGHAN.
23 Sept., 1916...Br.-Gen. W. H.
ANDERSON.
3 Feb., 1917...Br.-Gen. L. R. VAUGHAN.
15 May, 1917...Br.-Gen. H. H. S. KNOX.
12 Aug., 1918...Br.-Gen. G. H. N.
JACKSON (tempy.).
25 Aug., 1918...Br.-Gen. H. H. S. KNOX.

D.-A. and Q.-M.-G.

22 April, 1916...Lt.-Col. H. W. CLINCH
(acting).
8 May, 1916...Br.-Gen. R. FORD.**
2 Dec., 1916...Br.-Gen. G. D. JEBB.
15 Mar., 1917...Br.-Gen. G. R. FRITH.

G.S.O. 1.

....

B.-G.R.A.

22 April, 1916...Br.-Gen. E. W.
ALEXANDER, V.C.
22 Mar., 1917...Br.-Gen. B. R. KIRWAN.

C.H.A.***

22 April, 1916...Br.-Gen. W. J. NAPIER.
26 July, 1916...Br.-Gen. P. D.
HAMILTON (sick, 27/10/16).
19 Nov., 1916...Br.-Gen. C. W. CLARK.
9 May, 1917...Br.-Gen. C. W.
COLLINGWOOD.

---

* Transferred from command of XV Corps (Egypt), broken up at Port Said on 12/4/16 (see pp. 221 and 222).
** Transferred from staff of XV Corps (Egypt).
*** Formed in France on 22/4/16.

C.E.

22 April, 1916...Lt.-Col. C. COFFIN (acting).
 8 May, 1916...Br.-Gen. P. G. GRANT.*
11 Oct., 1916...Br.-Gen. J. A. S. TULLOCH
                    (tempy.).
28 Oct., 1916...Br.-Gen. P. G. GRANT.
15 Jan., 1917...Lt.-Col. R. J. B. MAIR
                    (acting).
25 Jan., 1917...Br.-Gen. S. D'A.
                    CROOKSHANK.
27 Feb., 1917...Br.-Gen. H. J. M.
                    MARSHALL.
29 Mar., 1917...Lt.-Col. A. ROLLAND
                    (acting).
 3 April, 1917...Br.-Gen. C. W. SINGER.

A.-D. Signals.

23 April, 1916...Maj. N. HARRISON.
20 Nov., 1916...Lt.-Col. N. HARRISON.

D.-D.M.S.

22 April, 1916...Col. F. R. NEWLAND.
29 Nov., 1917...Col. A. J. LUTHER.
31 Jan., 1918...Col. G. A. MOORE.

A.-D.V.S.

....
16 June, 1917...Lt.-Col. E. M. PERCY.

---

* Transferred from staff of XV Corps (Egypt).

XV CORPS
(FRANCE)

FORMATION.

XV Corps Headquarters began to form in France at Vignacourt (20 miles W. of Albert), on the 22nd April, 1916. Besides the Corps Commander, only three other Staff Officers (out of a transferable fifteen) joined from the Staff of that XV Corps which had been broken up in Egypt on the 12th April, 1916.*

On the 23rd April the organization of Corps Headquarters proceeded and Corps Troops and Signals arrived. Two days later, at 6.15 p.m. on the 25th, XV Corps Headquarters was ordered to take over the front held by the XIII Corps in the Fourth Army on the Somme. In accordance with these orders, XV Corps Headquarters moved to Heilly, opening there at 10 a.m. on the 29th April, and then took over the 7th and 21st Divisions from XIII Corps.

BATTLES AND ENGAGEMENTS.

1916

BATTLES OF THE SOMME.

1–13 July	**Battle of Albert** [7th, 17th, 21st, 33rd, and 38th Divs.—Fourth Army].
1 July	**Capture of Mametz** [7th Div.—Fourth Army].
2 July	**Capture of Fricourt** [17th Div.—Fourth Army].
7–11 July	**Mametz Wood** [38th Div.—Fourth Army].
14–17 July	**Battle of Bazentin Ridge** [7th, 21st, and 33rd Divs.—Fourth Army].
20–25 July	**Attacks on High Wood** [5th, 7th, 33rd, and 51st** Divs.—Fourth Army].
29 July	**Capture of Longueval** [5th Div.—Fourth Army].
31 Aug.–3 Sept. ...	**Battle of Delville Wood** [5th, 7th, 14th, 17th, and 24th*** Divs.—Fourth Army].

---

* D.-A. & Q.-M.-G., Chief Engineer, and B.M. Heavy Artillery (see p. 222 and fn.).
** Engaged from 21–30/7/16.
*** On 31/8/16 24th Div. was transferred from XIV Corps to XV Corps.

1916 *(Contd.)*

BATTLES OF THE SOMME *(Contd.)*.

3–7 September ... ... **Battle of Guillemont** [7th, 24th, and 55th, Divs.—Fourth Army].

9 September ... ... **Battle of Ginchy** [55th Div.—Fourth Army].

15–22 September ... **Battle of Flers-Courcelette** [14th, 21st, 41st, 55th, and N.Z. Divs. ; with 17 tanks D Coy.—14th (4), 41st (10), and N.Z. (3)—Fourth Army].

15 September ... ... **Capture of Flers** [41st and N.Z. Divs. ; with 1 tank D Coy.—Fourth Army].

25–28 September ... **Battle of Morval** [21st, 55th, and N.Z. Divs. ; with 1 tank D Coy. with 21st Div. (on *26/9*)—Fourth Army].

26 September ... ... **Capture of Gird Trench*** [110th Bde. (21st Div.) ; with 1 tank D Coy.—Fourth Army].

26 September ... ... **Capture of Gueudecourt** [110th Bde. (21st Div.) and 19th Lcrs. (1st Ind. Cav. Div.)—Fourth Army].

1–18 October ... ... **Battle of the Transloy Ridges** [12th, 21st, 29th,** 30th, 41st, and N.Z. Divs. ; with (on *17 and 18/10*) 2 tanks D Coy. with 30th Div.—Fourth Army].

1917

4 March ... ... **Bouchavesnes** [8th Div.—Fourth Army].

14 March–5 April ... **German Retreat to the Hindenburg Line** [8th, 20th,*** and 40th Divs.—Fourth Army].

---

21 ; 24 and 25 April ; and 5 May **Capture of Fifteen Ravine ; Villiers Plouich ; Beaucamp ; and La Vacquerie** [40th Div.—Fourth Army].

---

* First instance in the field of co-operation of Tank and Aeroplane.
** 88th Inf. Bde. under 12th Div.
*** At 2 p.m. on 25/3/17 the 20th Div. was transferred from XIV Corps to XV Corps.

1917 *(Contd.)*

21 June–18 November   **Operations on the Flanders Coast** [1st, 9th, 32nd, 33rd, 41st, 42nd, 49th, and 66th Divs.—Fourth Army].

10 and 11 July ... ...   **Defence of Nieuport** [1st and 32nd Divs.—Fourth Army].

1918

BATTLES OF THE LYS.

9–11 April ... ...   **Battle of Estaires** [31st, 34th, 40th, and 50th Divs., and 74th Bde. (25th Div.), 86th and 87th Bdes. (29th Div.), and 147th Bde. (49th Div.)—First Army].

12–15 April   ... ...   **Battle of Hazebrouck** [31st, 34th,* 40th, 50th,* and 1st Aus.* Divs., and 86th and 87th Bdes. (29th Div.), Comp. Bde. (39th Div.), and Comp. Force (Schools, Pioneers, Entrenching, and Rft. Bns.) ; with 2nd Cav. Div. in Reserve—First Army, until *Noon, 12/4,* then Second Army].

12–15 April   ... ...   **Defence of Nieppe Forest** [29th, 31st, and 1st Aus. Divs.—Second Army].

28 June   ... ...   **La Becque** [31st Div.**—Second Army].

19 July   ... ...   **Capture of Meteren** [9th Div.—Second Army].

---

* At 6 p.m. on 12/4/18 34th Div. had been transferred from XV Corps to IX Corps, Second Army. At 8 a.m. on 12/4/18 50th Div. was transferred from XV Corps to XI Corps, First Army. On 12 and 13/4/18 1st Aus. Div. (Aus. Corps) was transferred from Fourth Army to XV Corps.
** 31st Div. was placed under XI Corps, First Army, for this operation (p. 202).

1918 *(Contd.)*

THE ADVANCE TO VICTORY.

THE ADVANCE IN FLANDERS [9th, 29th, 31st, and 40th Divs.—Second Army].

18 August	**Capture of Outtersteene Ridge** [87th Bde. (29th Div.)—Second Army].
18 August	**Capture of Hoegenacker Ridge** [9th Div.—Second Army].
4 September	**Capture of Ploegsteert and Hill 63** [86th and 88th Bdes. (29th Div.)—Second Army].

THE FINAL ADVANCE.

IN FLANDERS.

28 Sept.—2 Oct. ...	**Battle of Ypres** [14th,* 31st, and 40th** Divs.—Second Army].
14–19 October	**Battle of Courtrai** [14th Div.—Second Army].

XV Corps (14th and 40th Divisions ; and 31st Division, until the last week in October) continued to advance on the right flank of the Second Army. But the Army Front gradually narrowed ; and, after the Schelde had been crossed, the XV Corps received orders to stand fast on the 10th November. That night the X Corps (right of the Second Army) and the XI Corps (left of the Fifth Army) joined hands in front of the XV Corps. The XV Corps (14th and 40th Divisions) was then withdrawn into Second Army Reserve ; and on the next day the Armistice brought hostilities to a close.

Since the Advance in Flanders opened on the 18th August, the XV Corps in 86 days had fought its way forward 50 miles across Flanders.

---

* At 10 a.m. on 2/10/18 the 14th Division was transferred from XIX Corps to XV Corps.
** On 3/10/18 the 40th Division secured the old British Front Line to the east of Armentières, and in this way the town (which had been given up to the Germans on 10/4/18) was recaptured.

XVI CORPS

G.O.C.

17 January, 1916 ... ... Lieut.-General G. F. MILNE.
17 May, 1916 ... ... Lieut.-General C. J. BRIGGS.

B.-G.G.S.

12 Jan., 1916...Br.-Gen. G. N. CORY.
21 Aug., 1917...Br.-Gen. H. L. KNIGHT.

D.-A. and Q.-M.-G.

19 Jan., 1916...Br.-Gen. H. J. EVERETT.
16 Aug., 1917...Br.-Gen. E. D. YOUNG.

B.-G.R.A.

18 Jan., 1916...Br.-Gen. A. W. GAY.
10 Mar., 1917...Br.-Gen. H. E. T. KELLY.

CORPS M.G.O.

....
27 Dec., 1916...Lt.-Col. W. G. F.
BARNARD.

C.E.

16 Feb., 1916...Br.-Gen. H. L.
PRITCHARD.*
12 July, 1916...Br.-Gen. G. WALKER*
(from C.E. XII Corps—tempy.).
11 Aug., 1916...Br.-Gen. H. L. PRITCHARD.

A.-D. Signals.

29 Jan., 1916...Maj. C. H. PRICKETT
(i/c Army Signals).
19 April, 1917...Lt.-Col. C. H. PRICKETT.

D.-D.M.S.

27 Jan., 1916...Col. M. P. C. HOLT.
1 June, 1917...Col. F. SMITH.
26 Jan., 1918...Col. E. T. F. BIRRELL.

A.-D.V.S.

....

---

* From 5/7/16–11/8/16 Br.-Gen. H. L. Pritchard acted as Chief Engineer at G.H.Q. British Salonika Army, but Br.-Gen. G. Walker returned on 26/7/16 to XII Corps.

NOTE.—There was no Corps Heavy Artillery Commander. The Heavy Artillery Groups were under Br.-Gen. P. L. Holbrooke, at G.H.Q. British Salonika Army.

XVI CORPS

FORMATION.

On the 14th December, 1915, the War Office sanctioned the formation of two Corps Headquarters in Macedonia, and on the 28th December XII Corps Headquarters was re-formed at Lembet Camp. The formation of the second Corps Headquarters was, however, temporarily postponed. At that time there were only two divisions available in this theatre of operations, and one of these divisions was in the General Reserve, which was directly under Army Headquarters. Nevertheless, the G.O.C. Eastern Mediterranean sent a direct order to form the second Corps Headquarters at once. As a result of this order, XVI Corps Headquarters began to assemble in the second week in January, 1916 at Avestokhorion (4 miles E. of Salonika).

BATTLES AND ENGAGEMENTS.

1916

OPERATIONS IN THE STRUMA VALLEY.

30 Sept.–2 Oct. ... ... **Capture of the Karajaköis** [10th and 27th Divs.].

2 October ... ... **Occupation of the Mazirko** [84th Bde. (28th Div.)].

3 and 4 October ... **Capture of Yeniköi** [10th and 27th Divs.].

31 October ... ... **Capture of Bairakli Jum'a** (14 miles W.N.W. of Seres) [28th Div.].

17 November; and ⎫
6 and 7 December ⎭ **Tumbitza Farm*** [82nd Bde. (27th Div.)].

1917

15 May ... ... **Capture of Ferdie and Essex Trenches****]28th Div.].

14 October ... ... **Capture of Homondos***** [27th Div.].

16 October ... ... **Capture of Bairakli**† **and Kumli** [28th Div.].

---

* 6 miles S.S.E. of Seres.
** N.W. of Bairakli Jum'a.
*** 5 miles S.W. of Seres.
† East of Bairakli Jum'a (Bairakli Jum'a is 14 miles W.N.W. of Seres.)

1918

THE OFFENSIVE.

18 and 19 September   **BATTLE OF DOJRAN** [28th Div.* and 228th Inf. Bde.,**
together with Greek Crete Div.].***

22–30 September   ...   **Pursuit to the Strumica Valley** [26th Div. and, from *27/9,*
27th Div.† ; together with Greek 14th Div.].

On the 25th September the 26th Division and the Greek 14th Division entered Bulgaria over the western end of the Belašica Planina, and on the next day the Greek Division crossed the Strumica at Dabilja and the British crossed three miles farther to the westward at Strumica town.

At noon on the 30th September, when the Armistice with Bulgaria came into force and brought hostilities to a close in Macedonia, the Anglo-Greek line on this part of the front ran through Barbarevo—Hamzali—Gradošor, some 5 miles to the northward of the River Strumica.

NOTE.—The moves of the British Divisions in Macedonia, from September, 1918, until the Armistice with Germany on the 11th November, are briefly detailed in G.H.Q. British Salonika Army (pp. 61, 62).

---

* In this Battle 83rd Inf. Bde. (less 2/E. York and 1/York and Lanc.) was with XII Corps (on the W. side of Lake Dojran).
** For composition, etc., of 228th Inf. Bde. (Br.-Gen. W. C. Ross), see p. 61 fn. The Bde. was in existence 1/3/17–6/1/19, and served with 28th Div.
*** The following British Heavy and Mountain Artillery was attached to XVI Corps for this Battle of Dojran :
    1, 6″ gun ; 1, 60-pdr. battery ; and 5, 2.75″ (10-pdr.) mountain batteries (III Mtn. Arty. Bde. ; and Argyll Mtn. Bty., and Ross and Cromarty Mtn. Bty.).
† 27th Div. served in XII Corps until 25/9 ; then was in Army Reserve until 27/9 ,when it joined XVI Corps. At Armistice 27th Div. had its head at Kosturino (6 miles S. of Strumica town).

XVII CORPS*

G.O.C.

9 December, 1915	Lieut.-General Sir C. A. ANDERSON**
	(sick, 12/2/16).
12 February, 1916	Major-General Hon. E. J. MONTAGU–STUART–
	WORTLEY (acting).
27 February, 1916	Lieut.-General Hon. J. H. G. BYNG.
25 May, 1916	Lieut.-General Sir C. FERGUSSON, Bt.

B.-G.G.S.

9 Dec., 1915...Br.-Gen. J. R. E.
CHARLES.**
16 July, 1918...Br.-Gen. W. D. WRIGHT,
V.C.

D.-A. and Q.-M.-G.

9 Dec., 1915...Br.-Gen. A. W. PECK.**
11 Feb., 1918...Br.-Gen. J. C. HARDING
NEWMAN.
27 Feb., 1918...Br.-Gen. R. F. A. HOBBS.

G.S.O. 1.

27 Mar., 1918
–5 May, 1918 } Lt.-Col. W. R. PINWILL.

B.-G.R.A.

20 Dec., 1915...Br.-Gen. C. G. HENSHAW.
10 July, 1916...Br.-Gen. C. R. BUCKLE.
7 July, 1917...Br.-Gen. S. F. METCALFE.
30 Sept., 1917...Br.-Gen. E. H. WILLIS.

C.H.A.

....
***
9 April, 1916...Br.-Gen. N. G. BARRON.

---

* When this Corps was formed on 9/12/15 it was given the number XV. On 9/1/16 the Corps number was changed to XVII.
** Transferred from Staff of Indian Army Corps.
(On 9/12/15 the Indian Army Corps was broken up in France, at Norrent Fontes. The Indian Army Corps had landed in France on 30/9/14, and since 7/9/15 had been commanded by Lt.-Gen. Sir C. A. Anderson.)
*** Formed between 9–14/4/16 in France.

C.E.

9 Dec., 1915...Br.-Gen. H. C. NANTON.*
3 May, 1917...Br.-Gen. W. D. WAGHORN
(tempy.).
4 June, 1917...Br.-Gen. H. C. NANTON.
19 Nov., 1917...Br.-Gen. W. D. WAGHORN.

A.-D. Signals.

9 Jan., 1916...Major F. V. YEATS-
BROWN.
20 Nov., 1916...Lt.-Col. F. V. YEATS-
BROWN.
20 Jan., 1917...Lt.-Col. H. C. SMITH.
2 Oct., 1917...Lt.-Col. A. C. CAMERON.
7 Nov., 1917...Major J. STEVENSON
(acting).
15 Dec., 1917...Lt.-Col. A. C. CAMERON.
18 Aug., 1918...Lt.-Col. C. H. WALSH.

D.-D.M.S.

9 Dec., 1915...Col. R. KIRKPATRICK.*
28 Dec., 1917...Col. H. A. BRAY.

A.-D.V.S.

16 June, 1917...Lt.-Col. B. L. LAKE.

---

* Transferred from Staff of Indian Army Corps (broken up in France on 9/12/15).

XVII CORPS

FORMATION.

On the 9th December, 1915, G.H.Q. (France) informed Indian Corps Headquarters (then at Norrent Fontes—4 miles south of Aire) that it would form a new Corps Head-quarters, which would be numbered XV; and, at the outset, the XV Corps was to take over the 14th* and 46th Divisions. As long as any units of the late Indian Corps remained in the First Army Area they were to be administered by the newly-formed XV Corps Headquarters. Between the 11th and 21st December the final appointments to the Headquarters Staff of the XV Corps were received at Norrent Fontes, and the Corps Commander together with 11 of the 19 transferable Staff Officers of the late Indian Corps were posted to and joined XV Corps Headquarters.

On the 9th January, 1916, the XV Corps had its number changed to XVII,** and on the 31st January the newly-numbered XVII Corps moved from Norrent Fontes to the Third Army Area (north of the River Somme). XVII Corps Headquarters was opened at Doullens, and, with the 36th, 46th, and 55th Divisions, took over the front previously held by XIV Corps.

In March, 1916. the Third Army (VI, VII, and XVII Corps) moved northward and took over the Arras Front from the French Tenth Army; and in this rearrangement the XVII Corps (25th, 46th, and 51st Divisions), between the 14th–30th March, took over the northern sector of the Army Front, from Roclincourt—Cabaret Rouge (Givenchy en Gohelle) from the French XII Corps. XVII Corps Headquarters now opened at Marieux.

Thenceforward and until the Advance to Victory in 1918, XVII Corps served on the Arras Front.

BATTLES AND ENGAGEMENTS.

1916

21 May ... ... **German Attack on Vimy Ridge** [25th Div.—Third Army***].

---

* The 14th Div. did not join XV (later XVII) Corps.
** On 12/1/16 another XV Corps H.Q. had formed at Port Said (p. 221); and a XVI Corps H.Q. was about to be formed at Salonika (p. 230).
*** Also see IV Corps and First Army.

1917

BATTLES OF ARRAS.

9–14 April ... ...   **First Battle of the Scarpe** [4th, 9th, 34th, and 51st Divs. ; with 8 tanks 7 Coy., C Bn., 1st Tank Bde.—Third Army].

23 and 24 April   ...   **Second Battle of the Scarpe** [37th and 51st Divs., and 103rd Bde. (34th Div.—with 51st Div.) ; together with 2 tanks, 1st Tank Bde.—Third Army].

28 and 29 April   ...   **Battle of Arleux** [34th and 37th Divs.—Third Army].

3 and 4 May   ...   ...   **Third Battle of the Scarpe** [4th and 9th Divs. ; with 17th Div. in Reserve—Third Army].

13–16 May ... ...   **Capture and Defence of Rœux** [17th and 51st Divs.—Third Army].

1918

FIRST BATTLES OF THE SOMME.

24 and 25 March   ...   **First Battle of Bapaume** [15th Div.—Third Army].

28 March   ...   .   **First Battle of Arras** [4th and 15th Divs.—Third Army].

THE ADVANCE TO VICTORY.

SECOND BATTLES OF ARRAS.*

26–30 August   ...   ...   **Battle of the Scarpe** [52nd, 56th, and 57th Divs.—Third Army].

2 and 3 September ...   **Battle of the Drocourt—Quéant Line** [52nd, 57th, and 63rd Divs.—Third Army].

---

* At Noon, 6/4/18 XVII Corps had been transferred (in the line) from Third Army to First Army.
  At Noon, 23/8/18 the Canadian Corps replaced XVII Corps in the First Army, and XVII Corps was then transferred back (in the line) to the Third Army.

1918 *(Contd.)*

THE ADVANCE TO VICTORY *(Contd.)*.

BATTLES OF THE HINDENBURG LINE.

27 Sept.–1 Oct. ... ... **Battle of the Canal du Nord** [52nd, 57th, and 63rd Divs.; with 15th Bn., 2nd Tank Bde.—Third Army].

8 and 9 October ... **Battle of Cambrai** [24th, 57th, and 63rd Divs.; with part of 12th Bn., 1st Tank Bde.—Third Army].

8 October ... ... **Capture of Niergnies** [63rd Div.—Third Army].

9 October ... ... **Capture of Cambrai** [57th Div.—Third Army].*

9–12 October ... ... **Pursuit to the Selle** [24th Div.—Third Army].

THE FINAL ADVANCE IN PICARDY.

17–25 October ... ... **Battle of the Selle** [19th and 61st Divs.—Third Army].

1 and 2 November ... **Battle of Valenciennes** [61st Div.—Third Army].

4 November ... ... **Battle of the Sambre** [19th and 24th Divs.—Third Army].

5–7 November ... ... **Passage of the Grande Honnelle** [19th and 24th Divs.—Third Army].

The XVII Corps continued to advance on the left of the Third Army. The 19th Division passed through Malplaquet on the 8th November, and on the next day the same division secured the Bois de la Lanière. By 6 p.m. on the 10th November the 24th Division had crossed the Maubeuge—Mons highway and established an outpost line between 1 and 2 miles to the east of this main road. After the Armistice had brought hostilities to a close at 11 a.m. on the 11th November, this Corps outpost line was

---

* Also see First Army.

NOTE.—On 31/10/18 20th Div. joined XVII Corps (from VIII Corps). On 1/11/18 20th Div. Arty. (XCI & XCII Bdes.) supported 19th Div.; and on 10/11/18 60th Inf. Bde. relieved two brigades of 24th Div. on Maubeuge—Mons road.

1918 *(Contd.)*

handed over to the 20th Division* at 4 p.m. on the 11th November, when the 20th Division relieved the 24th Division in the front line.

Since the 26th August the XVII Corps had fought in 7 battles, and had advanced in the face of obstinate resistance some 60 miles in 78 days.

---

* On 31/10/18 the 20th Div. had been transferred, from VIII Corps, First Army, to XVII Corps, Third Army.

XVIII CORPS

G.O.C.

15 January, 1917	Lieut.-General Sir F. I. Maxse.
22 June, 1918	} Lieut.-General Sir A. G. Hunter-Weston.*
–2 July, 1918	

B.-G.G.S.

15 Jan., 1917 }
–2 July, 1918 } Br.-Gen. S. E. Hollond.

D.-A. and Q.-M.-G.

15 Jan., 1917...Br.-Gen. P. M. Davies
(sick, 14/8/17).
14 Aug., 1917...Br.-Gen. B. Atkinson
(tempy.).
8 Nov., 1917 }
–2 July, 1918 } Br.-Gen. L. H. Abbott.*

G.S.O. 1.

29 June, 1918 }
–2 July, 1918 } Lt.-Col. G. Blewitt.*

B.-G.R.A.

15 Jan., 1917 } Br.-Gen. D. J. M.
–2 July, 1918 } Fasson.*

C.H.A.
**

15 Jan., 1917...Br.-Gen. H. E. J. Brake.
27 Mar., 1918 }
–2 July, 1918 } Br.-Gen. L. J. Chapman.*

C.E.

15 Jan., 1917 } Br.-Gen. H. G. Joly de
–2 July, 1918 } Lotbinière.*

A.-D. Signals.

15 Jan., 1917...Lt.-Col. G. E. B. Dobbs
(died of wounds, 17/6/17).
21 June, 1917 } Lt.-Col. W. L. de M.
–2 July, 1918 } Carey.*

D.-D.M.S.

15 Jan., 1917...Col. E. G. Browne.
12 Feb., 1918 }
–2 July, 1918 } Col. H. V. Prynne.*

A.-D.V.S.

....
16 June, 1917 }
–2 July, 1918 } Lt.-Col. W. H. Nicol.*

---

* On 2/7/18 transferred to VIII Corps.
** Formed on 15/1/17 in France.

Note.—On 2/7/18 XVIII Corps H.Q. merged with and became VIII Corps H.Q.

XVIII CORPS

FORMATION.

On the 15th January, 1917, XVIII Corps Headquarters began to form at Pas (7 miles east of Doullens), and at 10 a.m. on the 24th January XVIII Corps took over the 46th and 49th Divisions, forming the right of the Third Army. On the 31st January the 58th Division joined XVIII Corps. The Corps took over the front line southward of Arras and opposite Boisleux, with the V Corps on its right and the VII on its left.

BATTLES AND ENGAGEMENTS.

1917

14—19 March ... ... **German Retreat to the Hindenburg Line** [58th Div.—Third Army; transferred on 19/3 to VII Corps, Third Army].

BATTLES OF YPRES.

31 July–2 August ... **Battle of Pilckem Ridge** [39th and 51st Divs.; with G Bn., 1st Tank Bde.—Fifth Army*].

16–18 August ... ... **Battle of Langemarck** [11th and 48th Divs.; with part of 20 Coy. G Bn., 1st Tank Bde.—Fifth Army].

19 August ... . **The Cockcroft** [11th and 48th Divs.; with 12 tanks of 19 and 20 Cos. G Bn., 1st Tank Bde.—Fifth Army].

22 August ... ... **Fighting in front of St. Julien** [11th and 48th Divs.; with 12 tanks D Bn., 1st Tank Bde.—Fifth Army].

27 August ... ... **Fighting north of St. Julien** [11th and 48th Divs.; with 12 tanks 11 Coy. D Bn., 1st Tank Bde.—Fifth Army].

20–25 September ... **Battle of the Menin Road Ridge** [51st and 58th Divs.; with 34 tanks D and E Bns., 1st Tank Bde.—Fifth Army].

---

* At Noon on 13/6/17 XVIII Corps H.Q. left Fosseux (in Third Army area) and moved to the Convent at Vogeltje (2¼ miles N.W. of Poperinghe). ▌XVIII Corps came under Fifth Army on 13/6/17.

1917 *(Contd.)*

BATTLES OF YPRES *(Contd.)*.

26 Sept.–3 Oct.	**Battle of Polygon Wood** [11th, 48th, 58th Divs.—Fifth Army].
4 October	**Battle of Broodseinde** [11th and 48th Divs. ; with 12 tanks D Bn., 1st Tank Bde.—Fifth Army].
9 October	**Battle of Poelcappelle** [11th and 48th Divs., and 189th Bde. (63rd Div.)—Fifth Army].
12 October	**First Battle of Passchendaele** [9th and 18th Divs.—Fifth Army].
22 October	**Fighting east of Poelcappelle, in Houthulst Forest** [18th Div.—Fifth Army].
26 October–2 November	**Second Battle of Passchendaele** [58th and 63rd Divs.—Fifth Army].*

1918

FIRST BATTLES OF THE SOMME.

21–23 March	**Battle of St. Quentin** [20th, 30th, 36th, and 61st Divs. ; with part of 4th Tank Bde.—Fifth Army].
24 and 25 March ...	**Actions at the Somme Crossings** [20th, 30th, 36th, and 61st Divs., and 2nd and 3rd Cav. Divs. ; with part of 4th Tank Bde.—Fifth Army].
26 and 27 March ...	**Battle of Rosières** [20th, 30th, and 36th Divs. ; with part of 5th Bn. and L.-G. Coy. 13th Bn., 4th Tank Bde.—Fifth Army].

After the Battle of Rosières, at midnight 27th/28th March, 1918, General Humbert (Commanding the French Third Army, south of the R. Somme) placed the 30th and 36th Divisions under General Mesple, and the 20th and 61st Divisions under Lieut.-General

---

* At 10 a.m. on 2/11/17 XVIII Corps, Fifth Army, handed over the 58th and 63rd Divs. and its battle-front to II Corps, Second Army.

1918 *(Contd.)*

H. E. Watts (commanding XIX Corps). XVIII Corps Headquarters was thus deprived of any troops to command on the battle-front, and Corps Headquarters then withdrew down the Somme to Pont Remy. Here Headquarters remained until, in April, it moved to the neighbourhood of St. Pol, and took over the 20th and 24th Divisions. With these divisions, early in May XVIII Corps went into the line on the Lens—Vimy front in the First Army.

XVIII Corps still held this front when, on the 2nd July, Corps Headquarters merged with and became VIII Corps, under the original VIII Corps Commander who had joined and taken over command of XVIII Corps on the 22nd June.

In this fashion the XVIII Corps came to an end before the opening of the Advance to Victory.*

---

* On 2/7/18 XVIII Corps Headquarters was at Camblain l'Abbé (8 miles N.W. of Arras), and at this time the Corps was composed of the 20th, 24th, and 52nd Divisions.

Including the G.O.C. and his 2 aides-de-camp (who had been transferred from the VIII Corps to the XVIII Corps ten days before) of the 36 transferable staff officers of the XVIII Corps, 33 were transferred to the VIII Corps staff on 2/7/18.

XIX CORPS

G.O.C.

4 February, 1917 ... ... Lieut.-General H. E. WATTS.

B.-G.G.S.

9 Feb., 1917...Br.-Gen. F. LYON.
25 Sept., 1917...Br.-Gen. C. N.
MACMULLEN.
[27 Nov., 1918...Br.-Gen. E. N. TANDY.]

D.-A. and Q.-M.-G.

4 Feb., 1917...Br.-Gen. C. R. WOOD-
ROFFE.
23 Mar., 1917...Br.-Gen. A. J. G. MOIR.

G.S.O. 1.

....

B.-G.R.A.

4 Feb., 1917...Br.-Gen. W. B. R. SANDYS.

C.H.A.
*

4 Feb., 1917...Br.-Gen. R. H. F.
MCCULLOCH (sick, 27/6/17).
27 June, 1917...Lt.-Col. A. H. THORP
(acting).
2 July, 1917...Br.-Gen. C. G.
PRITCHARD.
15 April, 1918...Br.-Gen. F. A. WYNTER.

C.E.

4 Feb., 1917...Br.-Gen. A. G. BREMNER
(wounded, 22/3/18).
24 Mar., 1918...Br.-Gen. H. BIDDULPH.

6 June, 1918...Br.-Gen. E. N. STOCKLEY.

A.-D. Signals.

4 Feb., 1917...Lt.-Col. F. V. YEATS-
BROWN.
26 June, 1917...Lt.-Col. J. F. M.
STRATTON.

D.-D.M.S.

4 Feb., 1917...Col. O. R. A. JULIAN.
20 June, 1917...Col. C. E. POLLOCK
(tempy.).
24 July, 1917...Col. H. J. POCOCK.
7 June, 1918...Col. J. D. ALEXANDER.

A.-D.V.S.

....

16 June, 1917...Lt.-Col. C. E. STEEL.

---

* Formed in France on 4/2/17.

XIX CORPS

FORMATION.

On the 4th February, 1917, the XIX Corps Headquarters began to form at Flers (6 miles S.W. of St. Pol). At midnight on the 31st March the 58th Division joined XIX Corps from VII Corps, Third Army, but five days later this division passed on and joined V Corps, Fifth Army. On the 29th April the 30th Division (from VII Corps, Third Army) joined the XIX Corps, which was still in the back area, south of St. Pol.

At noon on the 12th June, 1917, XIX Corps went into the line to the north of Ypres. The Corps took over part of the battle front of the Fifth Army with the 55th Division ; the XIX Corps had the II Corps on its right and the XVIII Corps on its left.

BATTLES AND ENGAGEMENTS.

1917

BATTLES OF YPRES.*

31 July–2 August ...	**Battle of Pilckem Ridge** [15th, 16th, and 55th Divs. ; with C and F Bns., 3rd Tank Bde.—Fifth Army].
16–18 August	**Battle of Langemarck** [15th, 16th, 36th, and 61st. Divs. ; with part of 20 Coy. G Bn., 1st Tank Bde.—Fifth Army].
22 August	**Fighting south of Fortuin** [15th and 61st Divs. ; with 8 tanks C Bn. and 10 tanks F Bn., 3rd Tank Bde.—Fifth Army].
27 August	**Fighting north-west of Zonnebeke** [61st Div.—Fifth Army].
29 Oct.*–10 Nov. ...	**Second Battle of Passchendaele** [17th, 18th, 35th, 50th, and 57th, Divs.—Fifth Army].

---

* At noon on 7/9/17 XIX Corps handed over (in the line) to V Corps ; and at 2 p.m. on 29/10/17 XIX Corps took over (in the line) from XIV Corps, Fifth Army.

1918

FIRST BATTLES OF THE SOMME.

21–23 March ... ... **Battle of St. Quentin** [8th, 24th, 50th, and 66th Divs., and 1st Cav. Div. ; with part of 4th Tank Bde.—Fifth Army].

24 and 25 March ... **Actions at the Somme Crossings** [8th, 24th, 39th,* 50th, and 66th Divs. and 1st Cav. Div. ; with part of 4th Tank Bde.—Fifth Army].

26 and 27 March ... **Battle of Rosières** [8th, 16th, 24th, 39th, 50th, and 66th Divs., and Carey's Force ;** with part of 5th Bn., and L.-G. Coy. 13th Bn., 4th Tank Bde.—Fifth Army].

4 April ... ... **Battle of the Avre** [14th, 18th, and 24th Divs., and 2 Bns.,*** and 5th Aus. Bde. (2nd Aus. Div.), 9th Aus. Bde. (3rd Aus. Div.), 8th and 15th Aus. Bdes. (5th Aus. Div.), and 3rd Cav. Div.—Fourth† Army].

On 30/6/18 XIX Corps (6th and 41st Divisions) took over part of the Second Army front, relieving the Fr. XIV Corps (*D.A.N.*).

THE ADVANCE TO VICTORY.

18 Aug.–6 Sept. ... **THE ADVANCE IN FLANDERS** [6th, 34th, and 41st Divs., and 27th Am. Div.—Second Army].

THE FINAL ADVANCE IN FLANDERS.

28 Sept.–2 Oct. ... ... **Battle of Ypres** [14th,†† 35th, and 41st Divs.—Second Army .

14–19 October ... ... **Battle of Courtrai** [35th and 41st Divs.—Second Army].

25 October ... ... **Ooteghem** [41st Div.—Second Army].

31 October ... ... **Tieghem** [35th Div.—Second Army].

---

* At 4.30 a.m. on 25/3/18, 39th Div. (less 116th Bde.) was transferred (in the line) from VII Corps to XIX Corps, Fifth Army.
** For composition of Carey's Force see under Fifth Army (fn.** on p. 118).
*** 6/London and 7/London. These two battalions of 58th Div. were attached to the 18th Div.
† On 2/4/18 the Fifth Army had been renamed Fourth Army.
†† At 10 a.m. on 2/10/18 the 14th Div. was transferred to XV Corps, Second Army.

1918 *(Contd.)*

On the 6th November the XIX Corps, now on the left of the B.E.F., was in touch with the, French right,* and the British 41st Division was working in co-operation with the French 41st Division.

On the 9th November the Schelde was crossed, and by 11 a.m. on the 11th November, when the Armistice brought hostilities to a close, the XIX Corps had secured Grammont and the line of the River Dendre.

Since the 18th August, when the Advance in Flanders began, the XIX Corps had fought two battles and advanced 46 miles in 86 days.

---

* French VII Corps, Sixth Army (*Groupe d'Armées des Flandres*).

XX CORPS

G.O.C.

2 August, 1917	... ...	Lieut.-General Sir P. W. CHETWODE, Bt.
20 August, 1917	... ...	Major-General J. S. M. SHEA (acting).
31 August, 1917	... ...	Lieut.-General Sir P. W. CHETWODE, Bt.

B.-G.G.S.

2 Aug., 1917...Lt.-Col. S. H. KERSHAW
(acting).
22 Aug., 1917...Br.-Gen. W. H.
BARTHOLOMEW.
15 April, 1918...Br.-Gen. A. P. WAVELL.

D.-A. and Q.-M.-G.

2 Aug., 1917...Br.-Gen. E. EVANS.
26 Jan., 1918...Br.-Gen. C. W. PEERLESS.

B.-G.R.A.

2 Aug., 1917...Br.-Gen. A. H. SHORT.

C.H.A.

(formed 16/12/17)
22 Dec., 1917...Br.-Gen. P. DE S.
BURNEY.

C.E.

2 Aug., 1917... Br.-Gen. R. L. WALLER.

A.D. Signals.

15 Aug., 1917...Lt.-Col. A. N. PAXTON.

D.-D.M.S.

1 Aug., 1917...Col. R. H. LUCE.
19 Sept., 1918...Col. E. B. DOWSETT.

A.-D.V.S.

12 Aug., 1917...Lt.-Col. W. J. DALE.

LOCATION OF XX CORPS H.Q.*

2 August, 1917	... ...	**Deir el Balah** (on the beach)—Formation.
18 August, 1917	... ...	**Wadi es Selka** (S.E. of Deir el Balah).
3 September, 1917	... ...	**El Fuqari.**
30 October, 1917	... ...	**El Baqqar.**
2 November, 1917	... ...	**Beersheba.**
18 November, 1917	... ...	**Red House** (N. Bank of Wadi el Ghazze).
23 November, 1917	... ...	**Junction Station.**
28 November, 1917	... ...	**Latron.**
3 January, 1918	... ...	**Jerusalem.**
19 September, 1918	... ...	**Ram Allah.**
22 September, 1918	... ...	**Huwara.**
24 September, 1918	... ...	**Nablus** (Shechem).
29 October, 1918	... ...	**Haifa.**

Noon, 31 October, 1918. **Armistice with Turkey.**

---

* Including Advanced H.Q.

NOTE.—Deir el Balah to Haifa is 105 miles.

XX CORPS

FORMATION.

XX Corps Headquarters began to form on the 2nd August, 1917, at Deir el Balah (Palestine). On the 18th, Corps Headquarters moved south-eastward to the Wadi es Selka, and on the 3rd September was established at el Fuqari (6 miles east of Rafa). XX Corps took over 10th,* 53rd, 60th, and 74th Divisions, together with the XCVI Heavy Artillery Group,** and 30th and 85th Anti-Aircraft Sections.

XX Corps was responsible for the right section of the line, from Sheikh Abbas to the south (facing towards Beersheba).

BATTLES AND ENGAGEMENTS.

1917

THE INVASION OF PALESTINE.

THIRD BATTLE OF GAZA [10th, 53rd, 60th, and 74th Divs., and Impl. Camel Bde. ; with Berks. Bty., 10th Mtn. Bty., and XCVI H.A.G.**].

31 October	**Capture of Beersheba** [53rd, 60th, and 74th Divs., and Impl. Camel Bde., with Berks. Bty., 10th Mtn. Bty., and XCVI H.A.G.].
3–7 November	**Capture of Tell Khuweilfe** [53rd Div.].
6 November	**Capture of the Sheria Position** [10th, 60th, and 74th Divs., and 10th Mtn. Bty.].

JERUSALEM OPERATIONS.

Noon, 28 November –3rd December	**Turkish Counter-Attacks in Defence of Jerusalem** [52nd, 60th, and 74th Divs., and Yeo. Mtd. Div. and 7th Mtd. Bde.].
7–9 December	**Capture of Jerusalem** [10th, 60th, and 74th Divs., and " Mott's Detnt."***].
26–30 December ...	**Defence of Jerusalem** [10th, 53rd, 60th, and 74th Divs., and XX Corps Cavy.].

---

* H.Q. 10th Div. (from Salonika) reached Rafa at noon, 2/10/17, and came under XX Corps ; on 16/10/17 10th Div. completed its assembly at Rafa.

** 3 Heavy Bties. and 3 Siege Bties.—12, 60-pdrs. and 12, 6″ Hows.

*** Maj.-Gen. S. F. Mott's Detnt. included 53rd Div.,[1] XX Corps Cavalry (2/County of London Yeomanry), 91st Hy. Bty., and 11th L.A.M. Bty.

[1] Less 158th Inf. Bde., on duty between Beersheba and Hebron. Maj.-Gen. S. F. Mott commanded 53rd Division.

1918

OPERATIONS IN THE JORDAN VALLEY.

19–21 February ... ... **Capture of Jericho** [60th Div.; and 1st A.L.H. Bde., and N.Z. M.R. Bde. (A. and N.Z. Mtd. Div.)].

8–12 March ... ... **Tell 'Asur** (9 miles N. of Jerusalem) [10th, 53rd, and 74th Divs., and 181st Bde. (60th Div.); and 1st A.L.H. Bde., and Auckland Mtd. Rif. (A. and N.Z. Mtd. Div.); with 10th Mtn. Bty. and XCVI and XCVII H.A.G.s].

THE FINAL OFFENSIVE.

BATTLES OF MEGIDDO.

19–21 September ... **BATTLE OF NABLUS** [10th and 53rd Divs., and "Watson's Force"*; with 39th Ind. Mtn. Bty., Hong Kong and Singapore Mtn. Bty., and XCVII and CIII Bdes.** R.G.A.].

XX Corps attacked across the rugged hills of Mount Ephraim and drove the Turks northward and westward, and into areas in which enemy resistance had been overcome by the powerful attack of XXI Corps. All attempts at rallying were prevented by the swift advance and unceasing pursuit carried out by the Desert Mounted Corps.

At the end of the Battle of Nablus (on the 21st) the right of the XX Corps outpost line faced eastwards, through Qusra—Agrabe—Yanun—Beit Dejan (53rd Division), thus covering the right flank of the E.E.F. The corps front then swung westward from Jebel el Kebir to northward of and covering Nablus (10th Division). On the 23rd September the 30th Brigade (10th Division) advanced, and on the 24th occupied Tubas, and blocked the road to Beisan. This operation closed the active participation of XX Corps in the Final Offensive.

Thereafter the divisions were employed on salvage work and on improving the Nablus road. Towards the end of October the 53rd Division began entraining for Alexandria; and, when the Armistice with Turkey brought hostilities to a close, at noon on the 31st October, the 10th Division was around Tul Karm.

---

* *Lt.-Col. G. B. Watson's Force* consisted of 1/Worc. Yeo. (XX Corps Cav. Regt.), 1/155 P., 2/155 P., and Detachment from XX Corps Reinforcements Camp. Watson's Force occupied 5 miles of the line in the centre of XX Corps front.
** 1 Heavy Bty. and 6 Siege Bties.—4, 60-pdrs. and 24, 6" howitzers.
XCVII H.A.G. had become XCVII Bde., R.G.A. in April, 1918.
CIII Bde. R.G.A. :—B Group R.G.A. landed at Suez on 17/5/18, became B Bde. on 28/5/18 and CIII Bde. on 3/6/18.

XXI CORPS

G.O.C.

6 p.m. 18 August, 1917 ... ... Lieut.-General E. S. BULFIN.
13 June, 1918 ... ... Major-General Sir V. B. FANE (acting).
14 August, 1918 ... ... Major-General A. R. HOSKINS (acting).
19 August, 1918 ... ... Lieut.-General Sir E. S. BULFIN.

B.-G.G.S.

12 Aug., 1917...Br.-Gen. E. T.
          HUMPHREYS.
27 Feb., 1918...Br.-Gen. H. F. SALT.

D.-A. and Q.-M.-G.

12 Aug., 1917...Br.-Gen. St. G. B.
          ARMSTRONG.

B.-G.R.A.

12 Aug., 1917...Br.-Gen. H. A. D.
          SIMPSON-BAIKIE.

C.H.A.

(Formed 16/12/17).
16 Dec., 1917...Br.-Gen. O. C.
     WILLIAMSON-OSWALD (sick 27/4/18).
27 April, 1918...Lt.-Col. F. P.
          HUTCHINSON (acting).
19 July, 1918...Br.-Gen. O. C.
          WILLIAMSON-OSWALD.

C.E.

12 Aug., 1917...Br.-Gen. R. P. T.
          HAWKSLEY.

A.-D. Signals.

12 Aug., 1917...Lt.-Col. H. McLAREN.
19 Sept., 1917...Lt.-Col. H. C. B.
          WEMYSS.
1 Oct., 1917...Lt.-Col. A. B.
          CUNNINGHAM.
16 Nov., 1917...Lt.-Col. H. L.
          MACKWORTH.
13 Aug., 1918...Lt.-Col. J. R. MARRYAT.

D.-D.M.S.

12 Aug., 1917...Col. C. J. MacDONALD.
4 Mar., 1918...Col. E. P. SEWELL.

A.-D.V.S.

12 Aug., 1917...Lt.-Col. P. J. SIMPSON.
5 July, 1918...Lt.-Col. F. FAIL.

LOCATION OF XXI CORPS H.Q.*

12 August, 1917	**Deir el Balah**—Formation.
1 November, 1917	**Raspberry Hill** (W. of Wadi el Ghazze).
11 November, 1917	**Deir Sneid.**
14 November, 1917	**S. of Es Suafir el Gharbiye.**
19 November, 1917	**El Qubab** (N.E. of Junction Station).
28 November, 1917	**Bir Salem** (near Er Ramle).
4 January, 1918	**Jaffa.**
1 April, 1918	**Jerishe** (on the Nahr el Auja).
19 September, 1918	**Bulfin Hill** (3 miles W. of Mulebbis).
21 September, 1918	**Tul Karm.**
28 September, 1918	**Haifa.**
8 October, 1918	**Beirut.**

Noon, 31 October, 1918. **Armistice with Turkey.**

---

* Including Advanced H.Q.

Note.—Deir el Balah to Beirut is 185 miles.

XXI CORPS

FORMATION.

XXI Corps Headquarters began to form on the 12th August, 1917, at Deir el Balah (Palestine). XXI Corps took over 52nd, 54th, and 75th Divisions, together with XCVII and C Heavy Artillery Groups (and later CII H.A.G.), as well as 38th, 55th, and 102nd Anti-Aircraft Sections, and Detachment Tank Corps (8 tanks).** XXI Corps was responsible for the left section of the line from Sheik Abbas to the Sea (fronting Gaza).

When the Attack on the Gaza Defences (Third Battle of Gaza) opened, XXI Corps Headquarters moved forward to Raspberry Hill (2½ miles east of Deir el Balah and behind the Wadi el Ghazze).

BATTLES AND ENGAGEMENTS.

1917

THE INVASION OF PALESTINE.

THIRD BATTLE OF GAZA.

1–3 November	**Attack on the Gaza Defences** [54th Div. and 156th Bde. (52nd Div.) ; with XCVII, C, and CII H.A.G.s,* and 52nd Div. Arty. ; and Detnt. Tank Corps (8 tanks)**— with 54th Div.].
8 November	**Capture of the Wadi el Hesi Defences** [52nd Div.].

---

* 4 Heavy Batteries and 14 Siege Batteries—16, 60-pdrs. ; 2, 6″ Mk. VII guns ; 40, 6″ hows. ; and 12, 8″ hows.—total 70 heavy guns and howitzers.
C H.A.G. arrived at Alexandria on 1/8/17 ; and CII H.A.G. on 12/9/17.
(CI H.A.G. was in Mesopotamia).
** E Company Machine Gun Corps (Heavy Branch) became Detachment, Tank Corps, E.E.F., on 1/8/17.
On the night of 1st–2nd/11/1917 the 8 tanks moved up to their forward positions, and on 2/11/17 co-operated in the attack of the 54th Division : 4 tanks with the 163rd Brigade—3 reached the 1st Objective. 4 tanks then co-operated in the attacks of the 161st and 162nd Brigades—1 reached the Final Objective and 2 were in the 4th Phase.
After the Battle all the tanks returned to Deir el Balah ; they were all repairable, but they were not again used.

1917 *(Contd.)*

INVASION OF PALESTINE *(Contd.)*.

12 November ... ... **Burqa** (18 miles N.N.E. of Gaza) [156th Bde. (52nd Div.)].

13 November ... ... **El Maghar and**   { [52nd and 75th Divs. ; with 189th Hy. Bty. and 380th

14 November ... ... **Occupation of Junction Station** { Siege Bty., of XCVII H.A.G.].

JERUSALEM OPERATIONS.

17–24 November ... **Battle of Nabi Samweil** [52nd and 75th Divs.].

27 November—Noon { **Turkish Counter-Attacks in Defence of Jerusalem** [52nd, 54th,
28 November   { and 75th Divs.].

11, 15, and 20–22 { **BATTLE OF JAFFA** [52nd, 54th, and 75th Divs. ; with C and
December   { CII H.A.G.s].

21 December ... ... **Passage of the Nahr el Auja** [52nd Div.].

1918

8–12 March ... ... **Tell 'Asur** (9 miles N. of Jerusalem) [54th and 75th Divs., and XXI Corps Cav.* ; with XCV, C, and CII, H.A.G.s].

12 March ... ... **Fight at Ras el 'Ain** [162nd Bde. (54th Div.)].

9–10 April ... ... **Berukin** (20 miles E. of Jaffa) [7th (Ind.), 54th, and 75th Divs., and Aus. Mtd. Div.].

THE FINAL OFFENSIVE.

BATTLES OF MEGIDDO.

19–21 September ... **BATTLE OF SHARON** [3rd (Ind.), 7th (Ind.), 54th, 60th, and 75th Divs., D.F.P.S.,** 5th A.L.H. Bde. ; with VIII and IX Mtn. Bdes., and XCV, XCVI, C, and CII Bdes. R.G.A.***].

---

* Composite Regt. (A Sqdn. Duke of Lancaster's Own Yeo., and A and B Sqdns. 1/Herts. Yeo.).

** *Détachement Français de Palestine et de Syrie* (Col. P. de Piépape)—Régt. de Marche de Tirailleurs, Régt. de Marche de la Légion d'Orient, 1 Terrtl. Bn., 1 Coy. Syrians, 1 dismtd. Sqdn. Spahis, and 3 Mountain Bties. D.F.P.S. attacked on a 3½-mile front, on right of XXI Corps.

*** 5 Heavy and 12 Siege Batteries, with 20, 60-pdrs. ; 2, 6″ Guns, Mk. VII ; 4, 8″ Hows.; and 38, 6″ Hows.

XCV H.A.G. arrived at Alexandria on 20/10/17 ; XCV H.A.G. became XCV Bde. in April, 1918. C H.A.G. was re-designated C Bde. on 25/4/18 ; CII H.A.G. became CII Bde. on 27/4/18 ; and XCVI H.A.G. became XCVI Bde. in April, 1918.

1918 *(Contd.)*

In the Battle of Sharon XXI Corps broke through and overwhelmed the right of the strong Turkish defensive system from Bidya to the sea.

In an irresistible advance the Corps overran and secured Kufr Qa'sim, Qalqilye, et Tire, and, by 5 p.m. on the 19th, Tul Karm. This irruption rolled up the Turkish right and allowed Desert Mounted Corps to sweep forward along the Coastal Plain, complete the envelopment of the Turkish Army, and then press on northward in pursuit.

After the Battle of Sharon died down the divisions of XXI Corps were employed on salvage work and repair of the roads in the battle-area. Early in October the 54th Division concentrated at Haifa, 60th and 75th Divisions left the Corps and came directly under G.H.Q., and the 3rd (Indian) Division did garrison duty under D.M.C.

In the meantime, with the pursuit closing on Damascus, it was decided to secure the coast and ports of Syria, and the 7th (Indian) Division, which had reached Haifa on 29/9, was ordered to march to Beirut along the coast road. Two-and-a-half days were well spent in making the $\frac{1}{2}$-mile stretch of the stepped track of the Ladder of Tyre, which was cut along the cliff, into a road for motors and 60-pdrs. On 29/9 the Division started from Haifa and moved in 3 columns. The leading column entered es Sur (Tyre) on 4/10, Saida (Sidon) on 6/10, and marched into Beirut on 8/10. The 3rd, or Headquarters, Column, accompanied by 15th Heavy Battery (4, 60-pdrs.), left Haifa on 4/10 and reached Beirut on 10/10, covering the 96 miles in 7 days.

On 14/10 the 7th (Indian) Division began to advance from Beirut farther northward up the coast: the leading brigade (19th) reached Tripoli on 18/10, and the whole division concentrated there by 28/10. In 40 days the 7th (Indian) Division had advanced 270 miles.

Meanwhile, on 20/10, the 54th Division, at Haifa, was ordered to move to Beirut, marching by brigade groups at one day's interval. The advance began on 23/10, the brigades moved by Acre, the Ladder of Tyre, Tyre, and Sidon; and by noon on the 31st October, when the Armistice with Turkey brought hostilities to a close in the Near East, the leading troops of the division had reached Beirut; and the whole division completed its concentration in that ancient seaport city on the 5th November. In this way the Syrian coast and harbours were secured.

XXII CORPS

G.O.C.

[28 March, 1916]... ... ... Lieut.-General Sir A. J. GODLEY.*
27 August, 1918 ... ... Lieut.-General Sir W. P. BRAITHWAITE (tempy.).
12 September, 1918 ... ... Lieut.-General Sir A. J. GODLEY.

B.-G.G.S.

[28 Mar., 1916] Br.-Gen. C. W. GWYNN.*

D.-A. and Q.-M.-G.

[28 Mar., 1916] Br.-Gen. A. E. DELAVOYE.*

G.S.O. 1.

11 June, 1918 ⎱ Lt.-Col. P. B. O'CONNOR
–14 July, 1918 ⎰ (tempy).

B.-G.R.A.

[24 July, 1916] Br.-Gen. E. W. M. POWELL.*

C.H.A.
**

[5 Dec., 1916] Br.-Gen. A. S. JENOUR.*

C.E.

[27 Jan., 1917] Br.-Gen. A. E. PANET.*

A.-D. Signals.

[28 Mar., 1916] Major W. T. DODD.
[20 Nov., 1916] Lt.-Col. W. T. DODD.*
6 April, 1918...Lt.-Col. H. C. SMITH.
8 Nov., 1918...Lt.-Col. C. W. M. FIRTH.

D.-D.M.S.

[17 Oct., 1916] Col. C. M. BEGG.*
13 Nov., 1918...Col. E. W. BLISS.

A.-D.V.S.

[16 June, 1917] Lt.-Col. A. W. MASON.*

---

* At Midnight on 31st December, 1917, these officers were transferred from H.Q. II Anzac Corps to H.Q. XXII Corps. The dates in square brackets are the dates on which these officers joined H.Q. of II Anzac Corps. II Anzac Corps began to form in Egypt on 15/2/16, reached France on 7/6/16 and became XXII Corps at Midnight on 31/12/17.
** C.H.A. H.Q. was formed in France on 13/7/16.

XXII CORPS

FORMATION.

At Midnight on the 31st December, 1917, the II Anzac Corps (then holding the Becelaere—Zonnebeke sector of the Ypres front in the Second Army) became the XXII Corps.

Of the 33 transferable staff-officers in II Anzac Corps Headquarters, 29 were transferred forthwith to XXII Corps Headquarters.

The command of the 49th, 66th, and New Zealand Divisions as well as that of the Becelaere—Zonnebeke sector of the Ypres Front, previously under II Anzac Corps, now passed to XXII Corps. Corps Headquarters remained at Abeele (3 miles S.S.W. of Poperinghe).

BATTLES AND ENGAGEMENTS.

1918

BATTLES OF THE LYS.

13–15 April	**Battle of Bailleul** [9th Div. and 62nd Bde. (21st Div.) ; with part of L.-G. unit 5th Bn., 4th Tank Bde.—Second Army].
17–19 April	**First Battle of Kemmel Ridge** [9th and 21st Divs., and Comp. Bde. (39th Div.), and 146th Bde. (49th Div.), and French 28th Div., with part of L.-G. unit 4th, 5th, and 13th Bns., 4th Tank Bde.—Second Army].
25 and 26 April ...	**Second Battle of Kemmel Ridge** [6th, 9th, 21st ; 25th (on *26/4*), 30th, and 49th Divs., and Comp. Bde. (39th Div.), and XXII Corps Mtd. Troops ; with part of L.-G. unit 4th, 5th, and 13th Bns., 4th Tank Bde.—Second Army].
29 April	**Battle of the Scherpenberg** [[6th, 21st, 25th, 30th, and 49th Divs., and Comp. Bde. (39th Div.), and S. African Bde. (9th Div.) ; with part of L.-G. unit 4th, 5th, and 13th Bns., 4th Tank Bde.—Second Army].

1918 *(Contd.)*

THE ADVANCE TO VICTORY.

THE BATTLES OF THE MARNE.*

20–31 July ... ... **Battle of Tardenois** [51st and 62nd Divs.—French Fifth Army].

20–31 July ... ... **Fighting for the Ardre Valley** [51st and 62nd Divs.—French Fifth Army].

SECOND BATTLES OF ARRAS.**

29 and 30 August ... **Battle of the Scarpe** [51st Div. and 11th Div. (from 30/8)—First Army].

2 and 3 September ... **Battle of the Drocourt —Quéant Line** [11th and 51st Divs.; with part of 9th, 11th, and 14th Bns., 3rd Tank Bde. —First Army].

BATTLES OF THE HINDENBURG LINE.

27 Sept.–1 Oct. ... ... **Battle of the Canal du Nord** [4th and 56th Divs.—First Army].

8 and 9 October ... **Battle of Cambrai** [56th and 1st Cdn. Divs.—First Army].

9–12 October ... ... **Pursuit to the Selle** [56th and 1st Cdn. Divs., until *5 p.m. 11/10/18* ;*** then 49th, 51st, and 2nd Cdn. Divs.—First Army].

---

* XXII Corps (51st and 62nd Divs.) started southward for the French zone on 13/7/18 and detrained behind the Marne. Two days later the 15th and 34th Divs. followed ; and, on detraining, collected at Verberie and Senlis.
51st and 62nd acted directly under XXII Corps (as given above) in the French Fifth Army, and attacked the eastern face of the German salient.
15th and 34th Divs. operated against the western face of the German salient and fought under the French Tenth Army in the Battle of the Soissonais and of the Ourcq—15th Div. under French XX Corps and 34th Div. under French XXX Corps.
Between 31/7–7/8 the four British Divisions of XXII Corps left the Marne battle-area and returned to the British zone.
** On 29/8/18 XXII Corps took over the 51st Div. and the front line immediately north of the R. Scarpe. On the next day the 11th Div. came into the line, under XXII Corps, and took over the front immediately south of the R. Scarpe, in the First Army.
*** From 5 p.m. 11/10/18 the XXII Corps and Canadian Corps exchanged fronts.

1918 *(Contd.)*

THE FINAL ADVANCE IN PICARDY.

17–25 October ... ... **Battle of the Selle** [4th, 49th, and 51st Divs.—First Army].

1 and 2 November ... **Battle of Valenciennes** [4th and 49th Divs.—First Army].

4 November ... ... **Battle of the Sambre** [11th and 56th Divs.—First Army].

5–7 November ... ... **Passage of the Grande Honnelle** [11th, 56th, and 63rd Divs.—First Army].

The XXII Corps (on the right of the First Army) continued to press on rapidly eastward, and on the 9th November crossed the Maubeuge—Mons highway. When the Armistice brought hostilities to a close, at 11 a.m. on the 11th November, the right of the Corps was established along the railway to the east of Vieillereille le Sec, and its left was about a mile to the eastward of Villers St. Ghislain. At this time, XXII Corps Headquarters was at Sebourg (5 miles east of Valenciennes).

In the 115 days, since the Advance to Victory opened on the 20th July, the XXII Corps had fought in 8 battles ; and in the last 75 days, during which the XXII Corps fought in the First Army, it had advanced 50 miles.

All the divisions of the XXII Corps were represented on the 15th November at the Ceremonial Parade in the Grande Place, when the Commander of the First Army made his official entry into Mons.

The XXII Corps was one of the corps originally selected to advance to the German Frontier ; but the order was cancelled after Corps Headquarters had moved up to Mons on the 24th November. Corps Headquarters then remained at Mons and supervised the clearing up, etc., of the surrounding area.

XXIII CORPS
(HOME FORCES)

G.O.C.

16 February, 1918	Lieut.-General Sir W. P. Pulteney.
7 May, 1918	Lieut.-General Sir T. D'O. Snow (tempy.).
5 August, 1918	Lieut.-General Sir W. P. Pulteney.

B.-G.G.S.

16 Feb., 1918...Br.-Gen. W. G.
  Braithwaite.
15 Oct., 1918...Br.-Gen. A. W. Tufnell.

D.-A. and Q.-M.-G.

17 Feb., 1918...Br.-Gen. R. S. Oxley.

B.-G.R.A.

17 Feb., 1918...Br.-Gen. G. H. W.
  Nicholson.
29 July, 1918...Br. Gen. Sir D.
  Arbuthnot, Bt.

C.E.

17 Mar., 1918...Br.-Gen. G. D. Close.

A.-D. Signals.

17 Feb., 1918...Lt.-Col. R. M. Powell.

D.-D.M.S.

17 Feb., 1918...Col. L. J. Blandford.

A.-D.V.S.

17 Feb., 1918...Lt.-Col. E. D. Johnson.

A.-D.S. and T.

17 Feb., 1918...Col. E. F. Taylor.

NARRATIVE.

In the latter half of February, 1918, XXIII Corps Headquarters assembled at Brentwood and remained there until August, 1918. Corps Headquarters then moved to Bury St. Edmunds, and was still there on the 11th November, 1918, when the Armistice with Germany brought the Great War to a close.

XXIII Corps did not serve in any theatre of active operations.

XXIV CORPS

20–29 March, 1918 ... ... Lieut.-General G. DE S. BARROW.

B.-G.G.S.

20–29 March, 1918 ... ... Br.-Gen. A. P. WAVELL.

B.-G.R.A.		D.-A. and Q.-M.-G.
C.H.A.	Had not assembled by 29/3/18, when	D.-D. M.S.
C.E.	XXIV Corps H.Q. was dissolved	A.-D.V.S.
A.-D. Signals.		A.-D. S. and T.

NARRATIVE.

In the early spring of 1918 arrangements had been made to reinforce the E.E.F. with two Indian Divisions, and in consequence it became necessary to increase corps headquarters with the E.E.F. from two to three. On the 15th March the formation of XXIV Corps Headquarters was authorized, and the name of the suggested Corps Commander was submitted to and approved by the Army Council. General Barrow met his B.-G.G.S. in Cairo on the 20th March and started to work out details connected with the new formation.

On the 21st March, however, the Great German Offensive opened in France, and an urgent demand was made on the E.E.F. for immediate reinforcements to strengthen the Western Front. As a result, during April, two infantry divisions (52nd and 74th) left Palestine for France. The formation of a third Corps in the E.E.F. became unnecessary.

After ten days' existence XXIV Corps Headquarters was dissolved.*

---

* General Barrow returned to his original command :—G.O.C. Yeomanry Mounted Division ; and the appointment of Maj.-Gen. H. J. M. Macandrew to command that division (vice General Barrow) was cancelled on 9/4/18.
Br.-Gen. A. P. Wavell joined the Staff of XX Corps on 15/4/18 as B.-G.G.S.

RESERVE CORPS

G.O.C.

4 April, 1916 ... ... Lieut.-General H. DE LA P. GOUGH.

B.-G.G.S.

4 April, 1916...Capt. E. H. L.
          BEDDINGTON (acting).
14 April, 1916...Br.-Gen. N. MALCOLM.

D.-A. and Q.-M.-G.

4 April, 1916...Lt.-Col. F. D. RUSSELL
                    (acting).
27 April, 1916...Capt. A. J. HUNTER
                    (acting).

B.-G.R.A.

30 April, 1916...Br.-Gen. W. STRONG.

C.H.A.

....

C.E.

....

A.-D. Signals.

4 April, 1916...Major L. W. DE V.
                    SADLEIR-JACKSON.

D.-D.M.S.

4 April, 1916...Capt. A. J. A. MENZIES
                    (acting).

D.-A.-D. Remounts.

4 April, 1916...Lt.-Col. J. W. YARDLEY.

NARRATIVE.

Headquarters Reserve Corps began to form at Wailly (4 miles S. of Montreuil sur Mer) on the 4th April, 1916 ; and on the 12th May moved to Regnière Écluse (5 miles W.N.W. of Crécy). Headquarters Reserve Corps was still in the same position on the 22nd May, 1916, when the Corps Headquarters became Headquarters Reserve Army* (pp. 111–115).

---

* Reserve Army became Fifth Army on the 30th October, 1916.

MACHINE GUN CORPS (HEAVY SECTION)

LATER

MACHINE GUN CORPS (HEAVY BRANCH)*

THEN

TANK CORPS**

COMMANDER.

19 March, 1916	Colonel E. D. SWINTON.***
1 September, 1916	Lieut.-Col. R. W. BRADLEY.***
29 September, 1916	Colonel H. J. ELLES.
15 February, 1917	Br.-General H. J. ELLES.
16 April, 1918	Major-General H. J. ELLES.

DEPUTY TO MAJOR-GENERAL.

5 November, 1918 ... ... Br.-Gen. H. KARSLAKE.

Brigade-Major.

8 Oct., 1916 ⎫
–18 Dec., 1916 ⎬ Capt. G. LE Q. MARTEL.

D.-A.-A. and Q.-M.-G.

26 Sept., 1916 ⎫
–14 Feb., 1917 ⎬ Capt. T. J. UZIELLI.

G.S.O. 2.

26 Dec., 1916 ⎫
–23 April, 1917 ⎬ Maj. J. F. C. FULLER.

G.S.O. 1.

24 April, 1917...Lt.-Col. J. F. C. FULLER.
1 Aug., 1918...Lt.-Col. H. KARSLAKE.
7 Nov., 1918...Col. H. W. B. THORP.

A.-A. and Q.-M.-G.

15 Feb., 1917 ⎫
–4 Nov., 1918 ⎬ Lt.-Col. T. J. UZIELLI.

D.-A. and Q.-M.-G.

5 Nov., 1918...Col. T. J. UZIELLI.

---

* This title dates from 18/11/16.
** The Tank Corps was formed on 27/7/17 (A.O. 239/1917), and all officers and other ranks of the M.G.C. (Heavy Branch) were transferred to the Tank Corps (A.O. 240/1917).
On 17/10/18 H.M. The King became Colonel-in-Chief of the Tank Corps ; and on 18/10/23 H.M. conferred the distinction of " Royal " on the Tank Corps (A.O. 369/1923).
*** Col. E. D. Swinton raised, equipped, and trained M.G.C. (Heavy Section) and remained in command and at home until 9/11/16. From 4/4/16 Lt.-Col. R. W. Bradley was in command of the camp at Elveden and in charge of the training under Col. Swinton. On 1/9/16 Lt.-Col. Bradley went to France to command M.G.C. (Heavy Section) in the field ; and during his tenure of command in France his staff officer was Major W. F. R. Kyngdon.

A.-D. Signals.

27 August, 1917 ... ... Lt.-Col. J. D. N. MOLESWORTH.

Controller of Workshops and Salvage and Chief Mechanical Engineer.

24 Nov., 1916...Lt.-Col. F. SEARLE.

Central Workshops* and Stores.

24 Nov., 1916...Maj. J. G. BROCKBANK.
22 Nov., 1917...Lt.-Col. J. G. BROCK-
BANK.**

A.-D. Ordnance Services.

June, 1917...Capt. J. H. VERNALL
(D.-A.-D.O.S.)
27 Aug., 1917...Maj. J. H. VERNALL.
29 May, 1918...Lt.-Col. J. H. VERNALL.

A.-D. Transport.

16 April, 1918...Lt.-Col. W. BELFIELD.

D.-A.-D. Medical Services.

September, 1917 ... ... Capt. L. R. BROSTER.
25 February, 1918 ... ... Maj. L. R. BROSTER.

---

* Original title was " Central Repair Shops and Store ". It occupied about 27 acres and was situated a thousand yards west of the village of Erin (on the left bank of the Ternoise, some 7 miles to the N.W. of St. Pol.) The original establishment allowed for 13 officers and 394 other ranks. The Central Repair Shops and Store was started on 7/1/17 and was completed before 30/6/17; in this year the Workshops repaired and re-issued 227 tanks. Expansion soon became an urgent necessity; and on 29/3/18 new workshops were opened at Teneur (1 mile N.E. of Erin, and on the right bank of the Ternoise). In 1918 the number of tanks repaired (or altered) and re-issued was 2,523.
** On 19/12/18 Lt.-Col. Brockbank was promoted to Colonel and appointed Chief Engineer, Tank Corps (France).

1st BRIGADE, M.G.C. (H.B.).
(Formed 1/2/17).

15 Feb., 1917...Col. C. D'A. B. S. BAKER-
CARR.

On 27/7/17 1st Bde. M.G.C. (H.B.)
became

1st TANK BDE., TANK CORPS.

[15 Feb., 1917] Col C. D'A. B. S. BAKER-
CARR.
16 April, 1918...Br.-Gen. C. D'A. B. S.
BAKER-CARR.
[17 Nov., 1918...Br.-Gen. G. A. Mc L.
SCEALES.]

2nd BRIGADE, M.G.C. (H.B.).
(Formed 15/2/17).

5 Mar., 1917...Col. A. COURAGE.

On 27/7/17 2nd Bde. M.G.C. (H.B.)
became

2nd TANK BDE., TANK CORPS.

[5 Mar., 1917] Col. A. COURAGE.

31 Mar., 1918...Br.-Gen. A. PARKER
(on leave, 24/9/18 ; then sick).
24 Sept., 1918...Lt.-Col. G. A. Mc L.
SCEALES (acting).
18 Oct., 1918...Br.-Gen. H. K. WOODS.

3rd BRIGADE, M.G.C. (H.B.).
(Formed 24/4/17).

6 May, 1917...Col. J. HARDRESS-LLOYD.

On 6/8/17 3rd Bde. M.G.C. (H.B.)
became

3rd TANK BDE., TANK CORPS.

[6 May, 1917] Col. J. HARDRESS-LLOYD.
16 April, 1918...Br.-Gen. J. HARDRESS-
LLOYD.
[13 Nov., 1918...Lt.-Col. W. G. A. RAMSAY-
FAIRFAX (acting).
20 Nov., 1918...Br.-Gen. W. G. A.
RAMSAY-FAIRFAX].

4th TANK BDE., TANK CORPS.
(Formed 1/1/18).

1 Jan., 1918...Col. E. B. HANKEY.
20 April, 1918...Br.-Gen. E. B. HANKEY.
9 Nov., 1918...Br.-Gen. J. MICKLEM.

5th TANK BDE., TANK CORPS.
(Formed 3/3/18).

3 Mar., 1918...Col. A. PARKER.
31 Mar., 1918...Br.-Gen. A. COURAGE.
15 Aug., 1918...Lt.-Col. E. D. BRYCE (acting).
24 Aug., 1918...Br.-Gen. A. COURAGE.
2 Nov., 1918...Br.-Gen. S. H. CHARRINGTON.

6th TANK BDE., TANK CORPS.
(Formed 12/10/18).

12 Oct., 1918...Br.-Gen. R. PIGOT.

NOTE.—For Nos. 1, 2, and 3 Tank Groups see Appendix 5

TANK CORPS

FORMATION.

In 1915 sanction was given for the provision of " tanks,"* and in April, 1916, the first of the six fighting companies, which were to man them, began to form at Bisley. The first four companies (A, B, C, and D) were to be ready to move to France in August.**

The officer responsible for raising and equipping the new Corps was Colonel E. D· SWINTON, its first commanding officer.

The personnel consisted of officers and men transferred from the obsolescent Motor Machine-Gun Service. Many of the officers were appointed from the large numbers of N.C.O.s who had been sent back from France to England as cadets, to be trained for Commissions, and Colonel Swinton selected those with mechanical and motor knowledge

At the beginning of June, 1916, the companies moved from Bisley to Elveden (near Thetford) to secure a training ground free from observation ; and, on arrival, they took over the new machines and began to train with them. At Thetford Lieut.-Colonel R. W. BRADLEY joined and assumed command of the Heavy Section of the Machine Gun Corps, as it was then styled.***

The Companies took over Mark I Tanks, which on level ground had a speed of about 4 miles an hour and possessed a radius of action of about 10 hours, without a refill. Tanks were either " male " (2 Hotchkiss 6-pdrs. and 4 Hotchkiss machine guns), or " female " (4 Vickers machine Guns and 1 Hotchkiss machine gun). Each Company was organized in 4 sections, each section being armed with 6 tanks (3 male and 3 female). Each section was further subdivided into 3 subsections of 2 tanks each. In addition, each company was provided with one reserve tank. A tank crew consisted of 1 subaltern, 3 drivers, and 4 gunners (one was a non-commissioned-officer). In France the companies were served by 3 mobile workshops.

---

* This name was adopted for the landships on 24/12/15.
** A., B., C., and D. Companies were all formed in May, 1916. A Coy. reached France on 12/9/16 ; B Coy. on 16/10/16 ; C Coy. on 23/8/16 ; and D Coy. on 3/9/16.
 The provisional establishment allowed for the Headquarters of the Corps—then Heavy Section, Machine Gun Corps—was Colonel Commanding, Brigade-Major, Staff Captain, D.-A.-A. and Q.-M.-G., and an Intelligence Officer.
 E Tank Coy. M.G. Corps (Heavy Branch) landed at Alexandria on 9/1/17 and served in Egypt and Palestine. Its engagements are recorded in G.H.Q., E.E.F., and in XXI Corps (pp. 38 and 39 ; and 253).
*** Hereafter, throughout this narration, only the designation Tank Corps is used ; although it was not the official title of the Corps until 27/7/17.

270

On the 13th August, 1916, the first detachment of C Company left Thetford for France with 13 tanks; the remainder of the Company (with the remaining 12 tanks) followed on the 22nd. A few days later the right-half company of D entrained at Thetford, and the rest of the company reached France a week later. On arrival in the theatre of war C and D Tank Companies concentrated at the training centre established by Lt.-Col. J. Brough at Yvrench in Picardy.* In September Lt.-Col. Bradley reached Yvrench; Col. Brough then handed over command of the training-centre and returned to England. Shortly afterwards C and D Companies moved forward to a more realistic training-ground—The Loop, which lay to the northward of Bray on the Somme.

To this destination the tanks were moved by train, for secrecy; and by the 9th September the concentration was completed. Three days later A Tank Company reached France and on the 14th it was established at Yvrench.**

In the meantime, on the 11th September, C and D Tank Companies*** received operation orders for the Battle of Flers—Courcelette, in which they were to co-operate on the 15th September with the Fourth and Reserve Armies. In the Fourth Army: 17 tanks of C Company were to attack with XIV Corps, 17 tanks of D Company with XV Corps, and 8 tanks of D with III Corps. In the Reserve Army: 6 tanks of C Company were to co-operate with the Canadian Corps. (In addition, 10 tanks were allotted to Headquarters, but they were all unfit for action on the 15th.)

Unfortunately, the limited time available (after C and D Companies reached The Loop) had been insufficient to obtain adequate practice in driving tanks over shell-torn ground, nor was there time to make a detailed reconnaissance of the area of the impending attack. On the other hand, the fine, dry weather was favourable for tank operations; and though it was misty at daybreak on the 15th September, this soon cleared away, and for the rest of the day the visibility was good.

---

* 5 miles N.E. of Abbeville.
** The 4 Companies reached Le Havre as follows: A, 12/9/16; B, 16/10/16; C, 23/8/16; and D, 3/9/16.
*** C Company was commanded by Major A. Holford—Walker and D Company by Major F. Summers.

BATTLES AND ENGAGEMENTS.

1916

BATTLES OF THE SOMME.

15 and 16 September	**Battle of Flers-Courcelette** [48 tanks: 17 tanks C Coy. with XIV—56th (4), 6th (3), and Gds. (10); 17 tanks D Coy. with XV—14th (4), 41st (10), and N.Z. (3); 8 tanks D Coy. with III—15th (4), 50th (2), and 47th (2): Fourth Army; and 6 tanks C Coy., with 2nd Cdn. Div., Cdn. Corps: Reserve Army].
15 September	**Capture of Flers** [1 tank D Coy. with 41st and N.Z. Divs., XV: Fourth Army].
15 September	**Capture of Martinpuich** [4 tanks D Coy. with 15th Div., III: Fourth Army].
25 and 26 September	**Battle of Morval** [*25/9*: 2 tanks D Coy. with 23rd Div., III; and *26/9*: 2 tanks C Coy. with 56th Div., XIV, and 1 tank D Coy. with 21st Div., XV: Fourth Army].
26 September	**Capture of Gird Trench*** [1 tank D. Coy., with 21st Div., XV: Fourth Army].
26 September	**Battle of Thiepval Ridge** [2 tanks C Coy. with 3rd Cdn. Div., Cdn. Corps; and 6 tanks C Coy. with 18th (4) and 11th (2), II: Reserve Army].
26 September	**Capture of Mouquet Farm** [2 tanks C Coy. with 11th Div., II: Reserve Army].
17 and 18 October ...	**Battle of the Transloy Ridges** [5 tanks C and D Cos. with 4th (1), 6th (2), XIV; and 30th (2), XV: Fourth Army].
21 October	**Battle of the Ancre Heights** [4 tanks A Coy. with 18th, II: Reserve Army**].
13–18 November ...	**Battle of the Ancre** [*13/11*: 3 tanks A Coy. with 39th, II, and 2 tanks D Coy. with 51st, V; *14/11*: 3 tanks D Coy. with 63rd, V; *16/11*: 2 tanks D Coy. with 2nd, V; *18/11*: 5 tanks D Coy. with 32nd (4), and 51st (1), V, and 3 tanks A Coy. with 19th, II: Fifth Army**].

---

* The first instance of the co-operation of tank and aeroplane in the field.
** Reserve Army became Fifth Army on 30/10/16.

NOTE.—In the formations with which the Tanks co-operated: Divisions are indicated thus—Gds., 21st, 47th, etc.; and Corps are given in Roman numerals—II, V, XV, etc.

1916 *(Contd.)*

BATTLES OF THE SOMME *(Contd.)*.

13 November ... ... **Capture of Beaumont Hamel** [2 tanks D Coy. with 51st, V : Fifth Army].

14 November ... ... **Capture of Beaucourt** [2 tanks D Coy. with 63rd, V : Fifth Army].

Beginning in November a complete reorganization of the Tank Corps was undertaken, so as to meet the increased supply of weapons which had been authorized. Training establishments at home were expanded ; and a programme for the training of 14 new battalions was undertaken. All personnel were fused into one Corps. In France, on 18/11/16 the existing tank companies were expanded into battalions, by the formation of new companies. The battalions thus formed were designated by letters. In France, also, a large central repair shop and store was planned,* and General, Administrative, Engineering, and Technical Staffs were appointed.

1917

In February two Brigades were formed by grouping together the newly-formed tank battalions, and towards the end of April a third Brigade was added.

BATTLES OF ARRAS.

9–14 April ... ... **First Battle of the Scarpe**** [C Bn. and 10 Coy. D Bn., 1st Tank Bde., with VI, VII, and XVII : Third Army : and on *11/4*, 11 tanks of 11 Coy. D Bn., 1st Tank Bde., with V : Fifth Army].

11 April ... ... **Capture of Wancourt** [4 tanks 10 Coy. D Bn., 1st Tank Bde., with VII : Third Army].

11 April ... ... **Capture of Monchy le Preux** [7 tanks of 8 and 9 Cos. C Bn., 1st Tank Bde., with VI : Third Army].

9–14 April ... ... **Battle of Vimy Ridge**** [8 tanks of 12 Coy. D Bn., 1st Tank Bde., with Cdn. Corps : First Army].

23 and 24 April ... **Second Battle of the Scarpe** [20 tanks, 1st Tank Bde., with VI, VII, and XVII : Third Army].

3 and 4 May ... ... **Third Battle of the Scarpe** [4 tanks, 1st Tank Bde., with VII : Third Army].

3 May ... ... **Battle of Bullecourt** [12 tanks, 1st Tank Bde., with V : Fifth Army].

---

* See p. 268 and fn.
** At Zero on 9/4/17 C Bn. had 28 tanks and D Bn. 32 tanks—total, 60 tanks (35 male and 25 female).

1917 *(Contd.)*

7–14 June ... ... **Battle of Messines** [72 tanks of A Bn., and B Bn., 2nd Tank Bde., with II Anzac, IX, and X Corps : Second Army].

BATTLES OF YPRES.

31 July–2 August ... **Battle of Pilckem Ridge*** [G Bn., 1st Tank Bde., with XVIII ; A and B Bns., 2nd Tank Bde., with II ; C and F Bns., 3rd Tank Bde., with XIX ; D Bn., 1st Tank Bde., in Army Reserve : Fifth Army].

16 August ... ... **Battle of Langemarck** [20 Coy. G Bn., 1st Tank Bde., with Fifth Army].

19 August ... ... **The Cockcroft** [12 tanks, 19 and 20 Cos. G Bn., 1st Tank Bde., with 11th and 48th ; XVIII : Fifth Army].

22 August ... ... **Fighting south of Fortuin** [8 tanks C Bn. and 10 tanks F Bn., 3rd Tank Bde., with 15th and 61st, XIX : Fifth Army].

22 August ... ... **Fighting in front of St. Julien** [4 tanks, 2nd Tank Bde., with 14th and 47th, II ; and 12 tanks D Bn., 1st Tank Bde., with 11th and 48th, XVIII : Fifth Army].

22 and 23 August ... **Fighting on the Menin Road** [A Bn., 2nd Tank Bde., with 14th, 23rd, and 24th, II : Fifth Army].

27 August ... ... **Fighting north of St. Julien** [12 tanks 11 Coy. D Bn., 1st Tank Bde., with 11th and 48th, XVIII : Fifth Army].

20 September ... ... **Battle of the Menin Road Ridge** [34 tanks D and E Bns., 1st Tank Bde., with XVIII ; and 18 tanks C and F Bns., 3rd Tank Bde., with V : Fifth Army].

28 September ... ... **Battle of Polygon Wood** [15 tanks E Bn., 1st Tank Bde., with II Anzac : Second Army].

4 October ... ... **Battle of Broodseinde** [12 tanks D Bn., 1st Tank Bde., with XVIII : Fifth Army].

---

* On **31/7/17** there were 120 tanks, as well as **48** tanks in Army Reserve.

1917 *(Contd.)*

BATTLE OF CAMBRAI.

20 and 21 November   **The Tank Attack*** [1st Tank Bde. with IV, and 2nd Tank Bde. (less A Bn.) and 3rd Tank Bde. (with A. Bn.), with III : Third Army].

21 November ... ... **Capture of Cantaing** [12 tanks B. Bn., 2nd Tank Bde., with 51st Div. (IV) : Third Army].

21 November ... ... **Recapture of Noyelles** [2 tanks B. Bn., 2nd Tank Bde., with 6th Div. (III) ; Third Army].

23–28 November ... **Capture of Bourlon Wood**** [1st and 3rd Tank Bdes., with IV ; and 2nd Tank Bde. with III and IV : Third Army].

30 Nov –1 Dec. ... ... **German Counter-Attacks***** [1st and 2nd Tank Bdes. with III and 3rd Tank Bde. with IV : Third Army].

30 November ... ... **Attack on Gouzeaucourt** [22 tanks, 2nd Tank Bde., with Gds. Div. (III) : Third Army].

1 December ... ... **Attack on Villers Guislain and Gauche Wood** [19 tanks, 2nd Tank Bde. with Gds. and 12th Divs., and 4th (Ind.) and 5th (Ind.) Cav. Divs. (III) : Third Army].

1918

A considerable expansion of the Tank Corps took place early in this year : a fourth Tank Brigade was formed on the 1st January, and a fifth Brigade was added at the beginning of March. New designations were adopted during this expansion : Tank Battalions were numbered and Tank Companies were lettered.

---

* On 20/11/17 324 tanks attacked—A, B, C, D, E, F, G, H, and I Battalions—204 tanks co-operated with III Corps and 120 tanks with IV Corps.

** On 23/11/17 62 tanks were engaged ; on 25/11/17 there were 12 tanks ; and on 27/11/17, 32 tanks.

*** On 30/11/17 36 tanks co-operated ; and on 1/12/17, 39 tanks.

1918 (*Contd.*)

FIRST BATTLES OF THE SOMME.

21–23 March	**Battle of St. Quentin** [2nd Tank Bde. (less 1 Coy.) in Army Reserve, and 1 Coy. 8th Bn. with IV; 6th Bn., 3rd Tank Bde., with VI: Third Army—and 1st, 4th, and 5th Bns., 4th Tank Bde.: Fifth Army].
22 March	**Counter-attack at Beugny** [25 tanks 2nd Bn., 2nd Tank Bde., with IV: Third Army].
24 and 25 March ...	**Actions at the Somme Crossings** [Part, 4th Tank Bde. with Fifth Army].
24 and 25 March ...	**First Battle of Bapaume** [2nd Tank Bde.—8th Bn. with V, and 10th Bn. with IV; 3rd Tank Bde.—9th Comp. Bn., 4th Bn., part 13th Bn., and details and tanks, in defence of the Ancre and of the Camp, and part 4th Tank Bde. and 1 Coy. (L.G.s) of 13th Bn.: Third Army].
26 and 27 March ...	**Battle of Rosières*** [2nd Tank Bde.—3rd and 10th Bns. with IV; Comp. Bn., 3rd Tank Bde., with V: Third Army; and 5th Bn. and L.G. Coy. 13th Bn., 4th Tank Bde.: Fifth Army].
28 March	**First Battle of Arras** [Detnts., 2nd Tank Bde., and 1 Sec. 3rd Bn. and B Coy. 9th Bn. (L.G.s), 3rd Tank Bde., and 2nd, 8th, and 13th Bns., 5th Tank Bde.: Third Army].
5 April	**Battle of the Ancre** [1 tank 10th Bn. with IV, and 18 teams of L.G.s 4th Bn., 4th Tank Bde., with VII: Third Army].

---

24 and 25 April ...	**Villers Bretonneux** [1st and 3rd Bns., 3rd Tank Bde., with III and Aus. Corps: Fourth Army].

---

* Whippet Tanks (3rd Tank Battalion) were first used in action on 26/3/1918 on the Somme battle-front of IV Corps, Third Army, at Colincamps (between Hébuterne and Mailly Maillet). Whippets had a speed of 6 miles an hour and were armed with 3 Hotchkiss machine guns. Each Whippet carried one spare machine gun.

1918 (*Contd.*)

BATTLES OF THE LYS.

13–15 April	**Battle of Bailleul** [L.G. unit 5th Bn., 4th Tank Bde. : Second Army].
17–19 April	**First Battle of Kemmel Ridge** [4th, 5th, 13th Bns. (Lewis Guns), 4th Tank Bde. : Second Army].
25 and 26 April ...	**Second Battle of Kemmel Ridge** [4th, 5th, 13th Bns. (Lewis Guns), 4th Tank Bde. : Second Army].
29 April	**Battle of the Scherpenberg** [4th, 5th, 13th Bns. (Lewis Guns), 4th Tank Bde. : Second Army].

11 June	**Belloy*** [4 Armoured Cars of 17th (A.-C.) Bn., with French 133rd Div. : French Tenth Army].
Night 22/23 June ...	**Bucquoy**** [5 female tanks of C Coy. 10th Bn., 4th Tank Bde., and party Tank Engr. Bn. ; with 5 Pltns. 5/K.O.Y.L.I. (D Coy. and 1 Pltn. B Coy.), 62nd Div., IV Corps : Third Army].
4 July	**Capture of Hamel***** [62 tanks of 8th and 13th Bns., 5th Tank Bde., with 4th Aus. Div., Aus. Corps : Fourth Army].
23 July	**Action South of Moreuil** [36 Tanks of 9th Bn., tempy. under 5th Tank Bde.; with French 3rd Div., French IX Corps : French First Army].

---

* First engagement of 17th (Armoured-Car) Battalion.
** First night raid in which tanks were engaged.
*** Mark V Tank first employed in action in this engagement.

1918 *(Contd.)*

THE ADVANCE TO VICTORY.

8–11 August ... ... **Battle of Amiens** [430 tanks (96 Whippets). 3rd Tank Bde.—3rd (L.), 6th (L.), and 17th (A.-C.) Bns., with Cav. Corps ; 4th Tank Bde.—1st, 4th, 5th, and 14th Bns., with Cdn. Corps ; and 5th Tank Bde.—2nd, 8th, 10th, 13th, and 15th Bns., with Aus. Corps : Fourth Army].

SECOND BATTLES OF THE SOMME.

21–24 August ... ... **Battle of Albert** [1st Tank Bde.—3rd (L.), 7th, 10th, and 17th (A.-C.) Bns., with IV ; 2nd Tank Bde.—6th (L.), 12th, and 15th Bns., and 3rd Tank Bde.—9th and 11th* Bns., with VI : Third Army ; and 4th Tank Bde.—1st, 4th, and 5th Bns., with III ; and 5th Tank Bde.—2nd, 8th, and 13th Bns., with Aus. Corps : Fourth Army].

31 Aug.–3 Sept. ... **Second Battle of Bapaume** [1st Tank Bde.—3rd (L.), 7th, 10th, and 17th (A.-C.) Bns., with IV ; and 2nd Tank Bde.—6th (L.), 12th, and 15th Bns., with VI : Third Army].

SECOND BATTLES OF ARRAS.

26–30 August ... ... **Battle of the Scarpe** [3rd Tank Bde.—Comp. Coy. 9th Bn. and Comp. Coy. 11th Bn., and (from 27/8) 14th Bn., with Cdn. Corps : First Army].

26 August ... ... **Capture of Monchy le Preux** [2 tanks Comp. Coy. 11th Bn., 3rd Tank Bde., with 3rd Cdn. Div., Cdn. Corps : First Army].

2 and 3 September ... **Battle of the Drocourt—Quéant Line** [57 tanks 3rd Tank Bde.—9th, 11th, and 14th Bns., with XXII and Cdn Corps : First Army].

---

* On the 24th August three Mark V* tanks, which unsuccessfully attacked part of the Hindenburg Line, had by the end of the day covered over 40,000 yards in 26 hours.

1918 *(Contd.)*

BATTLES OF THE HINDENBURG LINE.

18 September ... ... **Battle of Epéhy** [5th Tank Bde.—2nd Bn. with III (8 tanks), IX (4 tanks), and Aus. (9 tanks) : Fourth Army].

21 September ... ... **Attack on The Knoll, Ronssoy** [9 tanks, 2nd Bn., 5th Tank Bde., with III : Fourth Army].

24 September ... ... **Attack on Quadrilateral and Fresnoy** [20 tanks, 13th Bn., 5th Tank Bde., with IX : Fourth Army].

27 Sept.–1 Oct. ... ... **Battle of the Canal du Nord** [1st Tank Bde.—7th Bn. with Cdn. Corps : First Army ; and 2nd Tank Bde.—11th Bn. with IV and V ; 15th Bn. with XVII, and 12th Bn. in Army Reserve : Third Army].

27 September ... ... **Capture of Bourlon and Wood** [2 tanks A Coy. 7th Bn., 1st Tank Bde., with 4th Cdn. Div., Cdn. Corps : First Army].

29th Sept.–2 Oct. ... **Battle of the St. Quentin Canal** [1st Tank Bde.—part 11th Bn. with V : Third Army ; 3rd Tank Bde.—5th, 6th (L.), and 9th Bns., with IX ; 1st, 4th, and 301st (Am.) Tank Bns. with Aus. and II Am. Corps (on *29/9* only) ; and 5th Tank Bde.—3rd (L.), 8th, 13th, 16th, and 17th (A.-C.) Bns., with Aus. Corps : Fourth Army].

29 September ... ... **Capture of Bellicourt Tunnel Defences** [3rd Tank Bde.—1st, 4th, and 301st (Am.) Tank Bns., with Aus. and II Am. Corps ; and 9th Bn., with IX : Fourth Army].*

3–5 October ... ... **Battle of the Beaurevoir Line** [3rd Tank Bde.—5th Bn. and detnt. 6th (L.) Bn., with IX ; and 5th Tank Bde.— 3rd (L.), 8th, 13th, and 16th Bns., with Aus. Corps : Fourth Army].

5 October ... ... **Capture of Beaurevoir** [6 tanks, 4th Bn., 4th Tank Bde., with 25th, XIII : Fourth Army].

---

* On 29/9/18 the Passage at Bellenglise was effected by the 46th Div. (IX Corps), with the co-operation of 2 Tank Cos., 9th Bn., 3rd Tank Bde. : Fourth Army.

1918 *(Contd.)*

BATTLES OF THE HINDENBURG LINE *(Contd.)*.

8 and 9 October ... **Battle of Cambrai** [1st Tank Bde.—2 Comp. Cos. 11th Bn., with V; and 12th Bn. with IV, VI, and XVII: Third Army; and 3rd Tank Bde.—5th Bn. with IX; and 4th Tank Bde.—1st, 3rd (L.), 4th, 6th (L.), 10th, 16th, and 301st (Am.) Bns., with XIII and II Am. Corps: Fourth Army].

9–12 October ... ... **Pursuit to the Selle** [17th (A.-C.) Bn., with Cav. Corps; and 3rd Tank Bde.—5th Bn. and detnt. 6th (L.) Bn., with IX: Fourth Army].

THE FINAL ADVANCE IN PICARDY.

17–25 October ... ... **Battle of the Selle** [1st Tank Bde.—11th Bn. (on *20/10*) with V, and 11th and 12th Bns. (on *23/10*) with IV and V: Third Army; 4th Tank Bde. (*17–19/10*)—6th (L.— 12 whs.) and 16th (12 tanks) Bns., with IX, 301st Am. Bn. (25 tanks) with II Am. Corps, 1st Bn. (12 tanks) with XIII, and 10th Bn. (23 tanks) in Army Reserve; 4th Tank Bde. handed over on *19/10* to 2nd Tank Bde.—6th (L.), 10th, and 301st Am. Bns., and 2nd Bde. on *23/10* co-operated with IX and XIII: Fourth Army].

20 October ... ... **Crossing of the Selle** [4 tanks 11th Bn., 1st Tank Bde., with 17th and 38th, V: Third Army].

23 October ... ... **Capture of Bousies** [6 tanks 10th Bn., 2nd Tank Bde., with 18th, XIII: Fourth Army].

23 October ... ... **Attack on Forest and Ovillers** [6 tanks 11th Bn., 1st Tank Bde., with 21st and 33rd, V: Third Army].

23 October ... ... **Capture of Grand Champ Ridge** [2 tanks 12th Bn., 1st Tank Bde., with 5th, IV: Third Army].

2 November ... ... **Attack S. W. of Landrecies** (Happegarbes Spur) [3 tanks 10th Bn., 2nd Tank Bde., with 32nd, IX: Fourth Army].

1918 (*Contd.*)

THE FINAL ADVANCE IN PICARDY (*Contd.*).

4 November ...	**Battle of the Sambre** [2nd Tank Bde.*—11 tanks, 10th and 301st (Am.) Bns., with IV and V : Third Army ; and 21 tanks, 9th and 14th Bns., with XIII, 5 tanks 10th Bn. with IX, and 6 cars 17th (A.-C.) Bn., with XIII : Fourth Army].
5–7 November	**Passage of the Grand Honnelle** [2nd Tank Bde.—6th (L.) Bn., with VI : Third Army ; and 9th and 14th Bns., with IX and XIII, and 6 cars 17th (A.-C.) Bn. with XIII : Fourth Army].
8 November–11 a.m. 11 November	**Final Operations** [2nd Tank Bde.—5 cars 17th (A.-C.) Bn. with XIII, until *9/11* ; and then, until Armistice, with Major-General H. K. Bethell's Force :** Fourth Army].

The 2nd Tank Brigade was the only Tank Brigade still in action on the 4th November when the final battle of the Great War was fought ; it was the only Tank Brigade to to be actively employed in the concluding operations between the Battle of the Sambre and the Armistice ; and the 17th (Armoured-Car) Battalion of the 2nd Tank Brigade was the first Tank Corps unit to enter Germany. The casualties incurred by the 2nd Tank Brigade during 1917 and 1918 were : killed, 39 officers, and 123 other ranks ; wounded 216 officers and 1,016 other ranks ; missing, 26 officers and 172 other ranks—total 1,592. Of the other Brigades, it will suffice to mention the 5th Tank Brigade. This Brigade only came into existence in March, 1918, nevertheless it took part in 15 battles and actions ; and in these engagements, of the 576 tanks which started no fewer than 310 reached their objectives.***

....

Owing to its continuous co-operation in the numerous battles and actions fought between the 8th August and the 11th November, in the appropriately named ' Advance to Victory,' the Tank Corps at the time of the Armistice had almost been fought to a standstill.† Since the 8th August nearly 2,000 individual tank actions had taken place,

---

* One section of tanks covered 26 miles to get into action on 4/11/18.
** *Bethell's Force* was formed on 9/11/18 and broken up after Armistice (for its composition see p. 213).
*** Only 26 of these tanks did not reach the starting line.
† The Tank Corps had co-operated in some 26 battles and engagements during "the Hundred Days."

1918 (*Contd.*)

and practically the whole of this number of tanks had been put out of action in one way or another. Of these 1,000 tanks passed through repair organizations and were made serviceable for further fighting.

At certain periods of the Advance to Victory tanks were operating between 30 and 40 miles from railhead, a serious handicap to models of that time. On the other hand the total number of casualties to the Tank Corps personnel was relatively small, and the presence and close co-operation of tanks must on many occasions have saved the Infantry from very heavy losses.*

To provide the necessary numbers for another continuous onslaught 18 newly-raised tank battalions were already undergoing the necessary training in England.

Meanwhile, it was decided that the six Tank Brigades would be organized in three Groups. The formation of these 3 Groups was ordered to begin on the 7th November, but the Groups were not to function officially until further orders. Each Group would consist of Group Headquarters and (normally) 2 Tank Brigades ;** but according to tactical requirements the number of Tank Brigades in any Group might vary.

If operations continued it was intended that the 1st Tank Group would co-operate with the First Army, the 2nd Tank Group with the Fourth Army, and the 3rd Tank Group with the Third Army.

On the 13th November the three Tank Groups began to collect in France, and by Noon on the 20th November the three Groups completed their formation.***

....

During its short life of two-and-three-quarter years, the Tank Corps had been continually in action on the Western Front in France and Belgium for upwards of two-and-a-

---

* Between 8/8–24/10/18, 1,848 tanks were engaged and 565 were knocked out. The casualties incurred by the tank crews in this period were : 472 killed, 2,347 wounded, and 367 missing. In the Advance to Victory the greatest number of tanks employed on one day was 430, on 8/8/18.

** Each Tank Brigade would have (normally) 3 Tank Battalions, each Battalion would be organized in 3 Companies, each Company in 4 Sections, and each Section would have 4 tanks.

*** For composition, etc., of the three Tank Groups see Appendix 5 (pp. 293–294).

1918 *(Contd.)*

quarter years; and whereas in 1916 approximately 88 tanks were engaged, in 1917 the number expanded to 988, and in 1918 it rose to 2,245 tanks.

During this period the machines underwent uninterrupted improvement, and the rapid growth and development of the Tank Corps is substantiated by its successive expansions: from companies to battalions in 1916, from battalions to brigades in 1917, and now in 1918 by this last expansion of all, from brigades to groups.

T

APPENDICES

1. HOME FORCES : COMMANDERS, CENTRAL FORCE.

2. G.O.C.s, COMMANDS AT HOME.

3. CORPS HEAVY ARTILLERIES, FRANCE.

4. NATURES OF ORDNANCE, B.E.F. (FRANCE), AUGUST, 1914, AND NOVEMBER, 1918.

5. NOS. 1, 2, and 3 GROUPS, TANK CORPS.

6. BRITISH SECTION, SUPREME WAR COUNCIL, JANUARY, 1918.

APPENDIX 1

HOME FORCES.

COMMANDERS.

CENTRAL FORCE.*

5 August, 1914	General SIR I. S. M. HAMILTON.**
13 March, 1915	}General SIR H. M. L. RUNDLE.
12 March, 1916	

FIRST ARMY.

5 Aug., 1914...General Sir B. M.
                  HAMILTON.
22 June, 1915...General Sir H. L.
                SMITH-DORRIEN.***
11 Dec., 1915 } Lt.-Gen. Sir A. E.
–12 Mar., 1916 }   CODRINGTON.

SECOND ARMY.

5 Aug., 1914...Lt.-Gen. Hon. Sir F. W.
                  STOPFORD. †
7 June, 1915 } Lt.-Gen. C. L.
–12 Mar., 1916 }   WOOLLCOMBE.††

THIRD ARMY.

6 Sept., 1914 }
               }Lt.-Gen. Sir A. E. CODRINGTON.†††
–11 Dec., 1915 }

NORTHERN ARMY.
(H.Q. Mundford; later, Norwich).

11 April, 1916 } General Sir B. M.
–16 Feb., 1918 }   ·HAMILTON.

SOUTHERN ARMY.
(H.Q. Brentford).

11 April, 1916 } General Rt. Hon. Sir
–16 Feb., 1918 }   A. H. PAGET.

---

* Central Force became a separate command on 19/12/15, when Field-Marshal Viscount French became C.-in-C. Home Forces (page 7). In March, 1916, Central Force was dissolved.
** Appointed on 11/3/15 to command M.E.F. (Gallipoli).
*** Appointed on 22/11/15 to command British Forces, East Africa.
† Appointed on 17/6/15 to command IX Corps, with M.E.F. (Gallipoli).
†† Assumed command of IV Corps, B.E.F. (France) on 1/12/16.
††† Transferred on 11/12/15 to First Army, and Third Army was broken up. On 12/3/16, Central Force and First and Second Armies ceased to exist.

APPENDIX 2

HOME FORCES.

G.O.C.s COMMANDS AT HOME.

ALDERSHOT COMMAND (H.Q.—Aldershot).

[1 March, 1912]...	Lieut.-General Sir D. HAIG.*
5 August, 1914	Major-General A. HAMILTON-GORDON.
8 May, 1916	General Sir A. HUNTER.**
1 October, 1917	Lieut.-General Sir A. J. MURRAY.

EASTERN COMMAND (H.Q.—Horse Guards, Whitehall, S.W.; later, 50, Pall Mall, S.W.).

[4 April, 1912]	Lieut.-General Sir J. M. GRIERSON.***
5 August, 1914	Lieut.-General C. L. WOOLLCOMBE.†
7 June, 1915	General Sir H. M. L. RUNDLE.
5 May, 1916	Lieut.-General Sir J. W. MURRAY.
1 September, 1917	Lieut.-General Sir H. H. WILSON.††
19 February, 1918	General Sir W. R. ROBERTSON.†††
29 June, 1918	Lieut.-General Sir C. L. WOOLLCOMBE.

IRISH COMMAND (H.Q.—Dublin).

[10 May, 1912]	General Rt. Hon. Sir A. H. PAGET.
5 August, 1914	Major-General Rt. Hon. L. B. FRIEND.
27 April, 1916	General Rt. Hon. Sir J. G. MAXWELL.
15 November, 1916	Lieut.-General Rt. Hon. Sir B. T. MAHON.
13 May, 1918	Lieut.-General Rt. Hon. Sir F. C. SHAW.

LONDON DISTRICT (H.Q.—Horse Guards, Whitehall, S.W.; later, Horse Guards Annexe, Carlton House Terrace, S.W.).

[3 September, 1913] ...	Major-General Sir F. LLOYD.
1 January, 1917	Lieut.-General Sir F. LLOYD.
1 October, 1918	Major-General G. P. T. FEILDING.

---

* Appointed to command L Corps B.E.F. (France).
** From 23/8/14–7/5/15 Commander of Aldershot Training Centre.
*** Appointed to command II Corps, B.E.F. (France) ; died in France on 17/8/14.
† Appointed to command Second Army, Central Force (H.F.), on 7/6/15.
†† Military Representative at the Supreme War Council, 8/1/18. Became C.I.G.S. on 19/2/18
††† Became C.-in-C. Home Forces on 30/5/18.

APPENDIX 2 (*Contd*).

HOME FORCES.

G.O.C.s COMMANDS AT HOME.

NORTHERN COMMAND (H.Q.—York).

[10 November, 1911] ...	Lieut.-General Sir H. C. O. PLUMER.*
1 January, 1915	Major-General H. M. LAWSON.
16 November, 1916	Lieut.-General Rt. Hon. Sir J. G. MAXWELL.

SCOTTISH COMMAND (H.Q.—Edinburgh).

[5 May, 1914]	Lieut.-General Sir J. S. EWART.
5 May, 1918	Lieut.-General Sir F. W. N. McCRACKEN.

SOUTHERN COMMAND (H.Q.—Salisbury).

[1 March, 1912]...	General Sir H. L. SMITH-DORRIEN.**
21 August, 1914	Lieut.-General W. PITCAIRN CAMPBELL.
8 March, 1916	Lieut.-General Sir H. C. SCLATER.

WESTERN COMMAND (H.Q.—Chester).

[31 October, 1910]	General Sir W. H. MACKINNON.
8 March, 1916	Lieut.-General Sir W. PITCAIRN CAMPBELL.
5 August, 1918	Lieut.-General Sir T. D'O. SNOW.

---

* Assumed command of V Corps B.E.F. (France) on 8/1/1915.
** Assumed command of II Corps B.E.F. (France) on 21/8/1914.

APPENDIX 3

CORPS HEAVY ARTILLERIES
(FRANCE).

No. 1 H.A.R. Group (G.H.Q. Artillery).

Formed 28/2/15.

28 February, 1915 ... ...   Br.-Gen. G. McK. FRANKS.
15 November, 1915 ... ...   Br.-Gen. F. H. CRAMPTON.

Became **XI Corps Heavy Artillery H.Q.** on 11/3/16.
Br.-Gen. F. H. CRAMPTON.

No. 2 H.A.R. Group (G.H.Q. Artillery).

Formed 28/2/15.

27 February, 1915 ... ...   Br.-Gen. H. C. C. UNIACKE.
16 November, 1915 ... ...   Br.-Gen. R. P. BENSON.

Became **V Corps Heavy Artillery H.Q.** on 9/4/16.
Br.-Gen. R. P. BENSON.

No. 3 H.A.R. Group (G.H.Q. Artillery).

Formed 28/6/15.

26 June, 1915 ... ...   Br.-Gen. A. C. CURRIE.

Became **Second Army H.A. Group** on 1/12/15.
Br.-Gen. A. C. CURRIE.

Became **III Corps Heavy Artillery H.Q.** on 5/4/16.
Br.-Gen. A. C. CURRIE.

APPENDIX 3 *(Contd.)*

CORPS HEAVY ARTILLERIES.
(FRANCE).

No. 4 H.A.R. Group (G.H.Q. Artillery).

Formed 25/7/15.

25 July, 1915	Br.-Gen. W. St. C. BLAND.
6 December, 1915	Col. A. E. J. PERKINS (tempy..)

Became **Third Army H.A. Group** on 9/12/15.

9 December, 1915 ... ... Br.-Gen. H. O. VINCENT.

Became **X Corps Heavy Artillery H.Q.** on 2/3/16.

Br.-Gen. H. O. VINCENT.

No. 5 H.A.R. Group (G.H.Q. Artillery).

Formed 18/8/15.

18 August, 1915 ... ... Br.-Gen. T. A. TANCRED.

Became **First Army H.A. Group** on 15/11/15

Br.-Gen. T. A. TANCRED.

Became **I Corps Heavy Artillery H.Q.** on 11/3/16

11 March, 1916 ... ... Br.-Gen. W. J. NAPIER.

No. 6 H.A.R. Group (G.H.Q. Artillery).

Formed 26/2/16.

7 March, 1916 ... ... Br.-Gen. C. R. BUCKLE.

Became **VII Corps Heavy Artillery H.Q.** on 1/4/16.

Br.-Gen. C. R. BUCKLE.

NOTE.—The other fourteen Corps Heavy Artillery Headquarters were formed in France, or Palestine for the particular Corps with which they served.

APPENDIX 4

NATURES OF ORDNANCE WITH B.E.F. (FRANCE).

23.8.14.

GUNS:
    13-pdr. Q.F. (Mk. I)
    18-pdr. Q.F. (Mk. I)
    60-pdr. (Mk. I)

A.-A. GUNS:

    ....

NOTE.—A.-A. Guns only reached the B.E.F. on the Aisne in September, 1914. These early A.-A. guns were POM-POMS.

HOWITZERS:
    4.5″ (Mk. I)

NOTE.—4 Bties. of 6″ (30-cwt.) Hows. only landed at St. Nazaire in September, 1914, and came into action on the Aisne Front on 24 and 25/9/14.

11.11.18.

GUNS:*
    13-pdr. Q.F. (Mk. I)
    18-pdr. Q.F. (Mks. II and IV).
    60-pdr. (Mks. I and II)
    6″ (Mks. VII and XIX)
    9·2″ (Mks. VI, X, XIII, and XIV)
    12″ (Mk. IX)
    14″ (Mk. III)

A.-A. GUNS:
    12-pdr.
    13-pdr. (6-cwt.)
    13-pdr. (9-cwt.)
    3″ (20-cwt.)

HOWITZERS:
    4·5″ (Mk. I)
    6″ (26-cwt.)
    8″ (Mks. VI and VII)
    9·2″ (Mks. I and II)
    12″ (Mks. I, II, III, IV, and V)
    15″ (Mk. I).

Between 4/8/14 and 11/11/18 the Output of new Guns and Howitzers was as follows :—1914—91 ; 1915—3,226 ; 1916—4,551 ; 1917—6,483 ; and 1918—10,680, TOTAL—25,031.

In all theatres (home and abroad) between 4/8/14—11/11/18 the strength of the ROYAL ARTILLERY (Regular, Temporary, Special Reserve, and Territorial Force) rose from :

    4,083 officers (2,552 regular)
    and 88,837 other ranks (50,808 regular) ;
        to
    29,990 officers (6,212 regular)
    and 518,790 other ranks.

In the same period the number of R.A. units rose from 554 (290 regular) to 1,872 (1,503 regular and special reserve); the number of A.-A. Batteries had risen from 0 to 289.

---

* On 11/11/18 there were also in France, 2, 4″ guns ; 810, 6-pdrs. ; 71, 9.45″ Trench Mortars ; 812, 6″ Newton Trench Mortars, and 1,636 Stokes Mortars (3″ and 4″).

APPENDIX 5

Nos. 1, 2, and 3 Groups, TANK CORPS.

No. 1 GROUP (Formed at Bryas—3 miles N.N.E. of St. Pol).

Commander:

13 November, 1918 ... ... Br.-Gen. J. HARDRESS-LLOYD.

G.S.O. 1:

15 November, 1918 ... ... Lt.-Col. G. L. CROSSMAN.

D.-A.-A. and Q.-M.-G.:

13 November, 1918 ... ... Major A. G. WOODS.

D.-A.-D. O.S.:

November, 1918 ... ... Major C. W. MESSER.

1st Tank Brigade.	6th Tank Brigade.
(Br.-Gen. C. D'A. B. S. BAKER-CARR) 7th, 11th, and 12th Tank Bns. 1st Tank Carrier Coy. M.T. Coy. (1086 Coy. A.S.C.)	(Br.-Gen. R. PIGOT) 16th and 18th Tank Bns. 6th Tank Carrier Coy. M.T. Coy (1127 Coy. A.S.C.)

No. 2 GROUP (Formed at Cavillon—10 miles W. of Amiens).

Commander:

13 November, 1918 ... ... Br.-Gen. A. COURAGE.

G.S.O. 1.:

November, 1918 ... ... Lt.-Col. P. NEAME, V.C.

D.-A.-A. and Q.-M.-G. :

November, 1918 ... ... Major M. W. BROOK.

D.-A.-D. O.S. :

November, 1918 ... ... Major A. D. CHISHOLM.

3rd Tank Brigade.	5th Tank Brigade.
(Br.-Gen. A. PARKER) 3rd, 6th, and 15th Tank Bns. 3rd Tank Carrier Coy. M.T. Coy. (1088 Coy. A.S.C.)	(Br.-Gen. S. H. CHARRINGTON) 2nd, 8th, and 13th Tank Bns. 5th Tank Carrier Coy. M.T. Coy. (1090 Coy. A.S.C.)

APPENDIX 5 *(Contd.)*

Nos. 1, 2, and 3 GROUPS, TANK CORPS.

No. 3 GROUP (Formed at Bavincourt—10 miles S.W. of Arras).

Commander:

13 November, 1918 ... ... Br.-Gen. E. B. HANKEY.

G.S.O. 1:

November, 1918 ... ... Lt.-Col. H. BOYD-ROCHFORT.

D.-A.-A. and Q.-M.-G.:

November, 1918 ... ... Major M. J. TAPPER.

D.-A.-D. O.S.:

November, 1918 ... ... Major G. SMITH.

2nd Tank Brigade.	4th Tank Brigade.
(Br.-Gen. H. K. WOODS)	(Br.-Gen. J. MICKLEM).
9th, 10th, and 14th Tank Bns.	1st, 4th, and 5th Tank Bns.
2nd Tank Carrier Coy.	4th Tank Carrier Coy.
M.T. Coy. (1087 Coy. A.S.C.)	M.T. Coy. (1089 Coy A.S.C.)

17th (Armoured-Car) Battalion was with the Second Army in Germany.

NOTES.—

Each Group Commander had an A.D.C.

Each Group H.Q. was also allotted one G.S.O. 2 and two G.S.O. 3 ; and 2 Staff Captains completed each A. and Q. Branch. An A.-D. M.S. was allowed for each Group.

TANK CORPS TROOPS at this time included :

No. 1 Gun Carrier Coy.
Training and Reinforcement Depot.
Tank Gunnery School.
Tank Driving Camp.
Tank Driving and Maintenance Schools.
Workshop for A.S.C. M.T. (711 Coy. A.S.C.)

CHIEF MECHANICAL ENGINEER—
Tank Field Battalion.
Central Workshops
Nos. 1 and 2 Tank Stores. }
Nos. 1 and 3 Advanced Stores.

APPENDIX 6

BRITISH SECTION—
SUPREME WAR COUNCIL

THE
(RT. Hor

One
(RT.

Military Representative
General Sir H. H. WILSON[2].
Private Secretary—Capt. LORD DUNCANNON

Chief of Staff (M.-G.G.S.)
Maj.-Gen. Hon. C. J. SACKVILLE-WEST.[2]

Allied and Neutral Branch	**Enemy and Neutral Branch**	**Material and Man-Power Branch**	**Maps**
Br.-Gen. H. W. STUDD[2] (B.-G.G.S.)	Br.-Gen. Sir H. WAKE, Bt.	Br.-Gen. F. H. SYKES (B.-G.G.S.)	Capt. J. M. B
Lt.-Col. EARL STANHOPE	(B.-G.G.S.)	Lt.-Col. I. O. DENNISTOUN (G.S.O. 1)	
(G.S.O. 1)	Lt.-Col. A. H. OLLIVANT (G.S.O. 1)	Lt.-Col. C. N. BUZZARD (G.S.O. 1)	
Lt.-Col. M. G. E. BELL (G.S.O. 2)	Maj. J. H. BEVAN (G.S.O. 2)	Lt.-Col. A. P. WAVELL (G.S.O. 1)	
Dominions (G.S.O. 2)	Dominions (G.S.O. 2)	Maj. R. H. BEADON (G.S.O. 2)	

NOTES:
[1] From 20/4/18, when he replaced Rt.-Hon. Earl of Derby as Secretary of State for War.

[2] On 19/2/18 General Sir H. H. Wilson became Chief of the Imperial General Staff,; Maj-Gen. Hon. C. J. Sackville-West then became Military Representative, Br.-Gen. H. W. STUDD became Chief of Staff, and Br.-Gen. C. B. Thomson became the head of the Allied and Neutral Branch.

The Supreme War Council was formed on the 7th November, 1917.

REME WAR COUNCIL

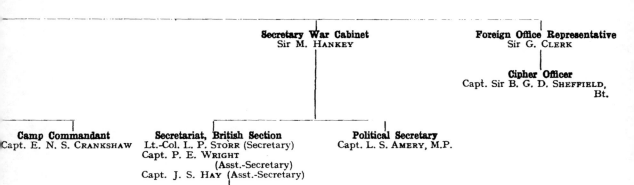

	Secretary War Cabinet Sir M. HANKEY		**Foreign Office Representative** Sir G. CLERK
			Cipher Officer Capt. Sir B. G. D. SHEFFIELD, Bt.

Camp Commandant
Capt. E. N. S. CRANKSHAW

Secretariat, British Section
Lt.-Col. L. P. STORR (Secretary)
Capt. P. E. WRIGHT
(Asst.-Secretary)
Capt. J. S. HAY (Asst.-Secretary)

Political Secretary
Capt. L. S. AMERY, M.P.

Head Clerk
Lieut. W. P. BRITTON.

The above Table is dated 8th January, 1918.

INDEX OF FORMATIONS

Infantry (*Contd.*).

34th, 20n.
36th, 84.
38th, 97 ; 102.
39th, 115.
40th, 104.
41st, 66 & n. ; 103 ; 201 & n. ; 218 ; 219.
42nd, 36 ; 49 ; 50.
46th, 76 ; 92 ; 116 ; 279n.
47th, 75 ; 103n. ; 104 ; 117.
48th, 66 & n. ; 67 & n. ; 68 ; 114 ; 117 ;
  201 & n. ; 219n.
49th, 83
51st, 20 & n. ; 74 & n. ; 93 ; 94 ; 115.
52nd, 36 ; 38 ; 39 ; 40 ; 53 ; 249.
53rd, 38 ; 39 ; 187n. ; 249 & n. ; 250.
54th, 38 ; 187n. ; 253 ; 254 ; 255.
55th, 76 ; 77.
56th, 92 ; 94 ; 104.
57th, 97.
60th, 40 ; 41 ; 60 ; 249 ; 250 ; 254 ; 255.
61st, 75 ; 117.
62nd, 20 & n. ; 95 & n. ; 98 ; 158 & n. ;
  191 & n. ; 277 & n.
63rd (Royal Naval), 17 ; 48 ; 49 ; 50 ; 53 ;
  75 ; 94 ; 97.
74th, 38 ; 249 ; 250.
75th, 253 ; 254 ; 255.
Composite (Helles), 50n.

FORMATIONS.

(1) Allied—

American (U.S.)—

II Corps, 106 ; 107 & n. ; 108 & n. ; 279 ; 280.
27th Division, 86n. ; 107n. ; 108n. ; 245.
30th Division, 86n ; 107 & n. ; 108n ; 142.
33rd Division, 105 ; 106n.
130th Inf. Regt., 106n.
131st Inf. Regt., 105 ; 106n. ; 150.
132nd Inf. Regt., 105.
301st Tank Bn., 98 ; 107 ; 108 ; 127 ; 128 ;
  129 ; 159 ; 167 ; 190 ; 212 ; 213 ; 279 ;
  280 ; 281.

Arab—

Forces, 37 & n. ; 40n. ; 43n. ; 44n.
Northern Army, 40n. ; 43 & n.
Battalion, 36.
Camelry, 40n. ; 43.

French—

G.Q.G. (Locations), 24 ; 25
G.Q.G.A. (Locations), 25.
First Army, 105 ; 109 ; 214 ; 277.
Second Army, 92, 195.
Third Army, 241.
Fifth Army, 20 ; 189 ; 259.
Sixth Army, 20 ; 102 ; 189 ; 195 ; 246n.
Ninth Army, 86n.
Tenth Army, 20n. ; 92 ; 177 ; 207 ; 235 ;
  259 ; 277 & n.
VII Corps, 246n.
IX Corps, 277.
XI Corps, 92.
XII Corps, 235.
XIV Corps, 86n. ; 92 ; 245.
XV Corps, 214.
XVI Corps, 86n. ; 196n.
XX Corps, 20 ; 259.
XXX Corps, 20n. ; 259.
XXXVI Corps, 85 & n. ; 86 & n. ; 189.
II Cav. Corps, 85 & n. ; 86 & n. ; 189.
3rd Division, 277.
28th Division, 189n. ; 258.
34th Division, 189 & n.
41st Division, 246.
51st Division, 214.

French (*Contd.*)—

122nd Division, 62n.
133rd Division, 189 & n. ; 277 & n.
154th Division, 189n.
1st Division (C.E.O.), 48n. ; 49 ; 50 ; 51.
2nd Division (C.E.O.), 48n. ; 49 & n. ; 50 ; 51.
2nd Cav. Division, 189 & n.
3rd Cav. Division, 189 & n.
6th Cav. Division, 189 & n.
C.E.O. (later C.E.D.), 46n. ; 48n. ; 49 ; 50 ;
  51.
D.A.N., 85n. ; 86n. ; 196n. ; 245.
D.F.P.S., 254 & n.
Groupe d'Armées des Flandres, 246n.
Groupe Provisoire du Nord, 11n.
R.M.M.C., 42n. ; 43.

Greek—

I Corps, 61n.
1st Division, 61n. ; 62n.
2nd Division, 61n. ; 62n.
13th Division, 61n. ; 62n.
14th Division, 61 ; 62n. ; 231.
Archipelago Division, 62n.
Crete Division, 61 ; 62n. ; 231.
Seres Division, 61 ; 62n. ; 208.

Italian—

Sixth Army, 67 & n. ; 219n.
Tenth Army, 67 ; 219.
VIII Corps, 219n.
XI Corps, 67 ; 219n.
XII Corps, 67 & n.
XXVII Corps, 219n.
Sicilia Bde., 62n.

Portuguese—

1st Division, 202.
2nd Division, 202.

(2) British Empire, Dominions, etc.

India—

Cavalry Corps, 74 ; 92 ; 126n.
Indian Corps, 17 ; 74 & n. ; 75 ; 140n. ;
  233 & n. ; 234n. ; 235.
4th (1st Indian) Cav. Div. (France), 74n ; 92n. ;
  94 ; 116 ; 126 & n. ; 127 ; 150 ; 275.
4th Cavalry Div. (E.E.F.), 42 & n. ; 43 ;
  44 ; 126 ; 127.
5th (2nd Indian) Cav. Div. (France), 74n. ;
  92n. ; 94 ; 103 ; 104 ; 126 & n. ; 127 ;
  150 ; 275.
5th Cavalry Div. (E.E.F.) 42 & n. ; 43 ; 44 ;
  126 ; 127.
10th Cavalry Bde., 42n. ; 43.
11th Cavalry Bde. 42 & n.
12th Cavalry Bde. 42n.
13th Cavalry Bde. 42 & n.
14th Cavalry Bde. 42n.
15th Cavalry Bde. 42 & n. ; 43 & n.
Impl. Service Cav. Bde. (later 15th Cav. Bde.),
  34 ; 35 ; 41 ; 42n.
Secunderabad Cav. Bde., 17.
3rd (Lahore) Division, 33 ; 41n. ; 74n. ; 82n. ;
  140n. ; 163 ; 254 ; 255.
7th (Meerut) Division, 41 & n. ; 44 ; 74n. ;
  75 ; 140n. ; 254 ; 255.
10th Indian Division, 34 ; 35.
11th Indian Division, 34 ; 35.
20th Ind. Inf. Bde., 41 ; 42n.
28th Ind. Inf. Bde., 35.
29th Ind. Inf. Bde., 35 ; 49 ; 50 ; 51 ; 52 & n. ;
  53 ; 181.
Ferozepore Inf. Bde., 125 ; 140 n.
Lucknow Inf. Bde., 34.
Sirhind Inf. Bde., 33 ; 34 ; 140n.
Bikanir Camel Corps, 34 ; 35 ; 36.

Printed under the Authority of His Majesty's Stationery Office
By C. Tinling & Co. Ltd., Liverpool, London and Prescot

Wt2790 2.46 500 CT&CoLtd Gp8.

S.O. Code No. 70.307.4*

302

FURTHER CORRIGENDA

HISTORY OF THE GREAT WAR, 1914—1918

ORDER OF BATTLE OF DIVISIONS

Part 2A

Page 78. Under 144th Bde. After 4th entry, Br.-Gen. H. R. Done, add these two entries :
  4 June, 1918...Lt.-Col. F. M. Tomkinson (acting).
  20 June, 1918...Br.-Gen. H. R. Done.
Under 145th Bde. After 7th entry, Br.-Gen. D. M. Watt, add these two entries :
  3 June, 1918...Lt.-Col. L. L. C. Reynolds (acting)
  20 June, 1918...Br.-Gen. D. M. Watt.

Page 139. Under **THE ADVANCE TO VICTORY.**
  1st entry—alter Fifth Army to First Army.
  2nd entry—alter Fifth Army to First Army.

Part 2B.

Page 54. To Footnote add in brackets
  (see Part 3B, pp. 117–128).

Part 3A.

Page 62. Under 49th Bde. After 2nd Entry Br.-Gen. P. Leveson-Gower.
  Delete fullstop and add (gassed, 15/8/17).
  Then add as new 3rd and 4th Entries
  15 Aug., 1917...Lt.-Col. K. C. Weldon (acting).
  23 Aug., 1917...Br.-Gen. P. Leveson-Gower.

Page 101. Under **THE ADVANCE TO VICTORY.**
  At the end of the only entry
  Alter Fifth Army to First Army.

FURTHER CORRIGENDA (*Contd*).

Part 3B.

Page 23. Under 133 Heavy Battery in line 1,
    Delete raised for and substitute attached to.
  ,,   In same line after 32nd Div. add in brackets (see p. 138, note 7).

Page 89. Under Battles of the Hindenburg Line add as 5th, and last, entry
    8 October   ...   ...   **Capture of Villers Outréaux.**

Page 127. Under **Battles of the Somme (1916)** add as 2nd, and last, entry
    14 November ... ... **Capture of Beaucourt.**

  Under **Battles of Arras (1917)**, add as 2nd entry
    23 April ... ... **Capture of Gavrelle.**

Part 4.

Page 66. Last para., last line, for Piave read mountain front.

2

Lightning Source UK Ltd.
Milton Keynes UK
UKOW03f1125141114

241613UK00001B/17/P